Planning and Develop
and Distance Learning

This book is aimed at those who are considering, or just starting to plan open and distance learning (ODL) courses. It offers practical advice on how to respond to your students' needs, expand your audience and become cost-effective without compromising quality. The main areas covered are:

- Different approaches to ODL and the principles upon which they build.
- Different types of self-study materials, media, and student support systems.
- How to develop self-study materials and student support systems for your courses
- Building quality assurance into the development process.
- Gaining support from your institution and external agencies.

With a wide range of practical, tried-and-tested examples and case studies, this book provides a comprehensive guide to planning and developing ODL courses.

Reginald F. Melton was Senior Lecturer in Educational Technology at the Open University where he worked for over twenty-five years. As a consultant, he also advised many overseas institutions on the planning and development of open and distance learning systems.

RoutledgeFalmer Studies in Distance Education
General Editors: Desmond Keegan and Alan Tait

Theoretical Principles of Distance Education
Edited by Desmond Keegan

Distance Education: New Perspectives
Edited by Keith Harry, Magnus John and Desmond Keegan

Collaboration in Distance Education
Edited by Louise Moran and Ian Mugridge

Otto Peters on Distance Education
Edited by Desmond Keegan

Theory and Practice in Distance Education
Borje Holmberg

Technology, Open Learning and Distance Education
A.W. Bates

Open and Distance Learning Today
Edited by Fred Lockwood

Foundations of Distance Education, 3rd Edition
Desmond Keegan

Opening Education
Terry Evans and Darren Nation

Staff Development in Open and Flexible Learning
Edited by Colin Latchem and Fred Lockwood

Globalising Education
Robin Mason

Convergence of Distance and Conventional Education
Alan Tait and Roger Mills

Open and Distance Learning in the Developing World
Hilary Perraton

Distance Training: Taking Stock at a Time of Change
Desmond Keegan

Using Learning Technologies: International Perspectives on Practice
Edited by Elizabeth J. Burge and Margaret Haughey

The Online Educator: A Guide to Creating the Virtual Classroom
Marguerita McVay Lynch

Planning and Developing Open and Distance Learning
A quality assurance approach

Reginald F. Melton

London and New York

First published 2002
by RoutledgeFalmer

11 New Fetter Lane, London EC4P 4EE

Simultaneously published in the USA and Canada
by RoutledgeFalmer
29 West 35th Street, New York, NY 10001

RoutledgeFalmer is an imprint of the Taylor & Francis Group

© 2002 Reginald F. Melton

Typeset in Times by Wearset Ltd, Boldon, Tyne and Wear
Printed and bound in Great Britain by TJ International Ltd,
Padstow, Cornwall

All rights reserved. No part of this book may be reprinted or
reproduced or utilised in any form or by any electronic, mechanical,
or other means, now known or hereafter invented, including
photocopying and recording, or in any information storage or
retrieval system, without permission in writing from the publishers.

British Library Cataloguing in Publication Data
A catalogue record for this book is available from the British Library

Library of Congress Cataloging in Publication Data
A catalog record for this book has been requested

ISBN 0-415-25480-9 (hbk)
ISBN 0-415-25481-7 (pbk)

Contents

List of figures vii
Foreword ix

Introduction 1

PART 1
Aims of open and distance learning 3

  1 Typical aims of ODL 5

PART 2
Characteristics of ODL 21

  2 The broad characteristics of ODL 23

  3 The design of self-study materials 41

  4 The use of media in ODL 85

  5 Student support systems 110

PART 3
The development of materials and systems 133

  6 Principles upon which development builds 135

  7 The first stage in the development process 141

8	The remaining stages in the development process	167
9	Collecting data for quality assurance and quality control	182

PART 4
Institutional support 201

10	The level of institutional support required	203

Bibliography 215
Index 219

Figures

1.1	Typical aims underlying approaches to ODL	19
2.1	Example of early introduction to courses on offer	25
2.2	Introduction to Course L130, *Auftakt*, as presented in Study Guide	28–29
2.3	Breakdown of Course L130, *Auftakt*, into parts, themes, sections (*Teile*) and study sessions	30
2.4	Introduction to a study session (*Lerneinheit*) in Course L130, *Auftakt*	32
2.5	The use of icons identifying the nature of activities in Course L130, *Auftakt*	33
2.6	The use of checklists indicating what students should be able to do	34
2.7	Sample time estimates for study of components in a 30-point course	38
2.8	Course materials and resources for ODL	39
3.1	An advance organiser for a study session	44
3.2	Aims included within advance organiser for study session	45
3.3	Advance organiser for an on-line mini-conference	48–49
3.4	The use of signalling devices	51
3.5	Activity relating issues discussed to student experience	52
3.6	Extract from description of an open-ended project	54
3.7	Use of photographs, illustrations, margins and bold print	55
3.8	Design characteristics for further study	57
3.9	Summary and checklist for a study session	59
3.10	Checklist for a study session	61
3.11	A framework for a study session	62
3.12	An advance organiser including a statement of aims for course	65–66
3.13	Preparatory activities contained within introduction to a course	68–69
3.14	Outline of assessment strategy for a course	72–73
3.15	Summary for a block/course	74
3.16	Detailed guidance for a block assignment	76

viii *Figures*

3.17	Detailed guidance for an end-of-course assignment	77
3.18	A framework for a course	79
3.19	Reference to fully developed self-study materials	81
4.1	Computer-conference strand encouraging students to reflect on topics for projects	92–93
4.2	Average cost per student per study hour of various media	107
5.1	Start of search on UK OU website for information on courses and qualifications	124
5.2	Introduction to computer-conference for a course on ODE	126–127
6.1	Some of the specialists who might be included in a course team	137
7.1	Some of the different types of aims to be considered	143
7.2	Functional analysis of management requirements	145
7.3	Hierarchical analysis of aims of course on 'Man and Energy'	147
7.4	A 'functional approach' used to link course structure to course objectives	149
7.5	A 'scenario-based approach' used to link course structure to course objectives	151
7.6	A 'project-based approach' used to link course structure to course objectives	153
7.7	Assessment criteria for an interactive speaking test	160–161
7.8	Items to be included in the outline for a course	165
8.1	Items to be included in the outline for a unit	170
8.2	Examples of core text for part of a study session	174–175
8.3	Items to be included in the core text for a unit	176
8.4	Items to be included in fully developed materials for a unit	177
8.5	Example of a course development schedule including developmental testing	179
9.1	Alternative question formats for making comparisons between student responses	188
9.2	A question format for identifying broad problem areas	193
9.3	A question format for identifying specific problem areas	195
9.4	Example of item and cell statistics for a multiple-choice test item	196
9.5	Theoretical variation of discrimination index (r) with facility index (f)	197
10.1	A framework for determining the support required for development of courses	209
10.2	A framework for determining the support required for presentation of courses	211
10.3	Checking the effectiveness of quality assurance procedures	213

Foreword

Over thirty years ago, when the United Kingdom Open University (UK OU) was established to provide undergraduate courses *at a distance*, there were many who were extremely sceptical – not only about the concept of Open and Distance Learning (ODL) but also about the quality of any learning materials to be studied at a distance. In the intervening years, evidence has been amassed to demonstrate that, not only is the concept valid, but high quality materials can be assembled that allow learners, of all ages and across all disciplines, to fulfil their potential. In his book, *Mega Universities and Knowledge Media* (London: Kogan Page, 1996), the then Vice Chancellor of the UK OU, Sir John Daniel, charted the development of ODL, commented on the potential of the new media and noted the millions of learners who were studying successfully.

The concept of ODL has been embraced by schools and colleges, corporate bodies and universities around the world. It is a concept that is being seized upon by governments to provide the education and training the population/workforce requires if nation states are to maintain and enhance the skills of their workforce and to remain competitive. Two simple illustrations serve to confirm this claim. First, in the UK, the government has set a target that the proportion of those under thirty years of age, to benefit from higher education, will increase from about 30 per cent today to 50 per cent by 2010. This target will not be achieved by building, staffing and funding more conventional institutions. It will simply not be possible to *scale up* the current provision – ODL methods will be required to supplement current teaching methods. Second, a recent report reveals that China, in meeting the needs of its learners, is developing its ODL and on-line capability with the target of between 4 and 6 million learners on-line by 2005; these are patterns replicated around the world.

It is evident that today few, if any, remain sceptical as to the potential quality of the learning materials studied *at a distance*. However, how to develop the required materials and support systems? In *Planning and Developing Open and Distance Learning: A Quality Assurance Approach*, Reg Melton provides us with a blueprint. It is a blueprint that is based on twenty-seven years' experience of working as an educational technologist within the Open University, amongst numerous course teams and across a range of subject areas. It is a blueprint that benefits from the considerable experience Reg has acquired not only in his teaching and research but in his extensive consultancy experience world-wide. In this book Reg systematically addresses the issues that we will need to consider as we develop quality materials and related support systems – taking us through a discussion of the aims and characteristics of ODL to the development process and institutional support required.

I was fortunate to work alongside Reg for over twenty-five years and can think of few who have his insights into the field of ODL, his breadth of experience, coupled with an ability to explain his ideas in terms that non-specialists can understand. Whether you are a novice or an experienced author of self-instructional material, there is much in this book for you and, as a result, much for your learners.

Professor Fred Lockwood,
Head of the Learning and Teaching Unit,
Manchester Metropolitan University

Introduction

If you are thinking about the possibility of making use of Open and Distance Learning (ODL), but need to know more about what is involved, or if you already have such work underway, but need advice on how to expand your offerings, how to reach out to increasing numbers of students, how to become more cost-effective, and how to improve the quality of your products and systems, then this book has been produced to meet your needs. The book is divided into four parts.

In Part 1 you will find an introduction to ODL, and what the different approaches to ODL strive to achieve. You will find that the designers of particular approaches to ODL often have different goals in mind, and the intent in this part of the book is to encourage you to reflect on the typical **aims of ODL** and then to determine for yourself what you might hope to achieve through the development of ODL within your own area.

Once you are clear about what you would like ODL to achieve in your own area, then you will be in a position to think more clearly about the type of approach to ODL that is likely to meet your particular needs. In Part 2 you will find a review of the **characteristics of ODL**: the type of self-study materials that might be developed, the variety of ways in which the media may be used, and the type of student support systems typically provided in ODL. The aim is to alert you to the wide range of options available to you, and to encourage you to determine for yourself the combination of components that is most likely to meet the needs that you have in mind for ODL within your own area.

It is, of course, one thing to decide on the type of study materials and student support systems that you would like to develop and quite another to actually produce high quality products that will stand up to public inspection, and it will make a great deal of difference if you adopt a development process that in itself will go a long way towards ensuring the quality of your products. In Part 3 you will find a description of a development process that includes quality assurance strategies within it as an integral part of the process. Again, you do not have to adopt precisely the same approach in your own situation. It is the principles underlying the process that are important, and you will be encouraged to reflect on these

2 Introduction

and develop your own approach to **the development of materials and systems** based on the same underlying principles.

One of the things you will soon realise is that the scale and success of any system of ODL that you hope to develop are likely to depend to a considerable extent on the level of support you can obtain from your own institution, and in Part 4 of the book you will be encouraged to give careful consideration to the level of **institutional support** you will need if your plans are to be realised. You will need to discuss with related colleagues the scale of the operation you envisage, the number of students to be targeted, their geographical location, the type of support they will need, the range of courses to be offered, and the variety of support systems that will need to be developed (for such functions as the publication of materials, the development of audio and video cassettes, student support facilities, student assessment, and so on), for this in turn will determine the level of institutional support you will need to obtain if the project is to be successful. The discussion of these issues is deliberately left to this late stage in the book, since it is much easier to appreciate the type of institutional support that is likely to be required once you have acquired a good understanding of the nature of open and distance learning and the related development process.

The whole book is in fact about *the building of quality assurance into the development process*, and a few words on this aspect might help place the process in a clearer perspective. Quality assurance depends on two essential requirements: the first is the specification of standards for whatever it is you want to produce – materials, services or systems – and the second is the development of systems or procedures that will enable you to produce what you have in mind to the standards specified. The first half of the book is in fact concerned with the development of a design specification for any approach to ODL that you might hope to develop, while the second half is concerned with determining the procedures that you will need to follow if you are to develop an approach to ODL that will meet the specified requirements.

Needless to say, a single book cannot hope to cover all aspects of ODL in depth, and this book is no exception. However, by placing emphasis on the basic principles underlying the planning, design, development, production and presentation of ODL, it should provide you with *a logical foundation on which to build*. At the end of some chapters you will in fact find references to related books that will help you to look in greater depth at the topics that have been addressed.

Finally, it is worth adding that, although the book has been designed to help those concerned with the planning and development of Open and Distance Learning (ODL), it should also be of value to anyone involved in teaching, training, staff development and management who is concerned with facilitating the development of teaching materials and student support systems, regardless of whether this is for teaching at a distance or not.

Part 1
Aims of open and distance learning

Although approaches to ODL may vary in the extent to which they place emphasis on what they strive to achieve and the ways in which they go about this, they tend to have a great deal in common, and in Chapter 1 you will find a review of **typical aims of ODL**. These are expressed in very broad terms, and include such ideals as 'opening up education to students wherever they might be located', 'increasing access to education by removing unnecessary barriers', 'encouraging lifelong learning', and so on. The intention is to draw your attention to the variety of aims underlying approaches to ODL, and to help you determine those that are most relevant to any approach to ODL that you might develop.

You will recognise that varying degrees of emphasis may be placed on these aims, and this is often reflected in the naming of an approach. For example, in the literature you will find references to 'open learning', 'distance teaching', 'open and distance learning', 'open and distance education', 'open distance and flexible learning', and 'open distance education and lifelong learning' to mention but a few – the terminology used typically seeking to draw attention to key characteristics of the approach adopted. Needless to say, the names of approaches to ODL would be impossibly long if they attempted to reflect all the aims underlying each approach, and, although the naming of an approach may be important in drawing attention to some of its key characteristics, it is more important to be clear as to the broad aims underlying the approach.

In reflecting on the aims you might hope to achieve through the development of ODL, you may find it helpful to think in terms of short-term and long-term aims, as this will help you to maintain a suitable balance between the realities of what can be achieved in the short term and the ideals of what might be achieved in the future.

1 Typical aims of ODL

Contents

Introduction	5
1.1 Opening access to education	6
1.2 Responding to student needs	8
1.3 The design of self-study materials	10
1.4 Student support	13
1.5 Cost-effectiveness	15
1.6 The quality of materials and systems	18
In perspective	18
Suggestions	20

Introduction

In this chapter you will find a review of the things that educators typically hope their approaches to ODL will be able to do. These are expressed in terms of broad aims, and include such ideals as those of 'opening up education to students wherever they might be located' and 'providing students with regular, ongoing support'. You will find the aims discussed under six headings, and a few words on each should help place them in perspective.

The first group of aims is about *opening access to education*, that is, opening up opportunities for students to learn what they want to learn wherever they might be located. This is very much what open and distance learning is all about, and is reflected in the choice of words in the title 'open and distance learning'.

The second group of aims is concerned with *responding to student needs*, and the use of the term 'learning' in the title 'open and distance learning' is a reflection on the extent to which related approaches place emphasis on the student-centred nature of ODL.

Within ODL self-study materials have an important part to play, and the effectiveness of such materials depends to a large extent on the strategies incorporated into their design. The third group of aims is therefore concerned with ways in which *the design of self-study materials* may facilitate student learning.

The quality of self-study materials is important, but their ultimate success will depend to a large extent on the provision of effective *student support*. Most laymen tend to think of ODL as operating at a distance with students studying in isolation, and to an extent this may be true, but one of the prime factors ensuring the success of ODL is the support provided in a variety of forms by tutors. This then is the focus of the fourth group of aims.

For educators and government officials contemplating the setting up of open and distance learning, one of the major attractions is its perceived *cost-effectiveness* when compared with traditional face-to-face teaching (FFT). You will in fact find that cost-effectiveness is dependent on ODL reaching out to relatively large numbers of students, and the next group of aims highlights some of the things that approaches to ODL must do if they are to be cost-effective.

Needless to say, although the cost-effectiveness of ODL may be important, it is equally important to ensure that the teaching provided is of the highest possible quality. Although it is important in any system of teaching to ensure that the quality of the teaching is as high as possible, it is even more important in ODL where teaching reaches out to large numbers of students and the teaching tends to be much more open to public inspection than traditional forms of face-to-face teaching. In any approach to ODL emphasis should therefore be placed on ensuring *the quality of materials and systems* to be used.

In the text that follows you will find discussion of the aims referred to above. Do reflect carefully on these, and identify those that appear relevant to any approach to ODL that you might hope to develop in your own area.

1.1 Opening access to education

Most developers of ODL are concerned with opening up education to a wider range of students. In the text that follows we will consider how ODL typically attempts to *open up education to students wherever they might be located* and how it tries to *increase access to education by removing unnecessary barriers*.

Open up education to students wherever they might be located

In its early days the UK Open University (the UK OU) gained particular recognition for the way in which it opened up opportunities for learning for UK students regardless of where they were located. It did this through the development of new, and more effective, methods of 'distance teaching'. The basic philosophy was to take teaching out to students in their homes, their place of work, or other easily accessible centres rather than to bring students to the teachers. Initially the UK OU concentrated on reaching out to students throughout the UK, but it was not long before it began reaching out to students beyond its national boundaries – initially to students on overseas military bases and in parts of the Commonwealth – and now, with the help of on-line teaching, it is reaching out to students from all corners of the globe on an increasing number of courses (for example, on the MA in Open and Distance Education).

Increase access to education by removing unnecessary barriers

Although distance teaching has an important role to play in opening up education to students, access to education can also be improved by removing unnecessary barriers. The way in which the UK OU has tried to remove such barriers may help stimulate your thinking on this subject.

When it was established in 1969, the UK OU believed that traditional university entry requirements were an unnecessary barrier for many of its potential students, and from the beginning, although it advised applicants on what they would need to be able to do in order to cope with particular programmes of study, it left the decision on whether or not to enrol in the hands of the student. The university wanted to open its doors as wide as possible to potential students, and its name reflects this policy of open access.

Some institutions fear such an open policy, believing that failure to filter out less qualified students will lead to an inevitable lowering of standards of achievement. The Open University's response was to set clear standards to be achieved on their courses, ensuring that the standards set compared with those on similar courses in other institutions of higher education. However, where there were considerable discrepancies in initial knowledge, it was inevitable that less qualified students would need more time and support to achieve the standards set, and this tended to place them under considerable pressure. One of the solutions developed was to produce preparatory courses for each of the foundation courses, so that less qualified students could acquire an agreed level of knowledge and skills at a more leisurely pace prior to enrolment on the related foundation courses. In doing this the university opened its doors to many less qualified students who would otherwise have been unable to benefit from a higher education.

Over the years the UK OU has been very much concerned with opening access to students through the removal of unnecessary barriers and through the development and exploitation of distance teaching methods. However, not all institutions involved in open and/or distance learning place the same emphasis on this aspect. For example, at the time of writing, both the National Autonomous University of Mexico (UNAM) and the National

Polytechnic Institute (IPN) in Mexico City have separate Open Education Units and Distance Teaching Units. In both institutions the prime purpose of the Open Education Units is to open up higher education to well-qualified students who have been unable to obtain traditional university places. However, the Open Education Units do very little teaching at a distance. Although students are provided with self-study materials, they are generally required to attend the central institution for tutorials and examinations, and the majority of students involved tend to live locally. In contrast, the Distance Teaching Units have used distance teaching to provide up-grading for professionals (such as social workers, nurses, managers, lawyers and engineers). However, their openness in terms of access has been somewhat limited in so far as the courses require traditional entry qualifications. Clearly the two institutions have developed different approaches to openness compared with that adopted by the UK OU.

1.2 Responding to student needs

Most institutions involved in open and distance learning place considerable emphasis on the importance of responding to student needs, and as such follow what is usually described as 'a student-centred' or 'learner-centred approach'. One way of responding to student needs is to *allow students as much freedom as possible to determine their own goals*. Needless to say, we cannot help individuals to achieve their goals unless they want to be helped and have identified the goals they want to achieve. We should therefore do all we can to *help students to recognise their potential* – encouraging them to think rationally about what they would like to achieve and the benefits they might derive from this process. We also need to encourage them to see the process of self-development as ongoing, and as such we should do as much as possible to *encourage lifelong learning*.

Allow students as much freedom as possible to determine their own goals

Students are more likely to be motivated to achieve specified goals if they perceive them as important and relevant to their needs (Stotland, 1969), and one of the best ways of ensuring this is to give students as much freedom as possible to determine their own goals (Rogers, 1969).

In its early days the UK OU offered students a very limited degree of choice – largely because it felt that it had to establish its credibility as a university among its peers, and it therefore concentrated initially on the development of a sound undergraduate programme. This meant that the only courses open to students were within specific degree programmes, and as such they appealed to a very limited group of students. A wider range of courses was subsequently developed outside the undergraduate programme under the umbrella of Continuing Education. Covering such areas as health and social welfare, the new courses provided students with a much wider range of choice, but to an extent this was initially limited by the fact that students were required to enrol either on courses within the continuing education area or on an undergraduate programme. The barriers between the two areas have since been largely removed with students being encouraged to enrol on whatever courses they wish to take – regardless of whether these lead to a degree or not. However, they are clearly advised as to which courses, or combination of courses, can be counted for credit towards certificates, diplomas and related degrees.

Further freedom of choice is encouraged through student projects which are to be found on a wide range of courses throughout the university. In encouraging students to identify their own goals, the hope is that this will encourage them to become involved in the process of learning, that they will gain satisfaction and pleasure from what they do, and will be encouraged to take their studies further.

Help students to recognise their potential

One way of way of encouraging self-development is to expose students to situations and problems that make them aware of their existing limitations and the benefits that might be derived from further self-development. For example, students might be exposed to new ideas and new ways of seeing things through television programmes, visits to new environments, through special articles, and group discussions which challenge their way of perceiving things. However, care must be taken to ensure that such activities take place in a supportive environment, ensuring that such challenges are not perceived as threatening (Smith, 1980).

The logic behind such an approach is provided by Hunt (1971) who argues that the conceptual understanding of individuals moves progressively forward from simple to more complex levels, but with the risk of development being arrested at any given level if individuals feel satisfied with their existing level of conceptualisation. Further development then depends on individuals feeling dissatisfied in some way with their existing concepts, and with this in mind he recommends exposing individuals to situations and problems which challenge their existing concepts without overwhelming them.

Encourage lifelong learning

There is no doubt that all our lives are affected by the process of change. We are constantly being asked to function in different ways in our jobs (new methods of management), to operate new types of equipment (computers and other high technology devices), and to digest new forms of information (research findings), and we need to continually update our knowledge, understanding and skills.

The idea that education and self-development over a limited period of early life can meet our lifelong needs is no longer valid. Instead, education and self-development need to be perceived as an ongoing process that enables us not only to cope with change but also to develop continuously throughout life in a process of lifelong learning. Self-development is not something that is achieved over a limited number of formative years in life, but is an ongoing process throughout life.

The UK OU has attempted to respond positively to the needs of lifelong learning by welcoming students of all ages and by offering them a wide range of courses to meet their perceived needs.

1.3 The design of self-study materials

Self-study materials have an important part to play in ODL, and their effectiveness depends to a large extent on the strategies incorporated into them. A whole range of strategies could be mentioned, but I will limit my comments to three particularly important ones. The first would appear to be self-evident, and that is that in developing self-study materials you should *ensure that self-study materials are structured in a logical manner*. The second strategy, very typical of ODL, is to *make use of a multi-media approach to facilitate learning* – selecting the most appropriate medium, or combination of media, for teaching and learning purposes. The intent is to enable students to use their senses to optimum effect. The third strategy is to build activities into self-study materials that will *encourage deep rather than superficial learning*. This strategy is particularly relevant to those involved in higher education.

Ensure that self-study materials are structured in a logical manner

All too often students are introduced to concept after concept without knowing where this is taking them. Cognitive theory (Ausubel, 1968) suggests that detailed learning should be presented within a logical framework, and that from the beginning students should be aware of the logical relationships between the various components. At no point in the learning process should students be unclear as to what they have achieved or how this will contribute towards the goals to be achieved. According to Ausubel, the provision of a broad framework along the lines indicated will in fact facilitate the assimilation of the more detailed learning to follow with the framework becoming an integral part of the cognitive structure.

Similarly, behaviourist theory (Tyler, 1949; Mager, 1962; Popham, 1969) suggests that the goals to be achieved and the means of achieving them should be clearly identified. Students should also be provided with help and guidance to achieve their goals, and their achievements should gain appropriate recognition. Students need to see that they are making progress and need to feel that the goals ahead are achievable if they are to make further progress.

Make use of a multi-media approach to facilitate learning

A great deal can be taught in any given medium, but the ability to use a variety of media can considerably strengthen the process of teaching and learning. The examples that follow illustrate two quite different ways in which this might be achieved.

In helping students to learn a foreign language it would be difficult to imagine how listening and speaking skills could be developed without students being able to listen to the language being spoken, and there is little doubt that some form of audio-medium would be required for this purpose. Likewise, it would be difficult to imagine how effective reading and writing skills could be developed without textual materials. In a language course we might therefore expect to see students moving backwards and forwards from one medium to another – from text to audio to video to text, and so on – but this is just one of the ways in which a variety of media might be used.

In contrast, there will be times when it makes sense for students to use a combination of media at one and the same time. For example, a student performing an experiment might find it helpful to be provided with instructions on an audio cassette, since this would leave his hands free to manipulate the equipment and to make notes and his eyes would be free to make careful observations. In this case the student is making use of a combination of media at one and the same time.

Courses, or programmes, that make use of a variety of media 'multiple media' – either sequentially or in combination – might be described as 'multi-media' in nature. In recent years the term multi-media has come to be increasingly associated with computer programs – highlighting the extent to which computers are able to make use of a variety of media (including text, graphics, pictures, sound and video). Unfortunately, the term has been somewhat abused with far too many computer programs being described as multi-media when they offer little more than on-line textual interaction. The use of a computer does not make a programme multi-media, and it is up to programme developers to demonstrate that their products are multi-media in the widest sense before making such claims. Daniel (1996, p. 121) places the subject in perspective in the following terms:

> Most of the mega-universities already call themselves multi-media distance teaching systems. Until now, however, the various component media of those teaching systems have come on separate supports. It is now possible to combine several of the media that deliver a particular set of course materials on a single support, CD-ROM being the leading current technology for this purpose.

Encourage deep rather than superficial learning

Where students are studying in isolation, as is often the case in open and distance learning, it is all too easy for them to adopt what Marton and Saljo (1976) describe as 'a surface approach' to learning – tending to concentrate on memorising facts and detailed information without reflecting on the underlying assumptions and arguments. What is required, particularly in higher education, is what Marton and Saljo describe as 'a deep approach' to learning – that is an approach where students concentrate more on understanding the overall message that is being conveyed and the assumptions on which it is based. Considerable efforts have been made in the UK OU to encourage a deeper approach to learning through the building of activities and projects into courses.

The building of activities and projects into courses will not in itself result in a deeper form of learning, for activities and projects may be designed in a variety of different forms to meet a variety of different needs. At the simplest level they may be designed to provide students simply with a means of checking their knowledge and understanding or their ability to apply newly acquired knowledge to new situations. They may be designed with a view to helping students develop specific skills – such as those of problem-solving, decision-making, and communication. However, at a more ambitious level, they may be designed with a view to encouraging students to take on more responsibility for what they do and what they learn – helping them to take greater control of their own learning.

According to the purposes for which they are intended, projects and activities may have a variety of different formats. At one extreme they may provide students with very precise guidance, leaving control very much in the hands of the teacher, while at the other extreme they may be very open-ended with control very much more in the hands of the student. In a careful study of the nature of activities Lockwood (1992) in his book *Activities in Self-Instructional Texts* provides numerous examples of different types of activity, while Henry (1994) in her book *Teaching through Projects* provides a wide range of examples of project formats. Both authors stress the importance of being clear as to the purpose of the activity or project to be developed, and both provide a wealth of advice on the actual development of activities and projects.

In recommending the use of activities and projects to encourage deep learning, it is recognised that students often have quite distinct preferences as to how they learn. Some may enjoy learning through activities and project work, while others may find such an approach difficult and frustrating. Some may be happy to read texts on their own, while others may find this tedious and boring. Some may prefer a more visual approach enjoying watching television or video programmes, while others may prefer the stimulus and learning that might be achieved through small group discussions. Where students are able to make use of their preferred learning styles it is recognised that learning can be enhanced (Dunn, 1984).

However, it is also recognised that students can develop new learning styles (Bargar and Hoover, 1984; Hyman and Rosoff, 1984; Joyce, 1984) thereby increasing the variety of ways in which they might learn, but where students are expected to develop new learning styles of learning they need to be given appropriate guidance and support. The UK OU attempts to provide this sort of guidance and support not only in helping students to develop project-related skills, but also in helping them to develop basic study skills.

1.4 Student support

However well designed self-study materials may be, there will inevitably be occasions when students will need further support. The most obvious form of support is that required to solve academic or personal problems, but for students studying in isolation moral support may be equally important. Although we might provide various forms of support through residential schools and local tutorials, this is likely to be on an occasional basis, and we also need make every effort to *ensure that appropriate support is available to students as and when they need it.*

You may well decide to develop the type of support systems that are used within the UK OU (see Chapter 4), making use of tutors, counsellors, and self-help groups. However, *ensure that the support provided takes into account local conditions* – the type of students involved and the local environment.

Ensure that appropriate support is available to students as and when they need it

Because of the requirements in terms of organisation and cost, some forms of support may be on an occasional basis. Thus within the UK OU assignments and tutorials on many courses may be offered no more than once a month, while residential schools may be offered only once during the presentation of a course and sometimes not at all. Such support may have a very important part to play in a course, but at the same time it may do little to respond to the ongoing, day-to-day needs of the student.

Additional support is needed on a more regular, ongoing basis. Don't forget that students are likely to spend the vast majority of their study time in their homes or in the place of work, and they need regular ongoing support. This might best be provided through interpersonal contacts with tutors, and fellow students – with these being sustained through such mechanisms as telephone contacts, telephone conferences, local meetings, computer links, computer-conferencing and video-conferencing to mention but a few.

A similar point may be made with regard to the actual availability of courses. Most institutions offer courses at fixed points in time, and if those enrolling on them have to wait substantial periods of time before commencing their studies, they may well lose much of their motivation and may well drop out before the course begins. Ideally students should be able to take up their studies as and when they see the need without encountering unnecessary barriers of time. The way in which things are gradually changing in the UK OU may help you to reflect on these issues. Most courses within the university are still presented at fixed points in time during the year (typically running from February through to October), but an increasing number are now being repeated at different times within the academic year. It is also possible for individuals to enrol on a few on-line courses at any time they wish, commencing their studies when they are ready to do so.

Ensure that the support provided takes into account local conditions

The UK OU was established with mature students in mind, and early studies by McIntosh and Woodley (1980) supported the view that student performance within this system increased with increasing maturity up to thirty years of age, levelling off beyond this point.

There are many reasons why mature students tend to prefer the type of opportunities offered by the UK OU. It may be that they wish to continue working for financial reasons or to avoid interrupting their careers. They may wish to remain at home to look after their children. They may be disabled and unable or unwilling to attend more traditional institutions of learning, or they may live in remote areas and are unable to pursue their studies by other means. Whatever the reason, the main point is that they have chosen to pursue their studies through the UK OU. This is their preference. They tend to be mature, well-motivated individuals, who are able to cope well with the type of learning environment provided by the UK OU.

The support systems provided within the UK OU are described in some detail in Chapter 4. However, they are not the only form of support systems that can be developed, and, if you are thinking of providing ODL for very young students, quite different forms of support systems may well be needed. An example may illustrate the point.

In the late 1970s the government of Indonesia determined to make nine years of basic education universally available. However, in 1979, recognising that there were not enough schools and teachers in the conventional Junior High School System to implement this policy within its existing five-year plan, the government decided to make use of open and distance learning to achieve its objectives, and set up a pilot system of Open Junior High Schools (Sekolah Nenengah umum Tingkat Pertama Terbuka, usually referred to as the SMPT). The unusual feature of this system (compared with systems for more mature students) was the way in which students were to be supervised in their work.

'Learning Centres' were set up in local communities – in whatever buildings were available, but often in existing primary schools with studies taking place outside normal primary school hours. Supervisors were recruited *to supervise* the students and to provide them with essential guidance, but *not to teach*, since the supervisors were not expected to be qualified Junior High School teachers. Instead students were expected to study centrally provided, self-study materials.

Small clusters of Learning Centres were each linked to a centrally located 'Mother School' – a conventional Junior High School – with each Mother School being responsible for all aspects of teaching within the related cluster. Once a week students were expected to attend classes in the Mother School – for group discussions, problem-solving, laboratory work, tape-slide presentations, television viewings, assessment, and so on. In turn the Mother School was responsible for ensuring that activities ran smoothly within the related Learning Centres, and two-way radio links were specially developed to provide ongoing support to both students and supervisors.

1.5 Cost-effectiveness

For educators and government officials contemplating the setting up of open and distance learning, one of the major attractions of ODL is the perception that it is much more cost-effective than face-to-face teaching (FFT) in traditional institutions. This is a very important claim to make, and needs to be justified, but as we shall see in the text that follows there is a wealth of data to support the claim, so long as the student numbers involved are relatively high. It follows that in developing systems of ODL it is important to *optimise student numbers* if the system developed is to be cost-effective.

As we shall see, increasing student numbers to the levels required is extremely difficult, if not impossible, if central academics are expected to undertake such tasks as the provision of tutorials, helping students to overcome their problems, undertaking student assessment, and so on. If student numbers are to be expanded to the levels that will ensure the cost-effectiveness of the system, careful consideration will need to be given to how this might be achieved. In the text that follows it will be argued that the way of achieving this is to *decentralise the student support systems*.

Optimise student numbers

The following should give you some idea of how the costs of ODL and FFT have been compared, and at the same time should provide you with

16 *Aims of open and distance learning*

some indication of the extent to which ODL appears to be more cost-effective than FFT.

One of the main differences between ODL and FFT is the fact that the fixed costs of ODL (course development costs, central institutional costs, regional institutional costs, and so on) tend to be much higher than those of FFT, while the variable costs of ODL (such as that of student support which depends on student numbers) tend to be much lower per student when the number of students involved is relatively high. In an early study that took this fully into account, Laidlaw and Layard (1974) concluded that when student numbers in the UK OU exceeded 21,691 it became more cost-effective than FFT in other British universities, with the cost benefits beyond this threshold increasing with increasing student numbers.

In a similar study Rumble (1987) noted that the minimum numbers required on UK OU courses to make them more cost-effective than their counterparts varied from course to course. For example, he noted that the break-even point on one of the early Foundation Courses (A100) occurred when student numbers reached 2,658 while the break-even point on one of the Post Foundation Courses (S22-) occurred when student numbers reached 800. This is not surprising, as the UK OU invests far more money in the development and subsequent support of Foundation Courses than on Post Foundation Courses – in part because it is assumed that students at Foundation Level need more support and in part because the greater numbers enrolled on Foundation Courses justify a greater investment.

Rumble's study provides confirmation of the fact that the cost of ODL courses depends very much on what is invested in them, and this suggests that in making comparisons between ODL and FFT we need to ensure that we are comparing courses of similar quality. One way of trying to achieve this is to compare the costs of students graduating within the respective systems, as this focuses attention on success rates and drop-out rates, and as such provides some indication of the relative qualities of the systems being compared.

From a study that took drop-out rates into account, Wagner (1977) concluded that the annual recurrent cost of supporting a full-time undergraduate in the UK OU was less than one-third of the cost of supporting an undergraduate in a traditional FFT university. In reviewing the data Wagner noted that students enrolling on undergraduate courses in FFT universities were likely to have at least two Advanced Level Certificates, whereas students enrolling with the UK OU were likely to be much less qualified. With this in mind he concluded that his figures underestimated the financial advantages of the UK OU, since more input was required to produce graduates within the OU than in its FFT counterparts.

Since cost-effectiveness is such an important issue, you may well want to look into it in much greater depth. If so, you will find an excellent introduction to the techniques of cost comparison in Keegan's book, *Foundations of Distance Education* (1996, pp. 165–183). You will also find data from a wide range of cost-effectiveness studies in Daniel's book *Mega-Universities and Knowledge Media* (1996, pp. 31, 60–65) and in Moore and Kearsley's book *Distance Education: A Systems View* (1996, pp. 71–74). All come to essentially the same conclusion, namely, that ODL can be extremely cost-effective, so long as it is delivered on a large enough scale to amortise the high costs of investment required.

Decentralise student support systems

One of the commonest mistakes in setting up ODL systems is to create a highly centralised system that is impossible to expand. Starting in a small way, central academics are often asked not only to develop self-study packages for students but also to provide tutorials and undertake subsequent assessment of students. The problem with such a system is that if student numbers increase, the academic workload increases, and central academics find themselves spending most of their time in course maintenance rather than in developing new courses. Central academics soon become overloaded, and further expansion of student numbers becomes impossible.

What is required is a system in which student numbers can easily be expanded without overstretching the resources available. The usual way of doing this is to recruit tutors in the regions to provide students with local support – undertaking such tasks as the provision of tutorials and the assessment of students in their locality. This leaves central academics free to concentrate on the development of further courses. This makes a lot of sense for a number of reasons.

Tutors can be recruited on a part-time basis at less expense than central academics. They often already have jobs as teachers or lecturers in the regions, and are likely to be taking on the job for a variety of reasons. It may be that it will open up further career opportunities, they may find it valuable to gain access to study materials developed by experts in the field, it could be that they are doing it for the extra financial benefits, but, whatever the reason, they do not have to be as highly qualified as the central academics developing the study materials, and can be recruited much more cheaply.

When student numbers increase, all one has to do is increase the student support staff in the regions – the tutors in particular – and central academics concerned with the development of study materials will remain largely unaffected by any such expansion.

The need to keep a clear distinction between central academics (involved in course development) and tutors (providing student support) applies even where all teaching and student support is on-line. It is still important to be able to increase student numbers if related courses are to be cost-effective, and, for all the reasons already given, one of the best ways of achieving this is to recruit tutors to provide student support. The

18 *Aims of open and distance learning*

only difference is that, since the support to be provided is to be on-line, the tutors may be located almost anywhere in the world. There may be a preference to recruit tutors in the home country, as it is useful to be able to get tutors together for training purposes, but even this can be undertaken on-line.

The issue of cost-effectiveness is of particular interest in that it highlights some major differences between ODL and FFT systems, and the following are worth noting:

- Setting up ODL courses requires a much higher initial investment than equivalent FFT courses, and this needs to be offset against the recurrent cost-benefits of teaching large numbers of students in ODL.
- Student support in FFT is highly centralised, but in ODL needs to be decentralised to facilitate student expansion and the cost benefits to be derived from this.
- In FFT most of the teaching time of central academics is devoted to providing students with face-to-face support. In contrast, most of the teaching time of central academics in ODL is spent on the development of new courses.
- So long as student numbers exceed the necessary threshold, the cost of supporting students in ODL is very much less than that of supporting students in FFT.

1.6 The quality of materials and systems

It is always important to try to ensure that teaching is of the highest possible quality, but this is even more important in the case of ODL where self-study materials go out to large numbers of students and are usually much more open to public inspection than teaching in FFT institutions. It is therefore especially important in ODL to ensure the quality of the self-study materials and student support systems.

Ensure that self-study materials and student support systems are of the highest possible quality

The best way of ensuring the quality of ODL is by building quality assurance and quality control procedures into the development process, and the way in which this might be achieved is discussed in detail in Part 2.

In perspective

The aims highlighted in this chapter are reflected within many approaches to ODL, and you should give them careful consideration in thinking about what you would like to achieve in developing your own approach to ODL. However, the aims should not be perceived as a definitive list excluding all

Opening access to education

   Open up education to students wherever they might be located

   Increase access to education by removing unnecessary barrier

Responding to student needs

   Allow students as much freedom as possible to determine their own goals

   Help students to recognise their potential

   Encourage lifelong learning

The design of self-study materials

   Ensure that self-study materials are structured in a logical manner

   Make use of a multi-media approach to facilitate learning

   Encourage deep rather than superficial learning

Student support

   Ensure that appropriate support is available to students as and when they need it

   Ensure that the support provided takes into account local conditions

Cost-effectiveness

   Optimise student numbers

   Decentralise student support systems

The quality of materials and systems

   Ensure that self-study materials and student support systems are of the highest possible quality

Figure 1.1 Typical aims underlying approaches to ODL

others. Educators involved in developing more traditional approaches to teaching and learning have for decades based their goals on principles derived from such fields as cognitive psychology, stimulus-response theory, social psychology, and from research into personal motivation and interpersonal behaviour. At a time when ODL was still in its infancy Hilgard and Bower (1975, pp. 608–609) identified over twenty principles of teaching and learning derived from such fields. Based on related research, these principles identify ways of facilitating learning, and are readily converted into goals to be achieved within approaches to ODL. Although only a few of these principles have been expressed in the form of aims within this chapter, it does not imply that they are not important, but simply that they are not perceived by the author as being critical to the development of ODL. Having said this, those involved in the development of ODL often have other goals in mind and you may well wish to include others in any approach which you might develop.

Suggestions

I would suggest that you make careful notes on the aims that appear to be relevant to your own particular needs, so that you can take these into account in thinking about the type of approach to ODL that you would like to develop in your own area.

I would also suggest that you encourage some of your colleagues to discuss with you the things that can be achieved through ODL (Figure 1.1), and that you reflect on the extent to which it might be relevant to your perceived needs. The point is that, if you hope to develop an approach to ODL in your own area, you will need the help and approval of your institution, and the sooner you get your colleagues involved in discussing the issues the better it will be. At this point in time some aims will appear more relevant to your situation than others, and it would make sense to talk about what you might realistically achieve in both the short term and the longer term.

Part 2
Characteristics of ODL

In this part of the book we will be focusing on such issues as the design of self-study materials, the ways in which media might be used, and the type of student support systems that are so essential to the success of ODL. In other words we will be looking at factors that need to be taken into account in designing materials and systems for ODL. Before getting into such detail it is important to ensure that we have a common understanding of what we are referring to when we talk about open and distance learning, and we will therefore begin in Chapter 2 by taking a look at **the broad characteristics of ODL**. We will then go on to look at the main components of ODL in turn, namely, the design of self-study materials, the type of media that may be used, and the type of student support systems that can be provided.

In Chapter 3 we will look at **the design of self-study materials**. This is not only about the structuring of the materials themselves, but also about providing students with essential guidance. Such guidance may be integrated together with the materials to be studied, it may be contained in a separate study guide, or it may be a combination of these options. However, the type of guidance required remains the same regardless of where it is located.

In the next chapter we will go on to talk about **the use of media in ODL** and the variety of ways in which it might be exploited to facilitate student learning. This will include discussion of both traditional media and more recent high technology developments. Although the review reflects on the strengths of individual media, attention is also given to the way in which the power of a medium might be considerably enhanced by using it in combination with other carefully selected media.

Although great emphasis is placed on the development of high quality self-study materials, there will always be students requiring help and guidance with their studies and students who will need help to sort out particular problems, and in Chapter 5 we will take a look at the type of **student support systems** that are typically developed in ODL to provide students with the type of support that is so essential.

The intent is to provide you with a picture of the range of options available to you and the logic behind the use of the various components discussed. Following your study of Part 1 you should already have a good idea of the main things you might achieve through the development of ODL in your own area, and this part of the book is intended to help you to determine the type of materials and systems you would need to develop in order to realise these aims.

2 The broad characteristics of ODL

Contents

Introduction 23
2.1 Enrolling on a course 24
2.2 The broad characteristics of courses 31
2.3 The type of parameters that need to be defined 37
In perspective 39
Suggestions 40

Introduction

The aim in this chapter is to introduce you to the broad characteristics of open and distance learning, doing this initially by following a student in the process of *enrolling on a course*. The idea is try to perceive ODL through the eyes of a student as she is introduced to open and distance learning for the first time. The course on which she enrols is one in German within the UK OU, and is chosen not so much because it is typical of the type of courses on offer, but rather because, once we have looked at the main characteristics of this particular course, it is much easier to talk about *the broad characteristics of courses* in general and the features they have in common.

We will then go on to look more closely at the way in which undergraduate courses within the UK OU are defined in terms of study time and credit ratings. In doing this the intent is not to suggest that you use the same parameters to define your own courses, but rather that you take note of *the type of parameters that need to be defined* from the outset. Without such definitions you will find that colleagues have very different ideas as to what constitutes a course: the amount of time that students might be expected to set aside for related study purposes, the credits that might be awarded for successful completion of a course, and the way in which such course credits might contribute towards academic awards.

2.1 Enrolling on a course

Let us take the case of Elizabeth, a teacher of eight to twelve year olds who has been asked to take on responsibility for teaching the older children in her school to 'Get by in German'. Having what she feels is a rather limited background in German, she has decided to improve her knowledge and skills by enrolling on the UK Open University's German language course 'Auftakt: get ahead in German'.

In the text that follows you will be able to see how she first learnt about the courses on offer and how she went about *obtaining initial information* about the UK OU and the course itself. You will see the extent to which she was given *support prior to registration* to help her to decide whether the course was likely to meet her needs and whether she would be able to cope with it. Following registration for the course, you will gain some insight into the type of *self-study materials* that she received through the post and the help she was given in sorting them out. One of the most important documents she received was a booklet which provided her with a very informative *introduction to the course*. We will join her just after she has read the introductory comments, and you will see that she now feels that she has a good idea of what the course is all about. In fact, she now feels ready to begin her studies, and at this point turns to *the study guide* which has a central role to play not only in providing her throughout her studies with the guidance she will need, but also including much of the core material that she will need to study.

Obtaining initial information

Elizabeth learnt about the course from a newspaper advertisement, and decided to obtain more information about what was involved. In response to her query she was sent an information pack about the university as a whole. Contained within it was a booklet identifying the full range of courses available across the university, the requirements for different types of qualifications, the broad characteristics of the courses and the type of support that would be provided, together with introductory information on each of the courses on offer. Apart from a summary of the range of courses offered by the Centre for Modern Languages, the booklet contained a brief description of the course in which Elizabeth was interested, and you will find a copy of this in Figure 2.1.

Support prior to registration

Not being sure whether she would be able to cope with the course, as it required some prior knowledge of German, Elizabeth sought further advice from her regional study centre, and was able to meet with a counsellor who talked her through what was involved. He also encouraged her

Modern languages

Our Level 1 language courses are for those who want to consolidate and build on their knowledge of French or German in order to communicate more effectively. They use printed, audio and video materials to develop the practical skills of listening, reading, speaking and writing, together with an understanding of aspects of French and German society and culture.

Your knowledge of the language should be roughly equivalent to O-level, GCSE or Scottish standard Grades 1 and 2, but it need not be formal and could come from time spent in French or German-speaking countries, regular contact with French or German-speaking people, adult education classes or other sources. You can get self-diagnostic tests from any of our Regional Centres to help you to assess your language level before you decide whether to register.

As well as marking and commenting on your oral and written work your tutor will conduct occasional evening or weekend tutorials, which you are strongly encouraged to attend since they will give you the best opportunities to practise your speaking skill. You will receive a study guide, which offers a great deal of support and teaches good study skills and language-learning strategies.

The course assessment consists of several pieces of written work and some audio work designed to test each language skill. The examination at the end of the course is specially designed, like the course work, to assess each of the four language skills, so it will be held at special examination centres and you might have to travel some distance to the nearest one.

Each course makes extensive use of illustrations and video images and there is a strong emphasis on spoken language, so, although full transcripts of the audio and video cassettes are provided, you might be at a disadvantage if your hearing is severely impaired, less so if you have impaired sight. You can get more information and advice by answering the question about special needs on the reservation form.

Auftakt: get ahead in German (L130)

The course's four books, video and audio cassettes develop your confidence in understanding, speaking, reading and writing German. You will also gain a better understanding of, and insights into, aspects of everyday life in modern Germany and issues of concern to German people, particularly since unification.

Each book deals with themes such as aspects of life and living in Germany, people's origins and community life, the worlds of work and leisure, health and fitness, the environment, and life before and after unification. Each book is accompanied by a half-hour video and two audio cassettes. These were largely filmed and recorded in Leipzig, in the east, and Tübingen, in the west. You will see the course's topics

and issues in the context of these towns as well as in relation to the country as a whole. With each book a feature and drama cassette offers activities designed to help you with both speaking and understanding German, and an activity cassette is integrated with the text of the book. Each book clearly specifies the learning objectives for its stage of the course and provides model answers (*Lösungen*) for all the tasks. There are also audio cassettes for assessment purposes.

> This course contributes 30 points at Level 1 and is particularly suitable for inclusion in a BA degree. There is no residential school and the course fee is £272.

Ouverture: a fresh start in French (L120)

Cadences, the first of the course's two parts, uses the routines and traditions of French life to revise and consolidate your knowledge and bring everyone up to the same level in French. The second part, *Valeurs*, builds on this foundation to teach more advanced language in the context of topical issues in French society. Each part consists of four books to be studied in close integration with audio and video recordings.

The materials will enable you to use the language as you learn. A series of printed and audio language exercises, called *Activités*, provides both teaching and practice in the four skills. Each *Activité* has an answer in the *Corrigés* section at the back of the book. Some of the *Activités* are open-ended and model answers are given for those.

> This course contributes 30 points at Level 1 and is particularly suitable for inclusion in a BA degree. There is no residential school and the course fee is £272.

Figure 2.1 Example of early introduction to courses on offer
Source: Courses, Diplomas and BA/BSc Degrees, UK OU, 1997, p. 11

to take a self-diagnostic test to help assess her existing language level, pointing out that it would still be her decision as to whether she registered on the course, but that the information obtained would help determine how well prepared she was and whether there were things she might do to prepare herself for the course.

The feedback she received suggested that she should be able to cope quite well with the course, and she registered for it. However, bearing in mind that it was a long time since she had undertaken any form of formal study, she felt that she needed to get back into the habit of studying and to develop the skills she would require for the course. She therefore sent for the package of 'preparatory materials' which were specially designed for this purpose, and found them very helpful in refreshing her skills and raising her confidence. Now, three months after registering for the course, she has just received her first package of course materials.

Self-study materials

The first package of materials to arrive included a letter, 'Herzlich Willkommen', welcoming Elizabeth to the course and explaining that the package included roughly half of the materials that would be needed for the course – the materials for the second half to be sent later. The package itself contained an introduction to the course (the 'course guide'), a study guide (in the form of two books, covering the first two parts of the course – two parts still to follow), two videos, nine audio cassettes, transcripts for all of the items included on the audio and video cassettes, an assessment book, and a number of other items such as a course calendar and forms for assessment purposes. At first glance it all appeared somewhat overpowering, but, having checked off the items and taken note of others that she would need to obtain for herself (the essential German grammar and German dictionary and a number of optional books about Germany and German literature), Elizabeth sorted out the newly arrived materials so that they would be easily accessible when she needed them.

Fortunately she had watched an introductory television programme for new students during her preparatory stage, and, in the light of advice received, had prepared a special area to study in peace and quiet. She had a desk, shelves, and drawers for her personal use, and soon had the various materials sorted out in readily accessible places. Although a computer was not an essential requirement on this particular course, Elizabeth was fortunate in having one (for notes, assignments, e-mail, and for Internet resource materials). She also had a telephone (to contact her tutor and fellow students), the all-important tape recorder, and easy access to a television and video recorder in the next room.

Introduction to the course

Following the advice included in the welcome letter, Elizabeth began by looking at the introduction to the course. It began by explaining the aims of the course and the language skills that it hoped she would be able to develop as a result of her participation in the course. It provided an overview of all the self-study materials she had received in the package, described the content of each, the roles that they would play within the course, and provided tips on how to get the best use out of the various resources provided. It identified the equipment that she would need in order to study the course (a television, video recorder, an audio cassette recorder, etc.), and provided details of relevant sources of information (such as Internet websites, German radio and television programmes, and the Goethe Institut). It also provided details on how she would be assessed and included details on the type of support she could expect from her tutor.

The introduction to the course also drew Elizabeth's attention to a course calendar that had been provided along with other materials in the package. This highlighted key events in the life of the course: when it was assumed the study of various components would begin and end, the dates of related TV transmissions, the deadlines by which assignments had to be submitted during the presentation of the course, and the dates for the end-of-course examination when her language skills would be assessed. To these Elizabeth added the dates for her tutorials. Recognising that the calendar would very much determine the rate at which she would need to progress, she pinned it to the wall in a prominent position to help her keep the various events and deadlines in mind.

Shortly after receiving the package of self-study materials Elizabeth received a letter from her tutor in which he introduced himself and provided her with details on the tutorials he would be offering and on how he could be contacted. She found this very reassuring, and felt that despite being 'at a distance' she was being welcomed into a supportive environment.

The study guide

Following the guidance provided, Elizabeth is now turning to the study guide (the first of four books provided for this purpose). It contains the ongoing guidance that she will need throughout the course and a great deal of the core material that she will need to study.

The opening pages (Figure 2.2) contain a brief introduction to the course focusing in on the actual content. She sees that each part of the course includes a 30-minute video and two audio cassettes. Each video includes 'clips' of people in Germany talking about their ways of life, their work, their interests, and their hopes for the future, one of the audio

What is *Auftakt*?

Auftakt is a German course for individual adult learners studying on their own without the support of a classroom teacher, but is also suitable for use in adult education classes. It aims to help you, the learner, develop confidence in speaking, listening, reading and writing German, so that you will be able to communicate effectively and accurately in German. When you have worked through all four books you should have achieved a language level equivalent to just below A level standard.

How much German am I expected to know?

At the beginning of the course it is assumed that you will have an elementary knowledge of German. This means that you should be able to get by when visiting a German-speaking country and understand simple German speech in everyday contexts. You should have achieved the approximate level of GCSE or the equivalent of a rusty O level, either through formal classroom teaching or through regular contact with native speakers of German.

What does *Auftakt* consist of?

Course books

Auftakt consists of four graded books, *Auftakt 1, 2, 3* and *4*. The books are carefully structured to assist the learning process and can either be used separately or studied in sequence. They are divided into two sections, each with a distinct theme (*Thema*), and each *Thema* consists of four parts (*Teile*). The *Themen* are numbered sequentially through the course. The first three *Teile* introduce and practise new topics, language structures and grammar items, while the fourth provides revision and consolidation. Each *Teil* is further divided into three units, with one unit (*Lerneinheit*) representing roughly two hours of study.

Clear introductions, study charts and precise instructions will guide you through each part and activity of the course. In *Auftakt 1* and *2* these instructions are in English, but in *Auftakt 3* and *4* most of them are in German. In addition, there are study tips (*Lerntips*) to help you learn the language more effectively, and cultural background notes (*Wissen Sie das?*).

You will find a *Checkliste* at the end of *Teile 1–3*, which summarises the key learning points. Answers for each activity are provided at the end of the book in the *Lösungen* section. Both the *Lösungen* and *Checkliste* are designed to help you assess your progress through the book or throughout the course.

Audio-visual material

A 30-minute **video** accompanies each book. Filmed in two German towns – Leipzig, an industrial city in the east, and Tübingen, a smaller university town in the south – the video features a wide variety of German people talking about their ways of life, their work, their interests, their hopes for the future. Occasionally, where the language may be slightly difficult, German subtitles have been added. All video sections are clearly numbered for ease of use.

v

Figure 2.2 Introduction to Course L130, *Auftakt*, as presented in Study Guide
Source: Course L130: *Auftakt, Get by in German*, Book 1, UK OU, 1996, pp. v–vi

Two **audio cassettes** accompany each book. Cassette One opens with an episode of the drama (*Hörspiel*), which runs throughout the course. This is followed by a documentary feature (*Hörbericht*) linked to the main theme of each *Thema*. Both the drama and feature sections are followed by simple fluency and pronunciation activities and can be used independently of the course book. Cassette Two (*Übungskassette*) consists of numerous speaking and listening exercises, which are closely integrated into the main course-book activities.

Transcript booklets

There is a separate transcript booklet, containing transcripts of both the video and audio cassettes which accompany each book. The language is transcribed as it is actually spoken, that is with hesitations, incomplete utterances, repetitions and, occasionally, incorrect German.

Additional resources

To study *Auftakt* you will need a grammar book and dictionary. The writers of this course have referred to *The Oxford German Grammar* by William Rowlinson (available in paperback and mini-reference form) and the new *Langenscheidt Standard German Dictionary*. Furthermore, you will find the Open University's *The Language Learner's Good Study Guide* full of useful advice on all aspects of language learning.

German spelling

The German federal states have agreed to introduce changes in the spelling of some German words from 1 August 1998. The reform, which aims to simplify German spelling, is based on recommendations of a commission set up in 1988 by the Austrian government. The commission consisted of experts from Germany, Belgium, Denmark, Italy, Liechtenstein, Luxembourg, Austria, Romania, Switzerland and Hungary. New rules for spelling will be taught in German schools and introduced in all official documents, in the media, commerce and other institutions. It is expected that the process of change will be completed by 1 August 2005. These rules have not been applied in this book.

Viel Spaß und Erfolg beim Deutschlernen!

Figure 2.2 (continued)

cassettes includes a modern drama running parallel to the course followed by a series of documentary features linked to the main theme contained in the related part of the course, while the second audio cassette contains numerous speaking and listening exercises. She sees that the package also includes audio cassettes for assessing her listening skills.

She sees that each part of the course is broken down into two themes, and on the next page (Figure 2.3) sees an introduction to the first theme

Thema 1

Zwei deutsche Städte

The first *Thema* of *Auftakt* is called *Zwei deutsche Städte*. The two German cities are Tübingen in Baden-Württemberg and Leipzig in Sachsen (Saxony). *Thema 1* introduces you to these towns and to some local inhabitants, including students, people who have lived there all their lives, newcomers and families, who will describe where and how they live.

In the first part of the book, *Teil 1, Ein erster Eindruck*, you will take a tour round the two towns with the help of the video. In *Teil 2, Meine vier Wände*, you will listen to the first episode of the audio drama (*Hörspiel*), *Begegnung in Leipzig*, and work on describing places where you and other people live. *Teil 2* also includes an audio feature (*Hörbericht*), *Kein Platz für Autos*. *Teil 3, Hier wohne ich*, develops the theme of describing homes and helps you to express positive and negative opinions about homes and places.

Teil 4, Wiederholung, is a revision section, which will help you revise and consolidate the most important aspects of the work done in *Teile 1–3*. By the end of *Thema 1*, you should be familiar with aspects of Leipzig and Tübingen. You will have revised the basic grammar which you will need to help you progress through the course and you will have practised useful skills such as finding your way and describing and expressing opinions about where you live.

Figure 2.3 Breakdown of Course L130, *Auftakt*, into parts, themes, sections (*Teile*) and study sessions

Source: Course L130: *Auftakt, Get by in German*, Book 1, UK OU, 1996, p. 1

which is centred around two German cities (*Zwei deutsche Städte*). Reading about this she is encouraged to see how the course makes use of social and cultural settings to stimulate learning. Reading further she notes that the themes are broken down into sections (*Teile*), and thereafter into study sessions (*Lerneinheiten*), with each study session requiring on average about two hours of study. She likes the idea of the study sessions, as this will help her to plan her time more effectively.

Continuing to read she sees that the introduction to each study session (Figure 2.4) contains a study chart identifying the topics to be studied, the activities to be undertaken, and the key aims (or key points) of each of these activities. The activities referred to include a documentary feature (*Hörbericht*) and a series of speaking and listening exercises (*Übungskassette*) contained on separate audio cassettes.

Turning the pages further she can see that each study session contains a substantial number of activities, and that these are not only clearly identified (numbered), but that icons are used to identify the resources (audio, video, etc.) needed for each activity (see Figure 2.5). In the case illustrated the activities identified relate to the documentary feature (*Hörbericht*) on audio cassette.

At the end of each study session she sees that there is a checklist (Figure 2.6) identifying not only the things that she should be able to do on completion of the session, but also identifying related activities that she can use to check whether she has achieved the knowledge and skills required.

The main point to note is that although Elizabeth has not yet embarked on the actual study of her course, she feels that she already has a good idea of how she will be going about her studies and what she might hope to achieve through them.

In providing extracts from the study guide the intent has simply been to provide an indication of the type of role it has to play in facilitating student learning. In the next chapter we will in fact be looking much more closely at the type of features that may be built into study guides, and at that point we will give careful consideration to how such features might be constructed and what they might aim to achieve.

2.2 The broad characteristics of courses

Needless to say, if you were to examine a whole range of courses within the UK OU you would find considerable variations between them, but you would also find that they have a great deal in common. Every course team will produce an *introduction to the course*, and this will contain very much the same type of information as Elizabeth's German course. Every course will include *study guidance*, and although this may be presented at times in somewhat different formats, there will be considerable similarities between the type of advice provided on different courses. Similarly,

Auftakt 1

Lerneinheit 6 Zu viel Verkehr

Lerneinheit 6 is based almost entirely around the *Hörbericht, Kein Platz für Autos*, which describes Tübingen's traffic problems and how the town is trying to solve them. One particular solution which they are trying in their attempts to minimise the impact of the car is a housing development called Schafbrühl.

The three topics *Lerneinheit 6* covers are *Working on the feature*, which outlines the situation and what the people of Tübingen think about it; *Discussing the problem and a solution*, where you will practise interviewing and being interviewed; and *Summing up the situation.*

STUDY CHART

Topic	Activity and resource	Key points
Working on the feature	1 Text	checking relevant vocabulary
	2 *Hörbericht*	listening to *Kein Platz für Autos*
	3 *Hörbericht*	transcribing extracts from the feature
	4 *Hörbericht*	checking you've understood the feature
Discussing the problem and a solution	5 *Übungskassette*	being interviewed about Tübingen's traffic problems
	6 *Übungskassette*	answering questions about Schafbrühl
	7 Text	writing questions for an interview
Summing up the situation	8 *Hörbericht*	writing a summary of the feature

1 Before listening to the *Hörbericht* about Tübingen's traffic problems, study the list on page 39 of words which are used in it. Read the list through twice, then cover the English side and see how many meanings you can remember. Repeat the process if you feel you need to. At this stage you don't need to be able to use the German words, just understand them.

In Tübingen gibt es zu viele Autos, so wie in vielen anderen Städten Deutschlands auch. Nur sind die Verkehrsprobleme in Tübingen besonders schlimm. Warum?

38

Figure 2.4 Introduction to a study session (*Lerneinheit*) in Course L130, *Auftakt*
Source: Course L130: *Auftakt, Get by in German*, Book 1, UK OU, 1996, p. 38

Thema 1 *Teil 2*

erwerbstätig *employed*	**der Durchschnitt (-)** *average*	**der Bach (¨e)** *stream*
in der Lage sein, etwas zu machen *to be able, or in a position to do something*	**der Stau (-s)** *traffic jam*	**das Gemeinschaftsgefühl (-e)** *community feeling*
	der Lärm *noise*	**der Nachbar (-n)** *neighbour*
der Grundstückspreis (-e) *cost of land*	**am Rande** *on the edge, outskirts*	**sich begegnen** *to meet one another*
	der Innenhof (¨e) *courtyard*	**toll** *great, fantastic; literally: mad*
der Pendler (-) *commuter*	**der Teich (-e)** *pond*	

2 Hörbericht 1

Now listen to *Hörbericht 1* right through. Don't worry if you don't understand all of it, just pick up what you can. Then listen to it again and write down the answers to the following questions.

1 What percentage of people who work in Tübingen commute to work?
2 Why do they commute rather than live in the town?
3 What is the average number of people travelling in each car?
4 Where are cars allowed in Schafbrühl?
5 What three things do you know about Frau Patzwahl and her family?
6 Where was the recording of Frau Patzwahl made?
7 What is there in the courtyard by her house?
8 List the advantages of Schafbrühl that are mentioned, seen from Frau Patzwahl's point of view.

3 Hörbericht 1

To fill in the gaps in these sentences you will need words and short phrases from *Hörbericht 1*. Some have already been given in the vocabulary list in Activity 1, others you will find on the tape. Write out the sentences in full and check your answers.

1 Die _____ in der Stadt sind besonders schlimm.

2 Die meisten Pendler sind _____ _____ _____

   _____ die Miet- und Grundstückspreise zu bezahlen.

3 Die Autos _____ _____ _____ mit 1,1 Personen

   besetzt.

4 _____ _____ ist Tübingen praktisch eine Großstadt durch

   die Einpendler.

5 Schafbrühl ist eine neue _____ . Die Autos _____

   _____ _____ der Siedlung bleiben.

39

Figure 2.5 The use of icons identifying the nature of activities in Course L130, *Auftakt*

Source: Course L130: *Auftakt, Get by in German*, Book 1, UK OU, 1996, p. 39

Auftakt 1

Checkliste

By the end of *Teil 2* you should be able to

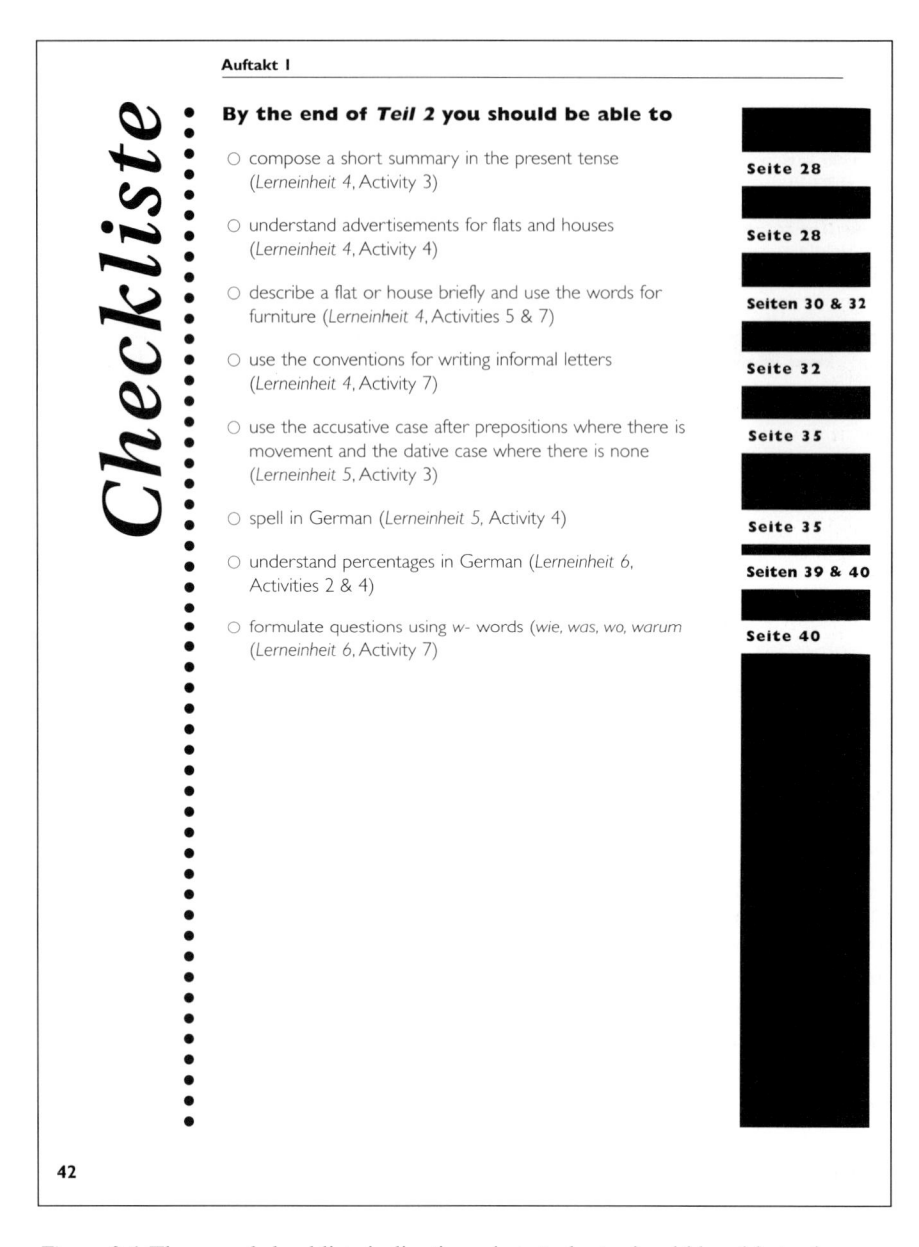

○ compose a short summary in the present tense (*Lerneinheit 4*, Activity 3) — **Seite 28**

○ understand advertisements for flats and houses (*Lerneinheit 4*, Activity 4) — **Seite 28**

○ describe a flat or house briefly and use the words for furniture (*Lerneinheit 4*, Activities 5 & 7) — **Seiten 30 & 32**

○ use the conventions for writing informal letters (*Lerneinheit 4*, Activity 7) — **Seite 32**

○ use the accusative case after prepositions where there is movement and the dative case where there is none (*Lerneinheit 5*, Activity 3) — **Seite 35**

○ spell in German (*Lerneinheit 5*, Activity 4) — **Seite 35**

○ understand percentages in German (*Lerneinheit 6*, Activities 2 & 4) — **Seiten 39 & 40**

○ formulate questions using *w-* words (*wie, was, wo, warum*) (*Lerneinheit 6*, Activity 7) — **Seite 40**

42

Figure 2.6 The use of checklists indicating what students should be able to do
Source: Course L130: *Auftakt, Get by in German*, Book 1, UK OU, 1996, p. 42

although every course team will determine for itself *the media to be used* and the *student support* to be provided, each team will choose from essentially the same wide range of options and will usually have access to the same range of expertise to put their ideas into practice. Let us consider each of these aspects in turn.

Introduction to the course

I am not aware of any course within the UK OU that has not produced an 'introduction to the course' along similar lines to that produced for Elizabeth's German course. The introductory material may be presented under some other title such as 'Course Guide', 'About the Course', and so on, it may make use of some other medium instead of the traditional brochure, but it will address very similar issues. For example, an introduction will normally provide an introduction to the more detailed learning to follow – highlighting the topics to be discussed and the relationships between them. It will identify the aims of the course, and will suggest possible study strategies that might be adopted to advantage. It will normally identify the type of resources that may be accessed, the equipment that may be needed, and will give instructions on how to use it. It will typically identify the type of support that students might expect from tutors, tutorials and so on, and will provide details on how students will be assessed. All of these aspects will be looked at much more closely in the next chapter.

Study guidance

Every course needs to provide students with appropriate guidance. In the case of the German course that we have just looked at, the guidance was integrated together with the actual materials to be studied. This has the advantage of guidance being provided as and when it is needed in close proximity to the material being studied.

Having said this, you will find times when the materials to be studied are not included in the actual study guide. It may be that students are advised to study a separate video, an audio cassette, an academic article, or some other such item, and on such occasions the guidance may be presented alone in the study guide (separate from the material to be studied). Conversely, the guidance may be integrated into the materials referred to, with the study guide simply referring students to the material. However, the main point to note is that the type of guidance required will be essentially the same regardless of where it is located.

In the next chapter we will be looking in some detail at the type of guidance that needs to be provided, but for the moment it is sufficient to say that it is likely to include many of the features that were contained in the study guide for the German course. Thus a typical study guide, apart from including much of the material to be studied, is likely to introduce students to each topic, identify the goals to be achieved, and include suggestions on possible study strategies. It will usually include a range of multi-media activities designed to involve students in the process of learning, and is likely to provide students with the means of monitoring their progress and determining whether they have achieved the intended goals. As you will see when we move on to the next chapter, these are simply some of the features that might be included in a study guide.

Once again, the guidance provided might be offered under some other heading. For example, in the case of Elizabeth's German course the study guides are simply referred to as books, but they have all the characteristics that one would expect to find in a study guide. Similarly, although the guidance provided in the case of the German course was in textual format, it could equally well be included in any preferred medium.

The above issues will all be expanded on in some detail in Chapter 3 in discussing the 'The design of self-instructional materials'.

The media to be used

In the case of Elizabeth's German course extensive use was made of textual materials (the four study guides/books, dictionaries, grammar books, etc.), audio cassettes, video cassettes and, to a more limited extent, television programmes. Within the UK OU it is up to course teams to determine the media that are most likely to meet their needs, and they have a wide range of media from which to choose. Other media that are widely used within the UK OU include academic articles, set books, home experiment kits, and computer software to mention the more obvious ones.

The variety of ways in which media might be exploited will be discussed in some detail in Chapter 4 in reflecting on 'The Use of Media' in ODL.

Student support

In the case of Elizabeth's German course student support was primarily provided through tutors, tutorials, and self-help groups. However, other forms of student support are used within the UK OU including audio-conferencing, computer-conferencing, residential schools, and so on. Once again, a wide range of options are available to course teams, and they have a degree of freedom in determining the type of support that they use.

Again, it is worth noting that on Elizabeth's German course students were advised on a range of resources that they might find helpful. These included recommended books, newspapers, magazines, German radio and TV programmes, and Internet resources. These are not the only possible resources that could have been used, and courses within the UK OU often encourage students to make use of other resources such as local libraries, the OU library website, and course websites.

The above issues will be addressed in much more detail in Chapter 5 in reflecting on the type of 'Student Support Systems' that are so essential to the success of ODL.

2.3 The type of parameters that need to be defined

When we left Elizabeth she was solely concerned with getting started on her German course and doing as well as she could. However, it is interesting to look ahead at some of the options that are available to her on completion of the present course if she would like to continue with her studies. She could in fact choose to study any of the courses available within the UK OU undergraduate programme, including other language courses, but three obvious options are worth noting. The first is for her to continue with further courses in German with a view to obtaining a Diploma in German. The second is to broaden her studies with a view to obtaining a Diploma in European Humanities with credit from her language courses contributing to the Diploma. The third option is to aim for either an Ordinary Degree or an Honours Degree, with her language courses contributing credit towards that end. To place these options in perspective let us take a look at how credits relate to awards within the UK OU system.

Undergraduate courses within the UK Open University are offered at three sequential levels, namely, levels 1–3. Elizabeth's German course is a first level course, and has what is referred to as a 30-point credit rating. In order to obtain a Diploma in European Humanities she would have to obtain 120 points from a selection of sixteen courses that are considered appropriate for this purpose. However, she would be limited to a maximum of 30 points from first level courses and a maximum of 60 from courses in modern languages.

Should Elizabeth ultimately decide to go for a degree she would need to accumulate a total of 360 points, with a maximum of 120 points being allowed to contribute towards the degree from first level courses. In other words, if she wishes, she could obtain the remaining 240 points from second-level courses. In contrast, if she should decide to go for an Honours Degree she would need to obtain a minimum of 120 of the remaining 240 points from third-level courses.

In common with most courses on offer in the UK OU (regardless of whether they are 30- or 60-point courses), Elizabeth's 30-point course is spread over a period of nine months from February to November, and is expected to involve the average student in 225 hours of study. Likewise, a 60-point course is expected to involve students in an average of 450 hours of study. Needless to say, all students are different and will require different amounts of time in which to complete their studies, but it is helpful for them to be aware of the time that the average student will need for the study of various course components. Every course team is in fact expected to estimate how much time the average student will need to spend on the

38 Characteristics of ODL

various course components, and this is normally checked out through subsequent evaluation. Course teams often produce quite different time estimates for very similar components, as this depends on the way in which these are to be used. However, it might be helpful to see an example (Figure 2.7) of the type of time estimates that are typically made for the main components in a course.

Study of units

2 hrs per study session
5 study sessions per unit
8 units within course
Time for basic study of 8 Units   *80 hrs*

Tutorials

5 tutorials in course
3 hrs per tutorial
Time for tutorials   *15 hrs*

Continuous examination and assessment

5 tutor-marked assignments (3 hrs each)
Examination (5 hrs)
Time for exams and assessment
Time for examination and assessment   *20 hrs*

Project work

Ongoing during second half of course
Time for project   *60 hrs*

Residential school

5 days for residential school during summer
8 hrs of contact per day
Time for residential school   *40 hrs*

Revision

Time set aside during final month for revision
Time for revision   *10 hrs*

Estimated Average Study Time for Course   **225 hrs**

Figure 2.7 Sample time estimates for study of components in a 30-point course

The broad characteristics of ODL 39

Bearing in mind that most students pursue their studies on a part-time basis, they usually do not undertake more than 60 points of study in a given year. They may take on more, but this tends to be discouraged, as experience indicates that this usually proves to be too much. This means that starting from scratch a degree is likely to take at least six years of study, although students who have gained credit from the University for prior qualifications can achieve a degree in a shorter period of time.

Before undertaking the design and development of courses for ODL, it is important to define the way in which credits will accumulate within the system you envisage and to be clear as to the relationship between credits and average study time.

In perspective

At this point it might be a good idea to stand back, and try to place the various components of ODL in perspective. I have tried to do this in Figure 2.8, where you will see that I have attempted to identify the inter-relationships between study guides/study guidance and the resources typically used in ODL.

In Figure 2.8 you will notice that I have used icons to represent the different media and resources typically used in ODL, but I have deliberately avoided using a book to represent the core learning and study guidance that might be contained in a study guide. This is because this may be contained in any preferred medium (textual, audio, video, on-line, etc.). However, once a medium has been chosen for this purpose, it makes sense

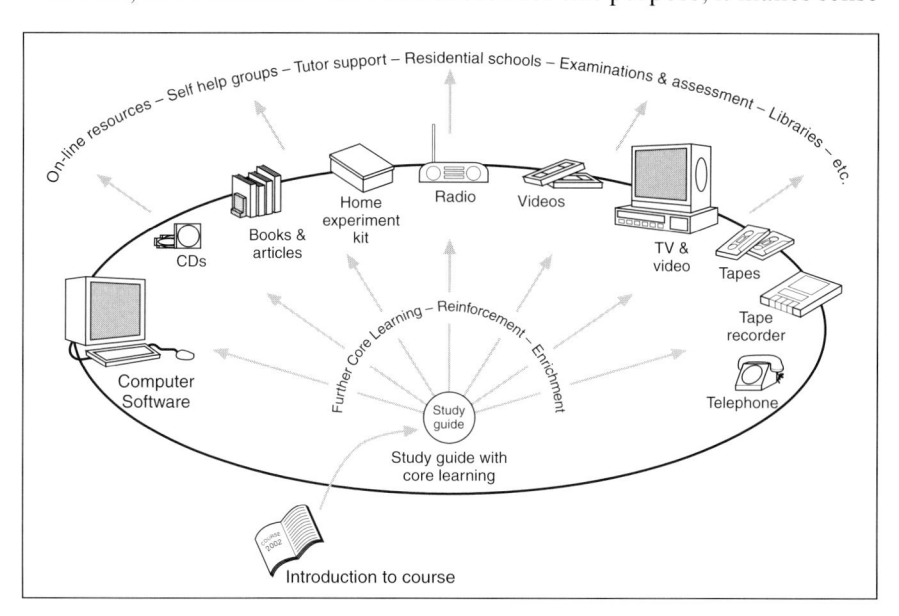

Figure 2.8 Course materials and resources for ODL

to stick to an obvious location within that medium for study guidance, so that students always know where to return for guidance. Within most courses within the UK OU that information still tends to be contained in textual format. However, where another medium is preferred (e.g. a computer-based medium) the same information might be placed within an appropriate location within that medium (e.g. accessed through an appropriate 'button' on the 'home page').

Within Figure 2.8 you will notice that I have referred to three types of learning: 'core learning', 'reinforcement', and 'enrichment'. We have already talked about the 'core learning' materials that might be included in the study guide, and these might be described as providing the basic knowledge, understanding and skills that we hope all students will acquire.

In contrast, 'reinforcement' materials are provided for students encountering difficulties in mastering the core content. The problem with such reinforcement is that it is time-consuming, and weak students are likely to fall even further behind with their studies. One way of reducing this problem is to encourage weaker students to undertake preparatory studies prior to the commencement of a course with a view to overcoming weaknesses that can be identified at that point in time.

At the other end of the scale, 'enrichment' materials are provided for students who have assimilated all the core learning without difficulty, and wish to pursue their interests in greater depth. The challenge in this situation is how to award such students credit for their additional studies. One possibility is to relate basic grades to the mastery of the core content and to relate higher grades to the mastery of the enrichment materials provided.

Suggestions

In the last few paragraphs I have tried to place what I perceive as key components of ODL in perspective – making use of a diagram to highlight the relationships between the various components. In reading through this chapter you may have perceived other things to be important, and I would suggest that you try to summarise these in a similar manner with the help of a flow diagram if that helps to place your thoughts in perspective.

3 The design of self-study materials

Contents	
Introduction	41
3.1 A framework for a study session	42
3.2 A framework for a course	60
3.3 Making use of existing materials	78
In perspective	84
Suggestions	84

Introduction

Within the UK OU courses have traditionally been broken down into units, and thereafter into sections of units or study sessions, with an extra layer often being added in the form of blocks of units, and these are the terms that I will use in talking about the design of courses. Other terms may be used to describe the various components, but the features that might be built into the design of courses remain the same regardless of the terminology used.

The aim in this chapter is to identify features that may be integrated into the design of self-study materials with a view to facilitating student learning. Within this chapter we will begin by looking at the type of features that might be included within *a framework for a study session*, as this will focus our attention on students and ways in which we might help them. We will then go on to see how study sessions may be integrated together within *a framework for a course*.

You will find that all the design features referred to here provide students with guidance to help them with their studies, and as such the guidance provided may be integrated with the actual materials to be studied or it may be included separately within a study guide and refer to the materials elsewhere. You will find examples of both these approaches in the pages that follow.

You will soon recognise that where materials are developed from scratch for ODL the guidance required will usually be integrated into the actual materials. In contrast, where existing materials are used there is every probability that further guidance will be required, and this is likely to be included in the study guide. Where existing materials are of a high quality and relevant to student needs it makes sense to consider the possibility of adapting them for ODL. Unfortunately, adapting such materials is not always as simple as one might wish, and in the final part of this chapter we will consider some of the factors that need to be taken into account in *making use of existing materials*.

3.1 A framework for a study session

Although here we will be talking about the design of a 'study session', precisely the same features may be built into the design of a 'section of a unit'. The only difference between a study session and a section of a unit is that it is assumed that students will be able to digest the contents of a study session within a single sitting, whereas a section of a unit may require several sittings. As you have already seen, a 'study session' is likely to make use of a variety of media and resources with a study guide linking all the components together. The same is true of a 'section of a unit'.

The design features that will be discussed here relate to *the introduction to a study session* where they are intended to place the detailed learning to follow in perspective, to *the content of a study session* to help students with their ongoing studies, and to *the conclusion to a study session* to help students to reflect on what they have learnt. Where all these features are combined together they are able to provide a logical *framework* for a study session. Let us consider each of these aspects in turn.

The introduction to a study session

Within an introduction to a study session you will usually find an outline introducing students to the contents of the study session (*an advance organiser*) and a broad statement of what students might achieve as a result of their studies (*a statement of aims*). However, you will often find information on *other aspects*, and we will also take a look at what these might be.

Advance organisers

The idea of the advance organiser is to introduce students to the detailed learning to follow – identifying the topics to be addressed and the relationships between them. The intent is to provide students with a meaningful and well-organised framework for the assimilation of more detailed knowledge. Without such an introduction students may be introduced to concept after concept without knowing where this is taking them or why they are studying the concepts concerned. The advance organiser provides us with an opportunity not only to introduce students to what is to follow, but also to point out the relevance and importance of what is to be learnt, and thereby to encourage student motivation.

It was Ausubel (1968) who first introduced the concept of advance organisers. In so doing he argued that a student's cognitive structure – that is the organisation, clarity and stability of the student's existing knowledge – is a prime factor affecting student learning of new material, and that if this is disorganised, ambiguous or unstable it will inhibit learning. He perceived the advance organiser as a way of facilitating the assimilation of knowledge – with the framework provided becoming part of the student's cognitive structure.

An example of an advance organiser for a study session is included in Figure 3.1. It is taken from a course designed to help health service workers develop their management skills, and the study session concerned (the first in the course) introduces students to the subject of 'coping with management'.

You will see that the main topics to be addressed within the study session are highlighted by means of italics, and the italicised words are then used as headings for the related parts, thus providing the framework for the detailed learning to follow. You will also notice that the author addresses the student directly as 'you', as though conversing in a one-to-one tutorial. This is a style that was recommended by Rowntree (1974) in the early years of the UK OU and one which has been widely adopted throughout the University since then.

Statement of aims

Advance organisers introduce students to the content of the study session, but they do not usually advise students on what they should be able to do on completion of their studies, and a broad statement of aims might be built into the introduction to the study session to do just this. You will find an example of how this might be achieved in Figure 3.2.

The advance organiser in the example introduces students to three local scenarios, namely: life at work in France, the telephone at work, and the right to work, while the statement of aims (identified by bullets) indicates what it is hoped students will achieve through their study of these three scenarios. In this case the stated aims are closely integrated within the advance organiser, but they could be presented as separate items if preferred.

The example reflects the way in which early language courses within the UK OU were designed to teach through the exposure of students to real-life situations. It was hoped that this would not only help to motivate students, but that the knowledge of the social and cultural environment

Session 1   Coping as a manager

Contents

	Introduction	6
1.1	Coping with the transition into management	6
1.2	Coping with pressure	11
	Summary	15
	Self-check	15

Introduction

Let us turn our attention to some very practical matters.

Book 1 offered you a variety of ways of looking at your job, with the aim of providing you with new insights and new perspectives to help you see your work more systematically and analytically. You considered some of the factors that can influence your effectiveness as a manager, and you determined your needs for improvement.

We are now going to highlight some of the problems that managers meet, and we will discuss some of the ways of coping with these problems.

One of the first problems encountered by a new manager is that of *coping with the transition into management*. The transition from 'being managed' to 'managing' can be a difficult one, and can be eased if those making it have some idea of what is expected of them, and of the problems they might encounter in making the transition. We will begin this session with a look at this process of transition.

Inevitably, you will encounter pressures and stresses in your work. You will probably find that a certain amount of pressure can be quite stimulating. However, too much pressure can be debilitating, and you need to recognize when pressure is excessive, and find ways of relieving it. *Coping with pressure* is important if you are to survive and be effective.

1.1   Coping with the transition into management

A very common problem that many new managers encounter when they first move into management is adjusting to the fact that their work as a manager is very different from the work they have been used to doing. There are two aspects of the transition into management that we will consider here. The first is what has been called the *player–manager syndrome*: some managers will find that in taking on management functions they are expected to give up those specialist roles which they have performed so well and with such satisfaction in the past, and they may be reluctant to do this. Others – particularly in the Health Service – will find that they are expected to retain some of their former specialist functions while taking on a management role as well, and finding an appropriate balance between these is not always easy.

The second aspect that we will focus on is the *transition process* itself. Here the problems highlighted are typical of those encountered by anyone moving into a new job, and not simply those of someone moving into management for the first time. They are likely to be encountered by your own staff when they take up new positions, and as a manager you will need to be sensitive to the problems staff face in adjusting to new and different demands. You may

Figure 3.1 An advance organiser for a study session
Source: Course B601 2, Managing Health Services, UK OU, 1993, p. 6

Study Session 3: Le Travail

Work plays an important part in all our lives – whether it is drilling for oil in the North Sea, washing the dishes at home, or learning to speak French – and this is true whether we are French or English. In this study session we will therefore be introducing you to the life of work in France, and you will hear French people talking about their work and some of the ways in which it affects their lives. In the process you will become aware of some of the ways in which work in France is organised differently from what is typically the case in the UK, and you will be introduced to some of the key issues raised by work in France – such as the right to work.

In *La Vie au Travail* you will be introduced to life at work in France, and on the video (3.01–3.35) you will hear French people talking about their work: describing their basic routines, and giving their views on what they perceive as the good and bad aspects of their jobs. Don't worry if you have some initial difficulties in understanding what is said. The activities that you will find in this section are designed to help you to:

- understand French people when they talk about their work, and
- imitate French people in describing the basic elements of your own work.

In carrying out your own work you will almost certainly need to use the telephone quite regularly, and in a foreign language this can be particularly difficult. In the next section *Le Téléphone au Travail* we will therefore introduce you to some of the language needed to use the telephone in the work environment, and we will use the audio-tape (3.49–3.71) to help you develop your confidence. It is hoped that the related activities will enable you to

- use the telephone to make appointments and arrange meetings.

In the final part of this study session we will go on to discuss another key issue, *L'Endroit du Travail*. On the video (3.35–3.75) you will hear French people not only talking about their rights, but also describing what they see as positive and negative aspects of their work. Once again the activities are designed to help you understand the issues and to talk about them yourself. It is hoped that this will enable you to

- describe some of the advantages and disadvantages of your own work, and
- express your opinion on the factors that are important in the making of an enjoyable working life.

Figure 3.2 Aims included within advance organiser for a study session

gained would also help students to communicate in a more meaningful manner with foreigners in their home environment.

It is worth noting that the advance organiser in the earlier management example (Figure 3.1) did not include a separate statement of aims, because it was already structured in terms of what students might hope to achieve – such as 'coping with the transition to management' and 'coping with pressure'. In contrast, the advance organiser in the more recent language example introduced students to local scenarios, and students needed to know what they might hope to achieve through their study of these situations – hence the inclusion of stated aims.

Although I indicated that a statement of broad aims might usefully be included in the introduction to a study session, I deliberately avoided suggesting the inclusion of a list of specific (behavioural) objectives. There are several reasons for this:

- Because of the need for specific objectives to be expressed in clearly measurable terms, they are often expressed in terms that have very little meaning for students until after they have completed the related studies.
- A list of specific objectives prior to the commencement of a study session can be quite daunting, and do little to help students to get to grips quickly with the learning to follow.
- There is evidence to suggest that specific objectives are more effective in facilitating learning when included at the end of a study session rather than at the beginning (Melton, 1978).

With the above factors in mind, it is in fact recommended here that specific objectives should be used at the end of study sessions. Used in this manner they may serve as checklists to help students determine for themselves whether they have achieved the objectives identified.

Other aspects

There is always a balance between how much information should be included in the introduction to a study session and how much should be made available later, as and when students need it, during the actual course of their studies.

Thus, although the introduction to a study session could include information on a number of further aspects (such as *study time* that needs to be set aside for the study of various components, the *resources* available to facilitate learning, *study strategies* that might be adopted, and the forms of *student support* that are available), in practice, much of this advice can be integrated into the ongoing study of the related study session, leaving little that needs to be added within the actual introduction. It is simply a question of asking how important it is for students to know about particular aspects in advance.

In contrast, you will find that introductions to courses (and to a somewhat lesser extent units and blocks of units) contain much more information and advice on these issues, since prior to launching into the study of a course (or related block of units) students need to make sure that they are well prepared for what is to be a major undertaking. As such, they will usually want to know in advance quite a bit about the resources required, the teaching strategies, the media to be used, and the support systems provided in order to ensure that they can prepare themselves well for what lies ahead.

The content of a study session

In the text that follows particular emphasis is placed on three aspects of design, namely, the *organisation and structure* of self-study materials, the use of *signalling devices* to help guide students through the maze of materials typically found in ODL, and the inclusion of *activities and projects* to ensure the involvement of students in the process of learning. Although these are perceived as particularly important aspects of design, they are not the only ones that need to be considered, and we will also take a brief look at a number of *other aspects*.

Organisation and structure

We have already seen examples of how advance organisers may be designed to provide students with broad frameworks for the assimilation of the more detailed learning to follow within a study session. The assimilation of knowledge within such frameworks may also be encouraged by ensuring that the knowledge within any given study session is presented within the same framework as that described in the related advance organiser. Figure 3.1 not only provides a good example of this relationship, but also illustrates how the structure of the study session may be highlighted by the use of related headings within the study session and by reference to these in the advance organiser.

At first glance there may appear to be a conflict between the desire to ensure that self-study materials are well structured and the desire to encourage students to determine their own goals and the means of achieving them. In fact there are several ways in which this conflict can be overcome, and Figure 3.3 provides us with an example of one way in which this might be achieved.

The example is taken from an on-line course on the 'Implementation of ODL' in which students are expected to undertake a related project as part of their studies. The example introduces students to a related mini-conference that was designed to help them develop their thinking with regard to their projects. In this case what is structured is the process of thinking about the issues involved rather than the knowledge and skills

> Msg #179 of 462 posted 4/8/00 by r. f. melton
> Plenary Area |Project Forum |Project Mini-Confe... |
>
> # 🐻 Project Mini-Conference 1
>
> Hello! I'm Reg Melton. My usual role on this course is as deputy chair, but during this mini-conference (1st to 15th April) I will be doing my best to help you develop your thinking about the type of project you might develop. If you want to know more about me click here
>
> I would suggest that you begin by reading the introduction to Block 5 which you will find in your Course Guide (pp 119-132). It begins with an introductory statement about *'Your Independent Project'* and then moves on to an article by Derek Rowntree in which he comments on some of *'The Perils and Pitfalls of Independent Projects'*. You will note that in his article Derek makes considerable reference to Jane Henry's book *'Teaching Through Projects'* which is published by Kogan Page, London 1994. If you would like to consider any of the issues highlighted by Derek in greater depth you will find Chapters 2 and 4-7 are particularly relevant.
>
> This mini-conference is intended to help you develop your thinking about the sort of project you might undertake, and you will find seven discussion threads to facilitate the process.
>
> The *first thread* is intended to facilitate an exchange of ideas on what might be *appropriate topics* for your project. It may be that you already have some clear ideas as to what you would like to do, but if you are feeling undecided, you may find an exchange of ideas helpful. However, do remember that the point of this conference is to help you develop your thinking, so don't feel that you have to stick to ideas expressed in the early stages.
>
> Once you have some idea of the topic you want to explore you will need to think more carefully about the type of project that is likely to be appropriate, and the *second thread* is intended to encourage you to think about the appropriateness of *different types of projects* - ranging from literature reviews to empirical studies.
>
> In developing your ideas there is always a risk that you might be carried away by your enthusiasm to try to take on too much, and in the *third thread* we will encourage you to think realistically about your project and *factors that need to be taken into account.*
>
> Recognising how long various types of activity take is crucial, and in the *fourth thread* we will encourage you to give careful consideration to the tasks to be undertaken and in particular to *planning and scheduling your time.*
>
> Under each of the above threads do feel free to discuss how the issues raised affect your thinking about your own project.

Figure 3.3 Advance organiser for an on-line mini-conference

Source: Course H804, Implementation of ODL, Project Forum, UK OU, 2000

The *fifth thread* is for the discussion of *other issues* not covered by the above threads, and this in turn may highlight the need for additional threads. Having reflected on the specific issues raised in the individual threads you may well wish to get feedback on *your emerging project*, and the *sixth thread* is added for this purpose.

As you develop your thinking about your project the chances are that you will become increasingly aware of ways in which we might help you to progress with the development of your project. Do keep these in mind, and at the end of the mini-conference use the *final thread* entitled *what next?*, to provide us with feedback on how we might help.

Add bookmark View bookmark

- #181 **Appropriate Topics** Friday, March 31, 2000, r.f.melton (34/34)
- #182 **Different Types of Projects** Wednesday, March 29, 2000, r.f.melton
- #183 **Factors that need to be taken into account** Wednesday, March 29, 2000, r.f.melton
- #184 **Planning and Scheduling your Time** Wednesday, March 29, 2000, r.f.melton (2/2)
- #185 **Other Issues** Wednesday, March 29, 2000, r.f.melton
- #186 **Your emerging Project** Wednesday, March 29, 2000, r.f.melton
- #187 **What Next?** Friday, March 31, 2000, r.f.melton (2/2)

| Comment | Outline | Parent | Jump | Delete | New replies | All in One Page | History | Search | Info | Copyright | File Area |

Moderator's Tools Edit Move Delete Simple search

Return to conference root   Return to H804 Welcome page

Figure 3.3 (continued)

50 Characteristics of ODL

that students are likely to acquire during the process of their projects. Within such a structure students have a great deal of freedom to identify their own goals and the issues that are of interest to themselves.

When we move on to consider design features that might be adopted within 'a framework for a course' we will reflect on other ways in which freedom of choice might be encouraged within well-structured materials.

Signalling devices

It is typical of ODL to expect students to make use of a wide range of resources, and it is easy for students to get lost in a web of confusion if they are not carefully guided through the maze. Signalling devices (such as icons) are therefore usually built into self-study materials to refer students as and when needed to related resources – videos, audio-tapes, science kits, on-line resources, and so on. These need to be consistently located in the same medium (e.g. in the unit study guide/text) using a commonly agreed referencing system (e.g. easily interpreted icons). They may vary somewhat from course to course, but need to be consistent within a course. In Figure 3.4 you will find an example of such usage. The three icons in the example indicate to students that in the activity concerned they will need to make use of three resources: the World Wide Web, a set of loose leaf readings supplied with the course, and a personal computer.

Activities and projects

Where students are studying at a distance it is all too easy for them to passively accept what is being presented without thinking too deeply about the issues involved. It is therefore common in ODL to try to involve students in the process of learning through the provision of activities and projects.

According to Lockwood (1992, pp. 22–49) activities may be designed to serve a variety of purposes such as those of helping students to do the following:

- monitor their own progress;
- check their understanding of issues;
- develop specific skills;
- apply what they have learnt to new contexts;
- relate issues studied to real life situations;
- think for themselves.

In Figure 3.5 you will find an example of an activity designed to encourage students to relate a number of issues to their own experiences. If you would like to see examples of various other forms of activities you might like to review some of those included in Lockwood's (1992) book *Activities in Self-Instructional Texts*.

back on the surprising phenomenon and, at the same time, back on itself.

2   Reflection-in-action has a critical function, questioning the assumptional structure of knowing-in-action. We think critically about the thinking that got us into this fix or this opportunity; and we may, in the process, restructure strategies of action, understandings of phenomena, or ways of framing problems.

3   Reflection gives rise to on-the-spot experiment. We think up and try out new actions intended to explore the newly observed phenomena, test our tentative understandings of them, or affirm the moves we have invented to change things for the better ... What distinguishes reflection-in-action from other kinds of reflection is its immediate significance for action.

(Schön, 1987, pp. 28–9)

Schön also uses the term 'reflection-on-action' – 'the process of making sense of an action after it has occurred and possibly learning something from the experience' – but 'reflection-in-action is usually (though not always) on the action as well' (Eraut, 1995, p. 16). Eraut proposes a third term, 'reflection-for-action', to indicate the purpose of any reflection. He also advances the view that reflection is different depending on the context in which it occurs and the speed of events. The time available for thinking makes a huge difference: classroom teaching generally allows for only very short bursts of reflection-in-action. Deliberation by professionals takes longer and usually occurs out of the action (Eraut, 1995, p. 21).

Activity 2.2 **2 hours**

Access http://educ.queensu.ca/~ar/schon87.htm on the Web and read Schön's address to the 1987 meeting of the American Educational Research Association in Washington DC. This summarises in an easy-going style his main ideas on education and, in particular, on educating the reflective practitioner.

Read Eraut's (1995) article 'Schön shock: a case for reframing reflection-in-action', which is reproduced in the Readings at the end of this file (they are arranged alphabetically by author). This is a challenging paper, written for people who may already know something about Schön's work. Answer the following questions in your personal notebook.

1   Eraut criticises Schön for 'straying from his own definitions' and ends up substituting another frame of analysis. His starting point for doing so is the effect on the mode of cognition of the time available for thinking. Why does he think this is important?

2   What do you understand now by the terms 'reflection-in-action', 'reflection-on-action' and 'reflection-for-action'?

3   Can you think of examples from open and distance education where practitioners (teachers) can promote each of these three? How would they do so?

Figure 3.4 The use of signalling devices
Source: Course H801, Foundations of ODE, Block 1, UK OU, 2000, p. 30

evaluation of it. Understandably, there is always some resistance to this kind of consideration.

To a significant extent, the educational values you hold are determined by your own personal history. You bring perspectives that are unique to you – the result of your particular journey through life. No doubt you could identify a number of events or circumstances that you know to be significant in the formation of your present values. Some of these values will have been carefully thought through, others will have been acquired without conscious awareness.

Though understanding the effects of the particular track you have taken through life is important, there is also a broader dimension that needs to be considered. Who you are is more than just the accumulation of your individual experiences. You are also a societal being: you are a member of cultural and social groups such as gender and age, you have national, ethnic or religious affiliations and you participate in various interest groups or professional organisations. Your situation needs to be considered in terms of the general social patterns evident in society as well as in terms of your individual life choices.

Membership of these social groups has shaped your life in profound ways. It has influenced (and continues to influence) not only what you know, but what you do not know; not only what you have experienced, but what you have not experienced; not only what skills you have, but what skills you do not have. At the same time as giving you a particular insight into aspects of your social and professional life, it may blur or obliterate your perspectives on others (Mezirow, 1990, p. 1). Although your perspective is unique, it is also clearly shaped by social forces.

Activity 2.11 **15 minutes**

In this activity, think about your own educational experience and the social influences on it. Figure 2.1 is a blank chart for you to fill in to show how social factors have affected you. On the x-axis, several social influences have been nominated. The y-axis ranges from positive to negative. Try to plot your overall perception of how each of these influences has affected your educational experience. If you feel there have been both positive and negative effects, mark them in.

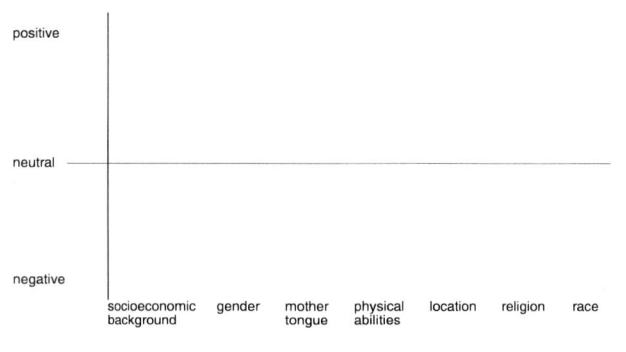

---

positive

neutral

negative

socioeconomic background | gender | mother tongue | physical abilities | location | religion | race

Figure 2.1 Personal profile of social influences on your educational experience

Figure 3.5 Activity relating issues discussed to student experience
Source: Course H801, Foundations of ODE, Block 1, UK OU, 2000, p. 46

According to Henry (1994, pp. 40–56) projects may also be designed to serve a variety of purposes including those of helping students to do the following:

- develop a wide range of skills and competences;
- develop specific learning skills;
- become more autonomous learners by giving them more control over the learning process and by helping them to make decisions for themselves;
- determine their own goals and the means of achieving them with a view to encouraging greater self-motivation.

Projects tend to be much more open-ended than activities with students being given considerable freedom to determine their own goals and the means of achieving them. An example of this open-ended aspect is provided in Figure 3.6, which contains part of the introduction to a project taken from an on-line course concerned with the *Implementation of Open and Distance Learning*. It is worth noting that although in this example students are given considerable freedom to determine the nature of their projects, the process is carefully structured. Thus students are expected to develop their thinking in stages – obtaining feedback on their early thinking from their tutors and fellow students. They are also expected to obtain approval from their tutors for their outline plans before launching into the full implementation of their projects.

Other aspects

The intent here is not to identify all the other possible features that might usefully be included in the design of self-study materials, but rather to focus on a few of the more obvious ones that should not be ignored.

In the early days of ODL it was recognised that blocks of uninterrupted text run the great risk of becoming boring and difficult to assimilate. A range of strategies were developed to overcome this, but as we move to other media – and in particular to on-line teaching – these are often overlooked, so let us take a look at some of the strategies that might be adopted.

Where the materials are textual in nature (as is often the case in unit study guides/texts and in on-line teaching), layout and presentation is still important. Text should not go on and on ad infinitum, but should be broken down into *easily assimilated parts* under related headings. Overcrowding of pages should be avoided, and consideration given as to how *white space* should be retained and used on a page. Figure 3.7 is interesting in this respect in that it illustrates how white space is often retained in the margins. In this case the *margins* are being used to include comments on the related figures, but they are also typically used for the location of icons (advising students of resources for further study), for important side notes

NEGOTIATING WITH YOUR TUTOR

So, your project may be of many kinds – a conceptual enquiry, a review of published research, a small-scale survey, an evaluation of some aspect of an ODL system, the development and piloting of learning materials, and so on. Your main concern should be to focus on a topic that is not only relevant to this course and worth spending your time on but also one that can realistically be tackled in the time available. As you probably know, dreaming up too large a project is a common mistake that new research students (and indeed all of us) are liable to make.

Remember, however, that you are *not* a research student – you are not doing a PhD or even a research MA, nor even doing a year-long dissertation as on H803. Although you may *choose* to spend more time on your project (especially if it is something you want to do anyway, perhaps for job reasons), we are allowing it only eight weeks of course time. At 12–16 hours per week, this adds up to around 96–128 hours – the equivalent of only about two or three weeks of full-time work (including writing up your project report).

As you may have noticed, TMA 03 asks you to write about the topic or issue you want to tackle in your project. This gives your tutor a chance to comment on your proposal, offer any relevant advice and even warn you of any potential problems. It is your tutor's job to confirm that your proposal suits the course, looks practicable within the time available and is sufficiently different from any assessed work you may have done already (e.g. on H801 or H802). If he or she sees any difficulties here, we expect you to be able to negotiate between you a project topic that will be satisfactory to you both.

Furthermore, your tutor will want to agree with you some kind of timetable for your project work and for sending regular email progress reports about how you are getting on, so, after receiving your tutor's comments on your TMA 03, you may expect some email discussion about the exact nature of your project and how you will be tackling it.

Figure 3.6 Extract from description of an open-ended project
Source: Course H804, Implementation of ODL, Block 5, UK OU, 2000, p. 110

(12.5×10^6 km^2) (units of area were discussed in Block 1, Box 4.2). Elsewhere, glaciers can be less than 1 km^2 in area. Some of the smallest are confined to valleys, although other valley glaciers spill out from the edges of ice-sheets (see title page).

Beneath the thickest parts of glaciers, the slowly moving ice scrapes against the bare rock, scouring debris away from the ground and carrying it along within the ice. The erosive power of a glacier moving slowly down a valley is enormous. Erosion acts over the floor and sides of the valley to carve a broad **U-shaped valley** (Figure 3.2b). A fast-flowing river, on the other hand, erodes the floor of a valley, resulting in a V-shaped valley (Figure 3.2a). The shapes of the valleys in Figure 3.2 are different because they formed in different ways — one by the action of flowing water, the other by the action of flowing ice.

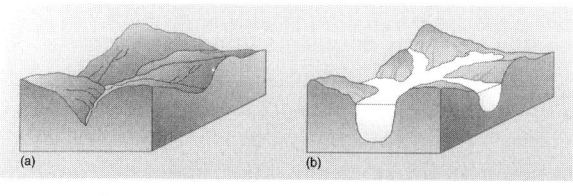

Figure 3.2 A mountainous region that experiences erosion by fast-flowing rivers develops a landscape characterized by V-shaped valleys (a). This contrasts with the case in a much colder climate (b) where valley glaciers are present and erode U-shaped valleys.

The zone of deposition

Towards the end of glaciers, large amounts of rock debris, ranging in size from house-sized boulders to dust a few thousandths of a millimetre across, are dumped from the ice and accumulate beneath the active glacier. This muddled mixture of rock particles is called **till** and occurs as mounds, sheets or sinuous ridges called **moraines**, which are left behind when the ice eventually melts; Figure 3.3 shows an example.

Figure 3.3 The moraine in the foreground of this picture was deposited when the valley was filled by a large glacier; the remnants of this Alpine glacier are seen in the background.

Figure 3.7 Use of photographs, illustrations, margins and bold print
Source: Course S103, Discovering Science, Block 2, UK OU, 1998, p. 31

(by authors and students), and for short anecdotes and pictures (to bring the subject to life). However, as in this example, great care is usually taken to avoid the overcrowding which can result if too much text is included in the margins.

The same example (Figure 3.7) contains a number of other features that are worth noting. *Highlighting* (bold print in this case) is used within the example to identify newly defined terms, and in most science courses in the UK OU you will find that *indexes* and *glossaries* are usually developed to facilitate rapid reference to the terms highlighted in this way. The page also highlights the way in which *illustrations* and *photographs* can often help to illustrate features in ways that may be extremely difficult to describe in words. *Diagrams*, *charts*, and *graphs* may also enrich explanations in a similar manner. Photographs are also a good, if expensive, way of relating issues under discussion to real life situations.

Anecdotes and *case studies* are another way in which concepts may be related to real-life situations, but as with most devices they may serve a number of purposes depending on the situation concerned. For example, a case study might provide an example of a concept being discussed, while at the same time it might help to increase student motivation by highlighting the relevance and importance of the issues being discussed. Where anecdotes or case studies are introduced into text, they are usually separated from the core text to avoid interrupting the main story line. This may be achieved by such devices as boxing around the related text, by using horizontal lines above and below it, by making use of different fonts and/or background shading

Take a look at Figure 3.8, and decide for yourself which of the features that we have so far discussed are illustrated in the example. The page may be somewhat overcrowded, but it does contain an interesting range of design characteristics.

- Can you pick out the basic story line? Is Box 3.1 part of this? If not what purpose does it serve? How is it separated from the story line? You will find two circular icons included within the box. What purpose do they serve?
- Is question 3.3 part of the basic story line? If not, how is it separated from the rest of the text?
- Do the illustrations of pollens enrich the related description of their characteristics? Can you identify the main advantages of including them?
- Assuming that you could let the story line spread over to the next page if necessary, are there ways in which you feel you could improve the layout?

Having gathered your thoughts together with regard to the design features built into Figure 3.8, you might like to reflect back on the range of

3.2.1 Pollen

Plant fossils range in size from tree trunks to microscopic pollen grains. Many plants shed pollen from the male parts of their flowers, and the pollen is carried on the wind or by insects to the female parts of flowers where fertilization occurs. It is by this process that the plants produce their seeds. The spring and summer air becomes heavily laden with pollen, as hay fever sufferers know only too well, and a mature tree may produce many tens of millions of pollen grains each year. Needless to say, a single pollen grain is tiny; its size can be measured in millionths of a metre (see Box 3.1, *The micrometre*).

Box 3.1 The micrometre

For things as small as pollen grains it becomes convenient to use a new unit — the micrometre, sometimes called the micron. The prefix **micro** indicates 'one millionth' in the way that milli means 'one thousandth' (Block 1, Box 3.1). The symbol for a micrometre uses the Greek letter µ (mu, pronounced 'mew'), to indicate the micro part, in front of m for metre: hence µm is the symbol for micrometre. There are several ways of expressing a micrometre:

$$1 \, \mu m = \frac{1}{1\,000\,000} \, m = \frac{1}{10^6} \, m = 10^{-6} \, m$$

● How many micrometres are there in a millimetre?

○ We know that $1 \, \mu m = 10^{-6}$ m, so there are 10^6 µm in 1 m. Likewise, $1 \, mm = 10^{-3}$ m, so there are 10^3 mm in 1 m. This means that 10^3 mm = 10^6 µm, so

$$1 \, mm = \frac{1\,000\,000 \, \mu m}{1\,000} = 1\,000 \, \mu m.$$

In words, there are one thousand micrometres in one millimetre.

Most pollen grains never reach the flowers for which they were intended, but instead fall to the ground or onto the surface of lakes and streams. Pollen grains can be deposited in the silt accumulating on the bottom of lakes or in peat accumulating in bogs and become preserved as fossils. Because plants produce huge numbers of pollen grains, just one spoonful of peat can contain many thousands of pollen grains from the trees, shrubs and grasses in the vicinity of the peat bog. Furthermore, because each type of plant produces pollen with a unique shape and surface pattern (Figure 3.9) it is possible to identify the range of plant types that have contributed to a given sample of pollen. Thus, whereas a rare fossil tree stump preserved in a bog reveals the identity of one type of plant that once grew in some ancient landscape, a mere handful of peat from the same bog contains a whole variety of pollen types, which reveals the range of plants that were present in that region.

Question 3.3 Figure 3.10 shows a number of pollen grains taken from a 140 000 year old sample of Essex clay. Compare their shapes with those of the pollen grains in Figure 3.9. Do you think that the local trees included oak and Scots pine, or elm and lime? ◀

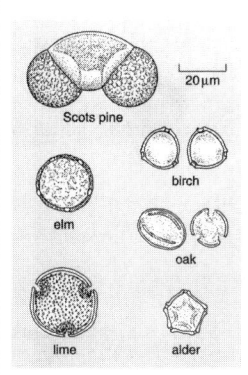

Figure 3.9 Drawings of pollen grains from different types of tree. Note the scale bar indicating that these small grains are only 20 µm or so across.

3.2.2 Pollen diagrams and ancient climates

The usefulness of fossil pollen to the scientist is that the types and proportions of pollen in a sample, such as Figure 3.10, can be compared with those produced by vegetation growing in present-day climates. The climate at the time the sample was formed can then be inferred. This brings us back to the main thread of this section, which is the pattern of temperature change on the Earth through time.

By collecting a series of pollen samples of different ages from a given area or site, and inferring the climate that produced each sample, we can arrive at a picture of how

36

Figure 3.8 Design characteristics for further study
Source: Course S103, Discovering Science, Block 2, UK OU, 1998, p. 36

examples concerned with 'helping students with their studies', and consider to what extent the ideas are relevant to other media. For example, is there all that much difference between a 'talking head' in a video (or TV) programme and a text that goes on and on without a break? Is it possible to use diagrams, charts, graphs, illustrations, photographs, film clips, anecdotes and case studies to illustrate issues in such programmes, and if so do you think that they might improve the quality of a video presentation in much the same way as with text?

ptsThe conclusion to a study session

In drawing a study session to a close it is common in the UK OU to include a *summary* that reflects on what has been learnt and a *checklist* that enables students to check what they have learnt and to determine whether they need to reinforce or enrich their learning in any way.

Summary

The summary provides an opportunity to reflect back on the learning that has taken place and this may be done in a variety of ways depending on the type of learning that has taken place in the study session. The detailed learning that has taken place during the study session might usefully be placed more clearly in perspective. The implications of new ideas for society, technology and the environment may be highlighted, while note may be made of the extent to which future knowledge and understanding might build on what has been learnt.

In Figure 3.9 you will find a summary taken from the course in management to which we have already referred. The study session to which it relates was all about coping with the transition into management and with the pressures of management. However, the summary does not churn out the obvious points once more, but reflects back refreshingly on what has been learnt in terms of 'maintaining control'.

Checklist

The idea of a checklist is to provide students with a key list of objectives that it is hoped that they will have achieved as a result of their studies, and to provide them with an opportunity to determine for themselves whether they have achieved the objectives specified for the study session.

A great deal has been written about the nature of objectives, and the intent is not to add to all that has already been said. Let it be sufficient to say here that they should identify as clearly as possible what students should be able to do and they should provide the means by which students can determine for themselves whether they have achieved the objectives identified. This might be done by providing students with test items or

Session 1 Coping as a manager

Summary

This session has highlighted some of the things you will need to think about as a manager. In conclusion, it is of interest to look at the pressures of managing from a reverse point of view.

When we experience pressure which is not excessive, we are left feeling *in control*: we know that through extra effort we can meet the deadline. When pressure is excessive and we feel under stress, there is a feeling of having *lost control*: there is too much to deal with, it is too complex, we cannot see our way clear to the goal, or we are not even sure what the goal is. Maintaining control depends on doing all the things that we summarized in *Activity 6*. If you don't do these things, you are likely to find it extremely difficult to cope with the mounting pressures.

Self-check

Spend a few minutes deciding how you feel about the work you have done in this session and what you plan to do next. The learning objectives are listed below. Make a note of:

- points on which you want to take action and pursue further with your line manager, mentor or tutor
- potential evidence for your portfolio from the work-based activities you have completed
- points about which you are still uncertain and need to go over again or seek help on from your tutor, mentor or line manager.

Objectives	Notes
You should now be able to:	
Predict some of the problems of adjustment that may be encountered as a result of job changes, and take steps to minimize their effects.	
Recognize stress and some of its causes, and suggest strategies for reducing the impact of stress arising from role problems and work overload.	

Figure 3.9 Summary and checklist for a study session
Source: Course B601 2, Managing Health Services, UK OU, 1993, p. 15

activities related to each objective, and it is these that provide additional clarity about what is required. You will find an example of a checklist in Figure 3.10 which is taken from a language course. The checklist is in two parts, and includes a statement of the objectives to be achieved (*Faites le bilan*) and a list of vocabulary to be remembered (*Vocabulaire à retenir*). In this case the understanding is that if students can successfully complete the related activities (*activités*) that they have in fact achieved the objectives indicated. You might compare the approach used here with the checklist included in Figure 3.9 where students are advised to reflect on the stated objectives and to determine an appropriate course of action in the light of their feelings.

It is also helpful to indicate how objectives relate to the means by which students will ultimately be assessed. Early on in a course many of the objectives may well be enabling objectives – the blocks on which required knowledge, understanding and skills are built – and students may ultimately be assessed against more complex objectives. Students need to know how the objectives specified relate to those against which they will ultimately be assessed.

If you would like to look more carefully into the subject of objectives, you may find my book (Melton, 1997) *Objectives, Competences and Learning Outcomes* of interest.

A logical framework

This is an appropriate point in time to stop and reflect on the design characteristics of a study session as a whole. You will now be aware that, regardless of the subject matter concerned, a wide range of features can be built into a study session to facilitate student learning. The features include the development of an introduction to the contents of the session (with the help of an advance organiser, a statement of aims, etc.), the presentation of the content in a stimulating and well-structured manner (with the help of activities, projects, case studies, diagrams, illustrations, etc.), and the addition of a conclusion (with a summary and checklist). The features may be integrated with the actual self-study materials, or included separately in a study guide and referring to materials located elsewhere. Where all these features are combined together they might be described as providing a framework for the presentation of a study session. The essential characteristics of this framework are summarised in Figure 3.11.

3.2 A framework for a course

We have already seen how courses are typically broken down into blocks of units, then into individual units within each block, and thereafter into sections or study sessions. We have also seen the logic of presenting each study session (or section) within a framework with a rather special type of

1 Professions et salaires

Faites le bilan

When you have completed this section of the book, you should be able to:

- Understand people talking about their jobs and salaries (*Activités 1* and *6*).
- Say what your job is and how much you earn (*Activités 3* and *5*).
- Use *faire* to describe what you are studying (*Activité 7*).
- Understand and use the future tense (*Activités 8, 9, 10* and *11*).
- Use *si* to express possibilities, with verbs in the correct tenses (*Activité 11*).
- Say whether something is easy or difficult (*Activité 12*).
- Recognize two uses of the demonstrative pronoun (*Activités 19* and *25*).
- Use *c'est celui qui, c'est quelqu'un qui, c'est un homme qui*, to give definitions (*Activité 19*).
- Summarize a text accurately to a prescribed number of words (*Activités 21* and *24*).
- Pronounce [s] or [z] correctly (*Activité 4*).

Vocabulaire à retenir

1.1 Les salaires

un stagiaire, une stagiaire
un enquêteur, une enquêteuse
une enquête
un projet d'avenir
un débouché
le marketing
l'informatique
la comptabilité
le droit
la gestion
la gestion de personnel
le secteur public/privé
gérer une entreprise

1.2 Les catégories professionnelles

la direction

un cadre, une femme cadre
un employé, une employée
un ouvrier qualifié, une ouvrière qualifiée
un ouvrier spécialisé, une ouvrière spécialisée

1.3 Les salaires des femmes

les droits de la femme
l'égalité des salaires
les heures supplémentaires (f.pl.)
un poste à moindre responsabilité/à plus haute responsabilité
minoritaire
majoritaire
être défavorisé,e par rapport à quelqu'un

41

Figure 3.10 Checklist for a study session
Source: Course L120, *Ouverture, Valeurs 2*, UK OU, 1998, p. 41

INTRODUCTION

Advance Organiser

Statement of Aims

Study Time, Resources
Study Strategies, Student Support

↓

CONTENT

Organisation and Structure

Signalling Devices

Activities and Projects

Easily Assimilated Sections
White Space, Margins
Highlighting, Indexes,
Glossaries,
Diagrams, Graphs, Charts,
Illustrations, Photographs,
Anecdotes, Case Studies

↓

CONCLUSION

Summary

Checklist

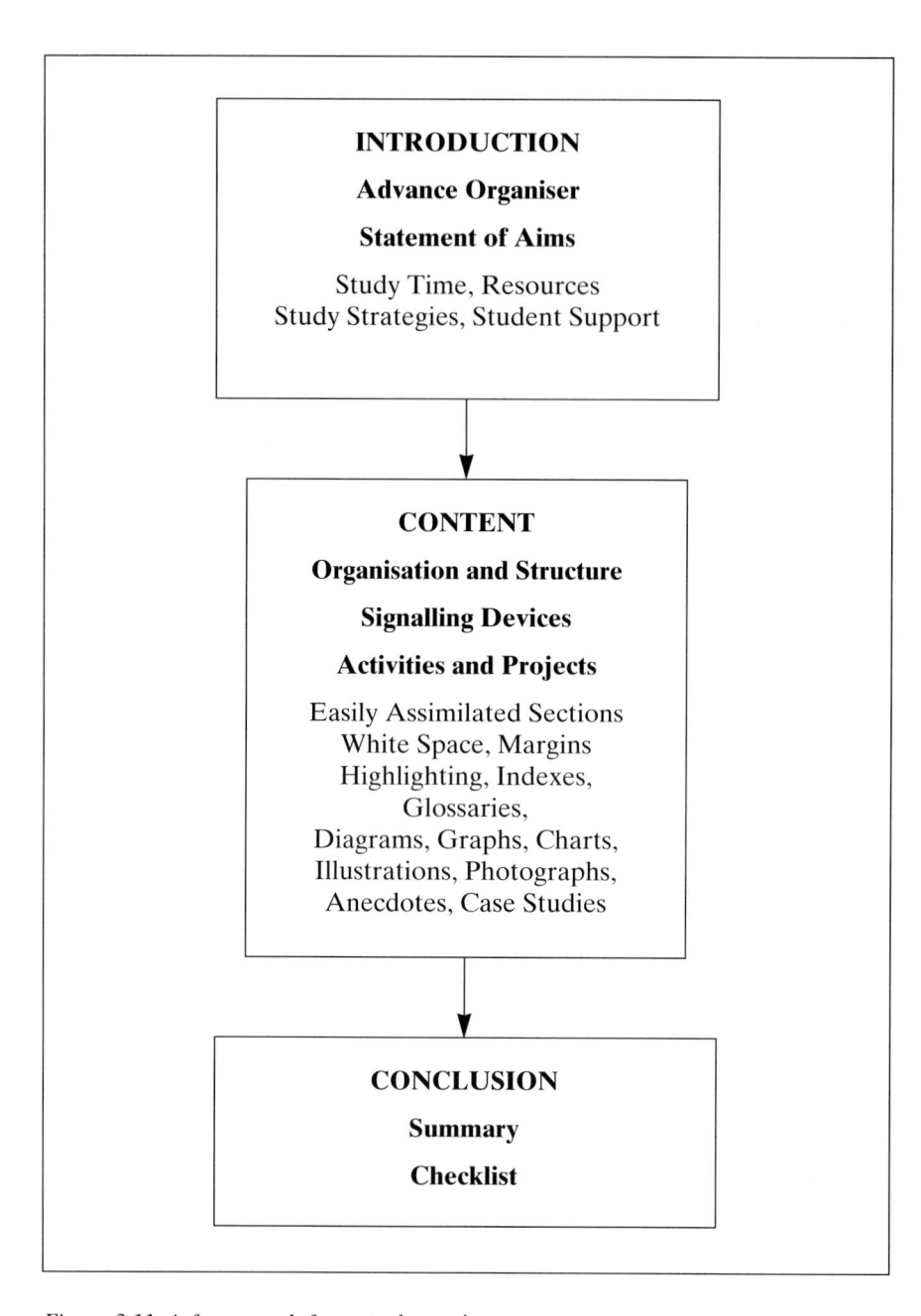

Figure 3.11 A framework for a study session

introduction (which includes within it an advance organiser and a statement of aims) and with a rather special type of conclusion (which includes within it a summary and a checklist).

Following the same logic we might expect each unit, each block of units, and a course as a whole to include introductions and conclusions along somewhat similar lines.

For example, just as we have noted how an advance organiser for a study session might be used to introduce the parts included within it, so we might expect an advance organiser for a unit to introduce the study sessions contained within it. We might also expect an advance organiser for a course to introduce the units within it.

Likewise, just as we have noted how a checklist for a study session should identify the objectives to be achieved on completion of the session, so we might expect a checklist for a unit to identify the objectives to be achieved on completion of the unit as a whole. In theory this could simply be the sum total of all the objectives specified for each study session. In practice, many of the study session objectives are likely to be enabling objectives, with a number of higher level unit objectives building on these in a variety of different ways.

In the paragraphs that follow we will look at the design features typically found in *the introduction to a course* and in *the conclusion to a course*, and we will take note of how these features might be combined together to provide *a logical framework* for a course. You will find that these features have a great deal in common with their study session counterparts, and you should have little difficulty in perceiving how the same characteristics might be built into introductions to units and blocks of units and, where appropriate, into conclusions for units and blocks of units.

The introduction to a course

As with the introduction to a study session, one would expect very much the same emphasis to be placed on the inclusion of a well-structured *advance organiser* and a clear *statement of aims* in the introduction to a course. However, in contrast to the limited emphasis placed on other features within the introduction to a study session, within the introduction to a course one would expect much more information to be provided on the *resources available* to students, on possible forms of *student support*, on *study strategies* that might be helpful, an outline of the *assessment strategy* to be employed, and *a schedule* highlighting key dates in the course calendar.

In the text that follows we will look at examples of each of these features taken from an MA course (H801) within the UK OU. The structure of this course *Foundations of ODE* is somewhat different from that of most UK OU courses in that it is broken down into four blocks and thereafter into sections (rather than into the more common blocks of units,

units and study sessions). However, it illustrates well the features that we want to review.

As you will now be reasonably familiar with the features we will be looking at, you might take this opportunity to look more carefully at the examples and decide for yourself how effective they are. Try to identify their strengths and weaknesses, and, where you perceive weaknesses, see if you can identify ways in which they might be eliminated.

Advance organiser

Let us begin by taking a look at an example of an advance organiser taken from the introduction to the UK OU course already referred to. Although the example (Figure 3.12) includes only the first two pages of the actual advance organiser you should have no difficulty in seeing how it is presented.

Place yourself in the position of a student, and decide for yourself whether the introduction gives you a good idea of the broad content of the course. You will notice that in describing the nature of each block a little information is provided on the sections into which each block is broken down. Do you find this helpful at this stage or would you prefer to have been given this information later? (Normally I would suggest leaving this to be included in the introduction to each block rather than in the introduction to the course.)

A statement of aims

The example in Figure 3.12 is also useful in that under the heading 'General course aims and structure' it contains (in paragraph 1) a broad statement of aims for the course. If you were a student, would this have given you sufficient insight into what you might expect to gain from the course? Would it have been sufficient to highlight the relevance and importance of the course to you personally?

Resources available

Before students commence their actual studies they will want to be assured that they are well prepared for it, and will certainly want to know about the resources that will be available to them. This will depend on the local situation and the system of ODL that has been established.

Students will need to know about the type of self-study materials to be provided. For example, will these include such resources as texts, audio-tapes, video-tapes, CDs, home experiment kits, radio programmes, and/or television programmes? Will they have access to library facilities either locally or elsewhere? Will they have access to on-line resources? Students

H801 Course Guide

A QUICK OVERVIEW OF THE COURSE

General course aims and structure

The course, H801 *Foundations of Open and Distance Education,* aims to give you a foundation of theory in relation to practice in this field, an understanding of the main teaching and learning issues, a knowledge of relevant research literature and a grounding in research methods applicable in open and distance education.

For each of the four blocks of this course you will receive a large loose-leaf file like this one, containing the study guide, selected readings and other items. You will also have set books to study, sent to you free of extra charge. The study guide, as you can see already, contains details of a substantial number of activities, possibly more than most students can cope with, to be carried out and recorded in your personal notebook and, if you wish, in the electronic TMA Workshop. The study guide also tells you when to turn to an audiocassette or videocassette.

You can print out the contents of any of the electronic pages if you find that easier. Your tutor will be keeping an eye on his or her students' contributions and may well respond if you raise queries or make good points. This is an important form of feedback and interaction between you and your tutor, so please use it.

You will see from the Assignment Guide that to complete your TMAs effectively you need to be an active contributor to the TMA Workshop in your tutor group. You will, therefore, need to give top priority to contributing to these discussions, in addition, of course, to reading the print materials, viewing the video and listening to the audio. You will also need to prioritise completing your TMAs by the cut-off date. If you do happen to drop behind the rest of your group, please consult your tutor about how to catch up.

Block 1 Theory and practice of open and distance education

During this block you will develop your understanding of major theoretical issues in open and distance education and of the theories underlying practice in this field. We cannot attempt to be comprehensive in a single block, but you should become able to relate distance education to its wider context by drawing on source material from a diverse range of backgrounds, including your own work and experience. Throughout, you will be encouraged to reflect critically on your own ideas and experience as a basis for practice.

David Hawkridge introduces Block 1, placing each section in context, and, in Section 1, explains terms and rationales. Most of this block is based on sections developed at the University of South Australia, in Adelaide, South Australia, and at Deakin University, in Geelong, Victoria. The Australasian flavour of many of the examples and readings enhances the international nature of the course. Section 2 'Becoming a critically reflective practitioner' begins with a brief history of critical reflection, prepared by David Hawkridge, then moves on to a substantial segment written by Rigmor George in Adelaide; she draws you into Australian education and culture as you consider further the nature of critical reflection in open and distance education. Then, in Section 3, Philip Juler, from Geelong, takes a broad international view in considering the theories underlying open and distance education, and discusses theoretical views on interaction between learners and teachers. In Section 4, Bruce King, Paul Finnane and Ian Mitchell take a close look at the learners. In Section 5, Philip Juler returns to consider the nature of interaction in open and distance education. In the final section, using

Figure 3.12 An advance organiser including a statement of aims for course
Source: Course H801, Foundations of ODE, Course Guide, UK OU, 2000, p. 11

Australia in the 1980s and 1990s as a case study, Nick Farnes, of the Open University, presents some important aspects of organisational structures and government intervention in open and distance education. A refreshing aspect about the Australian contributions to this course is that they range across primary, secondary and tertiary education and bring in examples from vocational as well as academic institutions. Other blocks focus on higher and adult education.

Block 2 Teaching and learning in open and distance education

Here again there is a variety of inputs and cultures, because the Open University collaborated with the University of South Australia and Deakin University in making this block too. The focus is on teaching and learning, though this block is far from being the only part of the programme in which these topics are discussed: they recur throughout it. First, in Sections 1 and 2, you will explore with Ellie Chambers of the Open University the nature of education, including open and distance education, from different philosophical perspectives that are the key to understanding how to approach teaching and learning in this field. Sections 3 and 4, prepared by Alistair Morgan at the Open University and Terry Evans at Deakin, respectively, will introduce you to the study environments of widely different learners. Morgan asks you to reflect critically on the experience of adult learners at a distance, while Evans focuses on distance education of children, with examples from various parts of the world.

Block 3 Researching the literature on open and distance education

Blocks 1 and 2 may seem quite theory oriented – this is intended. In our opinion, thinking about theory is an essential foundation for the study of open and distance education. You will find that foundation laying continues, but in more practical ways, in Block 3. This block was prepared entirely at the Open University, by Keith Harry, then Director of the International Centre for Distance Learning (ICDL), assisted by Nigel Blake, David Hawkridge and Alistair Morgan. ICDL runs the largest document collection in this field anywhere in the world, and this course gives you free access to it! You will learn the skills needed for searching this and other research literature databases by electronic means. For example, you will learn how to search online databases and how open and distance education are portrayed in specific classification systems. You will acquire a broad understanding of the main areas covered by the research literature in open and distance education, and the sources available. You will develop a critical appreciation of the research literature in a selected area of open and distance education, such as curriculum development, student support or evaluation. This block starts with the usual printed study guide sections, but before you have finished you will have worked with electronic updates and even electronic sections to the guide, as this is the only way to keep up-to-date in this rapidly changing field.

Figure 3.12 (continued)

should be provided with information on all these aspects in the introduction to a course.

Student support

Students will also want to know what forms of support will be available to them during their studies. It does not matter how good the self-study materials are, most students will need help and support at various points in time. Even the most able students value the existence of a support system. The type of support provided will again depend on the local situation and the system of ODL developed.

If tutors are available locally, students will need to know more about the type of support provided. For example, will students be able to gain individual access to their tutors by telephone, e-mail and/or computer-conferencing, and, if so, will they need to operate under specific conditions? Will there be regular group tutorials in their area, and, if so, where and when will these take place, and what will they aim to achieve?

Study strategies

Every course will have some advice to offer with regard to study strategies that might be encouraged, and this will depend in part on the nature of the course.

- Science courses might have a great deal to say about the role of various course components – such as the role of home experiment kits, computer-aided experiments, field studies, and laboratory work to be undertaken at residential schools.
- Language courses might have more to say about the way in which language learning is to be encouraged through the study of real life video clips, through the use of interactive audio-tapes, through listening to drama sessions, through telephone conferencing, computer-conferencing, and so on.
- On-line courses will have a great deal to say about the methodologies involved – particularly where the students will be encountering new ways of using the technology.

Information on *resources*, *student support* and *study strategies* may well be included in the introduction to a course under these headings, but it could equally well be provided under other headings. For example, in the UK OU course already referred to, the introduction to the course (Figure 3.13) provided such information under the following headings:

Meet your tutor by electronic mail
Visit the Institute on the World Wide Web

WELCOME TO H801

Welcome to H801 *Foundations of Open and Distance Education*. During the year, you will be studying the course in four parts or 'blocks'. Each block, which will probably take you 110–150 hours to study, is subdivided into sections of varying length. Block 1 takes seven weeks, Block 2 takes eight weeks, Block 3 takes seven weeks and Block 4 takes a maximum of ten weeks (see your Plan for the Year).

Special features of the course are your personal notebook and the electronic TMA Workshop. Your personal notebook is on your own computer and is where you respond to the activities scattered throughout the study guides. The electronic TMA Workshop, on a server at the Open University, complements your notebook. 'Personal notebook' may seem like just a fancy name for a new set of files, but it is actually a very important set, in which we suggest you record your learning, whether as rough notes or polished paragraphs. When you are coming up to a TMA we shall ask you to share some of your thoughts with other students in your tutorial group over the World Wide Web using the centrally provided electronic TMA Workshop.

You will want to refer back to your personal notebook and the TMA Workshop when the time comes to prepare assignments, because you can gain credit for answers that draw on what you wrote. You may also be given extra marks on assignments as a result of contributing to activities in the TMA Workshop.

You will experience for yourself in this course what it is like to learn at a distance, internationally, using the best available resources. You will have access to some of the latest research and thinking at the Open University and elsewhere. Your course team includes senior researchers and lecturers in the Institute of Educational Technology. No other university offers courses in open and distance education with such excellence behind them.

PREPARATORY ACTIVITIES

In order to prepare for the online component of the course, there are a few things you may need to do straight away. They are listed and described below.

Meet your tutor, by electronic mail

You will probably want to make contact with your tutor as soon as possible, if you haven't done so already. Now is a good time to check that you can easily get in touch with one another. Try it, using your own email system.

Activity 1

If you have your tutor's email address, test your system by trying to send a very short test message. Ask your tutor if they have received it.

Your expectations of your tutor should be informed by the knowledge that his or her contract is for an average of three hours per week of online tutoring for the tutor group as a whole and one hour per student on each assignment.

If you have studied H802, you will have been through some of the following activities already. All the same, you may want to look at them again, and a couple of them (Activities 5 and 6) relate just to H801.

Figure 3.13 Preparatory activities contained within introduction to a course
Source: Course H801, Foundations of ODE, Course Guide, UK OU, 2000, p. 4

H801 Course Guide 5

Visit the Institute on the World Wide Web

If this is your first course with us, you may like to find out more about both the Open University and its Institute of Educational Technology, which is responsible for this course. On this, as on all our courses, the Web will be a vital tool in most of your course work. If you are not already familiar with it, this next activity should be as good an introduction as any. Don't be put off if some of the names of the links, boxes or buttons are not exactly as we have given them here; the Web is a fast-changing medium and a printed guide such as this cannot hope to keep up with it.

Activity 2

Open your Web browser (in this Course Guide we are assuming you are using Netscape Navigator/Communicator or Internet Explorer). Type in the address: http://www.open.ac.uk/. This will take you to the Open University's home page. Explore if you like, by double-clicking on 'hot' words (hyperlinks), which are underlined and/or shown in a different colour, and using the **Back** and **Forward** commands.

Eventually you should click on Search, then on Institute of Educational Technology, which you will find in the list of faculties. Add a bookmark for this page. Again, explore the pages you can reach from here, adding further bookmarks if you wish. One of the links, you will see, takes you to details about our Postgraduate Qualifications in Open and Distance Education.

Visit the Virtual Campus

A great deal of your online work will be done in the Virtual Campus, so you should visit it now and become familiar with it.

Activity 3

Use your Web browser again to reach the Postgraduate Qualifications in Open and Distance Education page. Go via the Institute home page that you bookmarked in Activity 2 or type http://iet.open.ac.uk/ODLBrochure/ODL.html in the **Location** box and press Return or Enter. On that page click on the label Virtual Campus. This takes you into the entrance, but not yet as far as the pages where you will work with your tutors and fellow-students. Click on the label H801 Student Rooms and enter your user name and password (the ones you received by email from the Programme Secretary) in the dialogue box. Press Return and you will be right inside, looking at the names of areas used by H801 students.

Once you have entered the H801 pages, add a bookmark for the first one, then you can return to it easily.

Meet the other H801 students

Now is the moment to drop into the Madhouse Café, so named by students taking H801 in 1997! The Madhouse is where people gather to relax, let off steam, chat socially, meet old friends and make new ones. Everyone taking H801 this year is very welcome, tutors as well as students. It is also a place where you can read newspapers and pick up hot news about the course. Any time you come on to the campus, it is worth having a look at New Comments in the Café.

Figure 3.13 (continued)

Visit the Virtual Campus
Meet the other H801 students
Set up your personal notebook
Visit the TMA (tutor-marked assignments) Workshops
Call at the TMA Office
Surf the current titles on distance learning
Visit the Conference Area
Check the On-line Resource Centre

It is of interest to note that under these headings students were encouraged to obtain the information they required through a series of preparatory activities, and you will find details of the activities that were included under the first four of these headings in Figure 3.13.

Assessment strategy

On being introduced to a course, students will want to know whether they can choose to be assessed or not. Where they are to be assessed, they will want to know if this will be on a continuous basis throughout the course, in an examination at the end of the course, or in a combination of these. They will also want to know the criteria against which they will be assessed, how different assignments will contribute to their ultimate rating on the course, and details of any deadlines imposed on the submission of their assignments. You will find an example of what is required in Figure 3.14, which is taken from another MA course (H804) at the UK OU.

As students progress with their studies they will want more detailed information on the assignments that lie ahead, and we will look more closely at what is required in reflecting on the characteristics that might be built into the 'conclusion to a course'.

A schedule

You probably noticed that the assessment strategy outlined in Figure 3.14 included cut-off dates for the submission of tutor marked assignments and the final examinable component for the course. Most UK OU courses in fact provide students with a calendar highlighting the dates of important course events. This typically includes the dates for the submission of assignments, dates of related radio and television broadcasts, the time set aside for the study of blocks of units and other activities such as residential schools, and the dates for the end of course examination. There is usually plenty of space left in the calendar for students to record more personal information such as the dates of local tutorials, peer group meetings, and so on.

The design of self-study materials 71

The conclusion to a course

The conclusion to a course (just like a conclusion to a study session) needs *a summary* that places the course in perspective and *a checklist* indicating what students should be able to do by the time they have completed the course. If students are to be assessed against the criteria included in this ultimate checklist, the link between the criteria and the mode of assessment should be quite explicit. In other words, the checklist should clearly identify the *assessment details*.

In the text that follows we will look at examples of each of these features taken from the MA course (H804) to which we referred most recently in Figure 3.14. The structure of this course *The Implementation of ODL* is similar in format to that of the other MA course (H801) from which we have taken a number of examples in that it is broken down into blocks and then into sections. However, it is different in that it is structured with regard to process, rather than topics, giving students considerable freedom to pursue their own interests within this structure.

A summary

Just as with a summary for a study session, the summary for a course provides an opportunity to place what has been learnt in perspective. It is also an opportunity to identify ways in which new knowledge and skills may build on what has been learnt and to indicate how this in turn may have implications for society, technology and society.

In Figure 3.15 you will find an example of a summary taken from the MA course (H804) to which we have just referred. It is the summary for one of four blocks in the course, rather than for the course as a whole, but it nevertheless contains several of the characteristics that I have identified as being desirable in a course summary. The block concerned is about 'Knowing our learners in ODL', and as such highlights the variety of ways in which students are different. The summary takes this on board and goes on to reflect in a refreshing manner on the implications this has for course design.

A checklist

If we can talk about a hierarchy of objectives to be achieved on a course, we might refer to objectives in the lower regions of the hierarchy as enabling objectives and those in the upper regions as ultimate objectives to be achieved. It follows that, although a checklist for a course might be very similar in appearance to a checklist for a study session, they are different in that a checklist for a course identifies the ultimate objectives to be achieved on the course rather than lower level enabling objectives which are typically assessed by means of assignments during the presentation of a course.

CONTENTS

INTRODUCTION	3
How your work will be marked	3
General criteria for assessment	3
Referencing	4
Use of language	5
THE TUTOR-MARKED ASSIGNMENTS	6
Specific assessment criteria	6
TMA 01 (cut-off date 22 March)	6
TMA 02 (cut-off date 10 May)	6
TMA 03 (cut-off date 31 May)	7
TMA 04 (cut-off date 28 June)	7
TMA 05 (cut-off date 9 August)	8
Submitting TMAs 01–05	8
Late submission and extensions	8
THE EXAMINABLE COMPONENT	9
The project report (cut-off date 2 October)	9
Specific assessment criteria	9
Submitting your examinable component	9
Verification	10

Summary of the assessment structure for H804

	Word limit	Weighting	Cut-off date
Continuous assessment			
TMA 01	1500	15%	22 March
TMA 02	4000	30%	10 May
TMA 03	1000	0%	31 May
TMA 04	4000	30%	28 June
TMA 05	3500	25%	9 August
Examinable component			
Project report	6000	100%	2 October

Assessment strategy

There are two components of assessment: continuous assessment and the examinable component. **To be sure of a pass result you need to achieve scores of 40 in each component**. Similarly, to be sure of a distinction, a score of 85 must be achieved in each

Continuous assessment: TMA 01 is weighted at 15%; TMAs 02 and 04 are weighted at 30%; TMA 03 is ungraded; TMA 05 is weighted at 25%. No substitution will be allowed.

Examinable component: The project report constitutes 100% of this component.

Figure 3.14 Outline of assessment strategy for a course
Source: Course H804, Implementation of ODL, Assignment Guide, UK OU, 2000, p. 2

H804 Assignment Guide

INTRODUCTION

This guide explains the basis on which your tutor will assess your work during the year. It contains details of all five of the tutor-marked assignments (TMAs) as well as the final project report (the examinable component) for the course.

One element in the assessment strategy of the course is that students should have the same information as tutors about how answers are to be assessed. Therefore, this guide also contains the marking criteria that tutors will use in assessing your work.

Please read through the whole guide at the beginning of the course, as you will see that all of the assignments are closely integrated with your work on the blocks.

Finally, we encourage you to email your tutor with draft ideas about your TMAs and, particularly, about your project report, asking for his or her comments and suggestions.

How your work will be marked

Your tutor will comment on each TMA and, except for TMA 03, which is ungraded, give it a score out of 100 on the University Scale.

Scores out of 100 correspond to these levels as follows:

University Scale score	Performance standard
85–100	Pass 1
70–84	Pass 2
55–69	Pass 3
40–54	Pass 4
30–39	Bare fail
15–29	Fail
0–14	Bad fail

When you complete the course you will be awarded a final result – pass, fail or distinction – on the basis of a 50 per cent weighting on continuous assessment (the TMAs) and 50 per cent on your project report (the examinable component).

General criteria for assessment

In general, your tutor will be expecting you to write clearly, using correct spelling (please use your spell checker) and grammar. Your tutor will be looking for evidence that you have:

- reflected critically on issues raised in the course
- considered and appreciated a range of points of view, including those in the course, and developed your own view
- stated your argument clearly with supporting evidence and proper referencing of sources
- drawn on your own experience.

The specific criteria by which your TMAs and the examinable component will be assessed are listed later in this guide.

Figure 3.14 (continued)

FINAL REMARKS

Perhaps we can end with a metaphor from the world of horse-racing – one that turns on a different meaning of 'course'. Do we place our bets – that is to say, decide our teaching strategy – in terms of horses for courses or courses for horses? The former approach aims to select the horses that are most likely to cope well with the conditions prevailing on a given course (track). The latter approach starts with the strengths and weaknesses of a known horse and considers what sort of course conditions it needs if it is to have its best run.

Traditionally, in education, our attitude has been 'horses for courses'. We have developed a course and then selected those learners whose prior qualifications suggest they should have the skills required to cope with its demands. Or, we may have let anyone start the course, knowing that only those with the appropriate prior skills (not all of whom will have the prior qualifications to prove it) will clear all the fences.

As you may have gathered, I favour the alternative 'courses for horses' approach. Here we try, as far as possible, to adapt our courses to meet the needs of each individual learner. That is, to pursue the ideal of openness. Admittedly, such accommodating openness is costly, especially in support time and in the demands it makes on us as teachers and trainers. But trying to make our courses client-centred rather than producer-driven is, for me, the supreme challenge of ODL.

You may or may not find such a switch of emphasis easy to accept. Even if you accept it as an ideal, you may not see how you can implement it within your context. It is not easy, I know, especially if you are dealing with distance learners and large numbers of them – not to mention recalcitrant colleagues and an inflexible assessment system. However, even if you are restricted to offering courses that *look* the same for all learners, perhaps you may wish to individualise them along the lines suggested by Nathaniel Cantor more than fifty years ago:

> No two students will learn in the same way. Every individual will take out of the course what he feels he wants or needs and will put into it whatever efforts his capacity and willingness to learn allow. The [teacher] who is aware of these differences in learning will permit different students to use him, and the material of the course, in their own unique ways. As long as the student is sincerely trying to do something with himself and struggling to learn, he should be permitted to move at his own speed and on his own level.
>
> (Cantor, 1946)

Figure 3.15 Summary for a block/course

Source: Course H804, Implementation of ODL, Block 1, UK OU, 2000, p. 23

A checklist at the end of a course should not only enable students to determine for themselves whether they have achieved the objectives specified, but it should also provide academics with the guidance that they need to independently determine whether students have in fact achieved the objectives specified.

Assessment details

Knowing what is to be achieved is not the same as knowing how assignments may be used to measure student achievement. However, we would expect the introduction to a course to indicate how assignments will be used to determine the ultimate achievement of students on the course as a whole. What is now required is more detailed information on the actual assignments, and where this is located will depend on the form of assessment.

If student assessment is in the form of an end-of-course examination, then it would be appropriate to provide the additional detail on what is required in the conclusion at the end of the course. However, if assessment is undertaken through a combination of assignments at the end of each block (or unit) together with an end-of-course examination, then it would be appropriate to provide more detailed information on the block (or unit) assignments at the end of each block (or unit) and the information on the end-of-course examination in the conclusion at the end of the course.

An alternative approach is to include information on all aspects of assessment (introductory outlines together with essential details) in an assessment guide – referring students to related parts of this during the presentation of the course. This is very much the same type of choice that exists in developing adjunct aids (that is, aids to learning such as advance organisers, activities, and checklists), where these may be either integrated into self-study materials or included in a separate study guide.

The following examples of the type of assessment information that is required are taken from a course where assignments were set at the end of each block of study, while the usual end-of-course examination was replaced by a project – with project reports being submitted for assessment. The project report was referred to as the 'examinable component'.

We have already seen an outline of the assessment strategy that was adopted for this course (see Figure 3.14), and you will find an example of the more detailed information that was provided for each block-related assignment in Figure 3.16. You will also find a sample (the first of two pages) of the more detailed information provided on the 'examinable component' in Figure 3.17.

At this point it is important to emphasise that I have not attempted to recommend any particular approach to assessment, nor have I attempted to describe the variety of different approaches to assessment. Rather, I

THE TUTOR-MARKED ASSIGNMENTS

You will be expected to submit five TMAs on this course. Four of them are graded and one (TMA 03) is not, but it is still obligatory.

Specific assessment criteria

For each of the four graded TMAs, we are asking tutors to allocate marks on the following basis:

- The extent and quality of your contributions to the relevant online discussions during the preceding block (10 per cent).
- The way in which you use appropriate resources: the course books, other books or articles, the online discussions, Web resources (30 per cent).
- The quality of your insights into the distinctive features of your own ODL context and the appropriateness and inventiveness of your proposals for acting effectively within it (25 per cent).
- The clarity and coherence of your written argument or discourse (25 per cent).
- The appropriateness of your written presentation, e.g. style, grammar, spelling, paragraphing, referencing (10 per cent).

Notice from the first point that, however excellent one of your TMAs may be, it will not score more than 90 per cent unless you have contributed to the online discussions during the weeks that preceded its cut-off date. Your online contributions will be judged in terms of their cogency, relevance, helpfulness, courtesy, timeliness and frequency.

TMA 01 (cut-off date 22 March) 1500 words

In the light of the issues raised in Block 1, re-examine what you know about the learners for whom you might be planning an ODL programme and identify the implications for the kind of course and support you need to provide them with. We would expect your TMA to fall into two equally weighted parts:

1. A profile of your learners (as described in the overview essay for Block 1), indicating their nature, needs and learning circumstances.
2. A section in which you identify two or three (no more) of the most crucial things you know about your learners and explain what you see as significant about these particular aspects in the context of implementing ODL.

You may find it possible and useful to talk with some learners or work colleagues about this assignment before you complete it. What ideas do they have? Would they agree with your understandings and interpretations? You may also want to rehearse some of your ideas online with your tutor group.

Figure 3.16 Detailed guidance for a block assignment

Source: Course H804, Implementation of ODL, Assignment Guide, UK OU, 2000, p. 6

H804 Assignment Guide

THE EXAMINABLE COMPONENT

The H804 project report takes the place of an examination for this course. It carries 50 per cent of the overall course grade and is submitted at the end of the course. Like your TMAs it will be marked by your tutor; unlike your TMAs it will also be marked by a second tutor who will not know whose project report she or he is marking or what mark the first tutor gave it.

The project report (cut-off date 2 October) 6000 words

The final eight weeks of this course have been set aside for you to complete an independent learning project in which you explore an aspect of ODL that is of particular interest to you. (You may, of course, have been working on your project earlier in the course as well.) The examinable component is your written report on that project.

Specific assessment criteria

Regardless of the aspect of ODL that you have explored, markers are asked to bear in mind the following criteria:

- Does your introduction provide a clear indication of what your project is about, why you consider your subject important and how you set about exploring it?
- Does the body of your report involve analysis as well as description and does it demonstrate that you have been able to construct, explain and justify your own perspective on the subject?
- Are the facts and data you mention and the argument you build upon them clearly and coherently organised and expressed?
- Does the report relate the facts and data you mention to a range of the concepts and issues discussed elsewhere in the course, drawing on a variety of sources: reading, discussions and experience?
- Do your concluding paragraphs summarise all the main points, acknowledge any gaps, mention any relevant insights, recommendations or decisions, indicate any further work that might usefully be undertaken and show evidence that you have reflected on your experience and that the course has made a difference to the way you see it or might act upon it?
- Is the report clearly one that could have been written only by someone who has taken H804? And, further, does the report as a whole demonstrate that the course has had some influence on your thinking, that it has somehow illuminated your conception of ODL and possibly also your professional practice?
- Is the report as a whole written and presented in an appropriate manner, e.g. with regard to style, grammar, spelling, paragraphing, referencing?

Figure 3.17 Detailed guidance for an end-of-course assignment
Source: Course H804, Implementation of ODL, Assignment Guide, UK OU, 2000, p. 9

have simply indicated that whatever assessment policy is adopted that this should be explained as clearly as possible to students – either at appropriate points within self-study materials or in a separate assignment guide.

A logical framework

This is an appropriate point in time to stop and reflect on the design characteristics of a course as a whole. You will now be aware that, regardless of the subject matter concerned, and regardless of whether this is presented in terms of topics or processes, a wide range of features can be built into the presentation of a course to facilitate student learning. These include the development of an introduction (with the help of an advance organiser, statement of aims, and information on resources, student support, etc.) and the addition of a conclusion (with the help of a summary, and details of assessment). Where these features are combined together they might be described as providing a framework for the presentation of a course, and you will find the essential features of this framework summarised in Figure 3.18.

Where these features are physically located may vary, and the following are three commonly used options. The first option is for 'the introduction to the course' and the 'concluding comments' (including both assessment details and a concluding summary) to be presented respectively at the beginning and end of the related 'Study Guide'.

An alternative is to include the 'Introduction to the Course' in a separate document that can be circulated in advance to students. Similarly, assessment details might be included in a separate 'Assessment Booklet' that can be referred to at appropriate times during, and towards the end of, the course. Within such a scenario the most appropriate location for any concluding summary is likely to be at the end of the 'Study Guide'.

Another commonly used option is to include all the features referred to in a separate 'Course Guide' with students being referred to it at appropriate points in time. As such, part of it would provide students with an introduction to the course, but it would also contain details of the assessment process to be followed, and students would be referred to these as and when appropriate during the course. It is not difficult to find good examples of all the options referred to above.

3.3 Making use of existing materials

You will have already noted that existing materials such as books, academic articles, tapes, and videos may be adopted for use in ODL with the help of appropriate adjunct aids included within a related study guide. However, depending on the type of materials involved, it sometimes makes sense to make use of existing materials and at other times it does not. In the text that follows we will therefore take a look at three

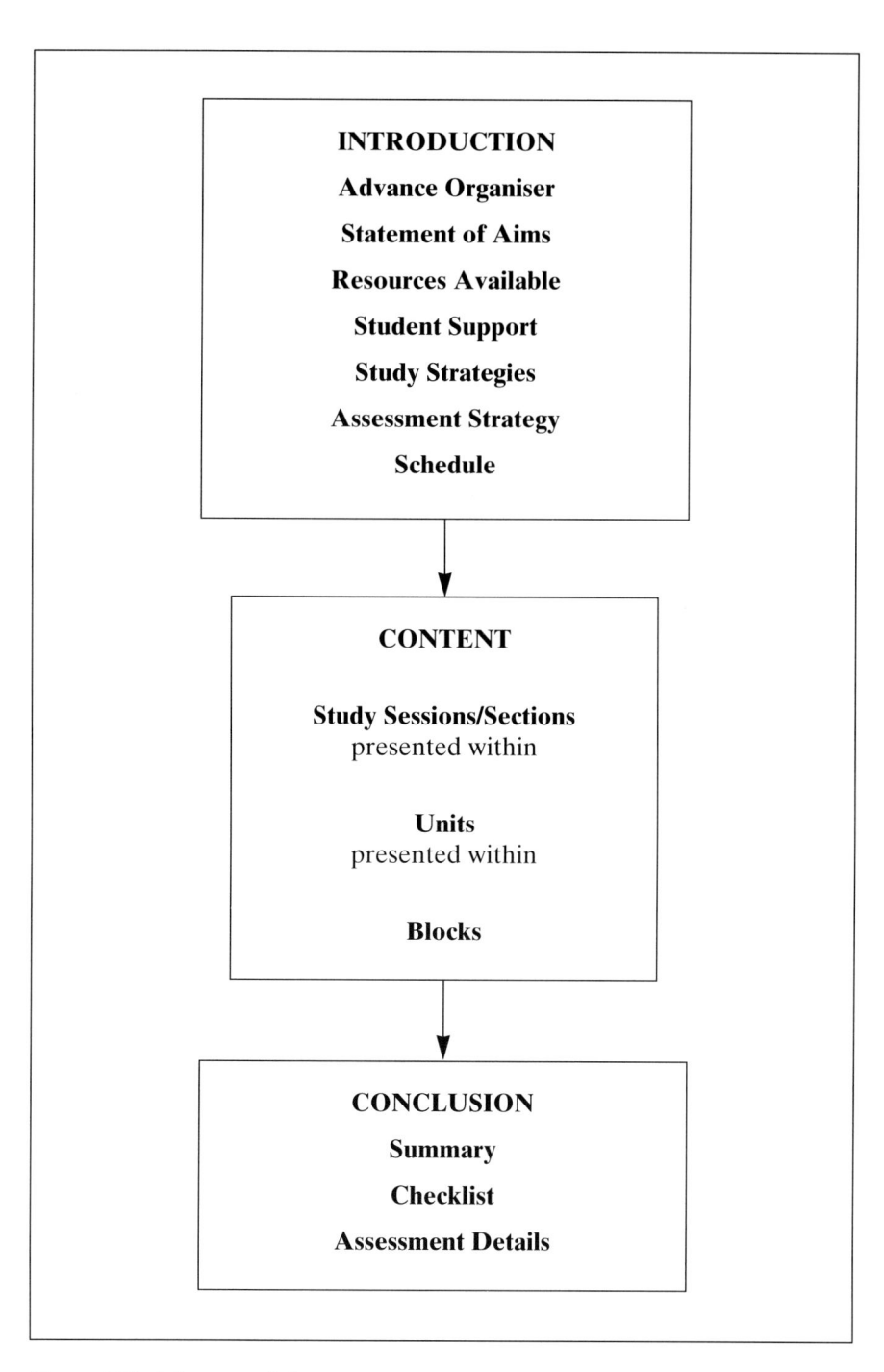

```
INTRODUCTION
Advance Organiser
Statement of Aims
Resources Available
Student Support
Study Strategies
Assessment Strategy
Schedule
          │
          ▼
CONTENT

Study Sessions/Sections
   presented within

       Units
   presented within

       Blocks
          │
          ▼
CONCLUSION
Summary
Checklist
Assessment Details
```

Figure 3.18 A framework for a course

different scenarios, and consider what is involved in adopting such materials for ODL.

In the first of these scenarios we will assume that the materials are well-developed self-study materials, and that the *materials may be used as they are*. In the second scenario we will assume that the content is perfectly acceptable, but that *adjunct aids will need to be developed* before the materials will be acceptable for self-study purposes. In the final scenario, we will assume that the development of adjunct aids in itself would not convert the materials to good self-study materials, and that the *content itself needs to be changed*. This is in fact the most difficult situation to deal with.

Materials may be used as they are

If the existing materials have appropriate adjunct aids built into them, they may be used in their existing form so long as they can help students to achieve specific course objectives, have been presented at the right level for the students concerned, and are well structured and clearly presented.

This scenario is most likely to be encountered where the materials have been specially developed for use in the course concerned. The materials might be in a variety of different forms such as audio-tapes, videos, home experiment kits, computer programs, CDs, and so on.

In such situations all that is required is to use the study guide to refer students to the self-study materials at appropriate points in time. You will find an example of this approach in Figure 3.19 which is taken from a science course in the UK OU.

One of the advantages of the approach illustrated is that, although each activity is separated from the core text by means of an introductory title and an end arrow (with an icon in the margin identifying the type of resource required), it is still easy to follow the chain of the core text. In fact, so long as the activities are not crucial to further progress, if students prefer to do so, they should have no difficulty in continuing with their study of the core text – returning to complete omitted activities at a later point in time.

Adjunct aids will need to be developed

Where existing materials have not been specifically developed for self-study purposes, they may still be adopted for use in ODL so long as they can help students to achieve specific course objectives, have been presented at the right level for the students concerned, and are well structured and clearly presented. They may include articles, books, audio-tapes, videos, home experiment kits, computer programs, CDs, and so on. All that is required is the development of appropriate adjunct aids for inclusion in a related study guide.

[A temperate Earth? Block 2]

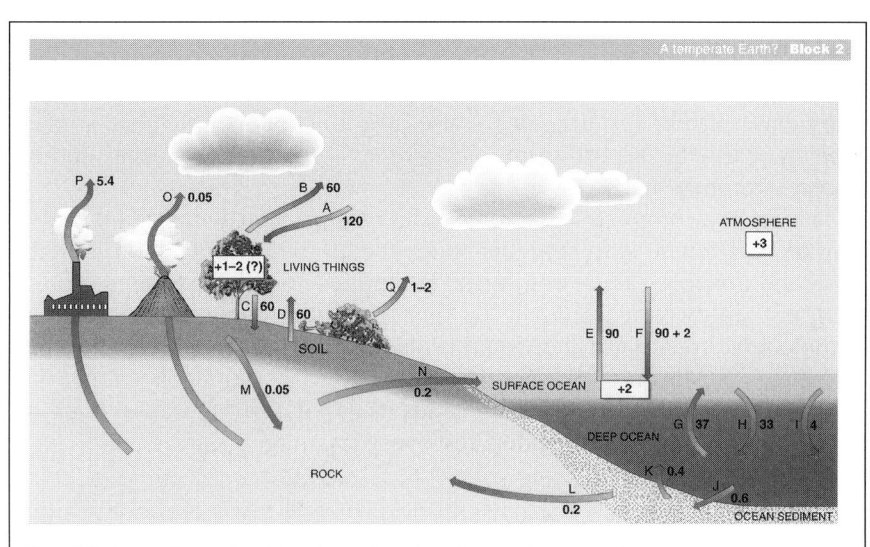

Figure 8.11 gives our final version of the carbon cycle — the modern one. Note the two new human-caused releases of carbon into the atmosphere: arrow P, which shows the burning of fossil fuels as an extra transfer process from rock to the atmosphere; and arrow Q, which shows the clearing and burning of forests as an extra transfer process from living things to the atmosphere. The resulting annual increases in the reservoirs of carbon in the atmosphere, surface ocean, and living things are shown in boxes. The largest change has been in the atmosphere — the 1996 level of about 760×10^{12} kg C (Table 8.1) was about 30% higher than the 'pre-industrial' level of about 590×10^{12} kg C estimated from ice-cores.

Carbon dioxide is a greenhouse gas, and the effect on the GMST of the increase in atmospheric CO_2 will be taken up in Section 10, where we will also look to the future. Before that, in the next section, we will see if we can understand climate changes in the recent and distant past, and this will involve looking at factors additional to CO_2. This attempt to explain the past should help scientists to predict the future.

Now that you have made a full trip around the global carbon cycle, you are ready to explore it more fully in Activity 8.5.

Activity 8.5 An element on the move
In this first CD-ROM activity of the course, 'An element on the move', you will 'be' a carbon atom, and will move through and explore an expanded number of reservoirs in a sequence of your own choosing. Remember that important notes for this activity can be found in the Study File. ◀

Figure 8.11 A pictorial representation of today's carbon cycle — rates of input and output do not balance, and some reservoirs (atmosphere, surface ocean, living things) are not in a steady state. Estimated annual changes in the sizes of these reservoirs are shown in boxes. The rates P and Q represent human-accelerated release of carbon from the rock reservoir to the atmosphere (P) and from the living things reservoir to the atmosphere (Q). Rate F has increased by about 2×10^{12} kg C y^{-1}.

Figure 3.19 Reference to fully developed self-study materials
Source: Course S103, Discovering Science, Block 2, UK OU, 1998, p. 135

The materials adopted in this way do not become the course, but rather become valuable resources to which students can be referred for very specific purposes. The wide use of such resources is particularly appropriate for post-graduate courses where students need to read widely and need to view issues from a variety of different perspectives. For example, on one of the MA courses to which we have already referred (Course H804: *The Implementation of ODE*, MA in ODE, UK OU, 2000) the resources provided included fourteen set books. Students were also provided with a course guide, a study guide, and a wide range of on-line resources, while computer-conferencing was used to provide support and stimulate discussion of a wide range of issues concerned with the implementation of ODL. The same range of resources were also used to support individual student projects, with the report from each project replacing the usual end-of-course examination.

The on-line computer-conferencing had a particularly important role to play on this course with students being encouraged to reflect on how the ideas and concepts addressed might be applied to the implementation of ODL in their own environment. As such, computer-conferencing was used in the course to support individual problem-solving through collaborative activities. As Mason (1998, pp. 34–35) indicates in her book *Globalising Education*, computer-conferencing lends itself particularly well to this type of facilitative approach to guided, discovery learning.

Content itself needs to be changed

If you are developing self-study materials for the first time, you may wish to make use of materials that have been used either by yourself or your colleagues in traditional face-to-face teaching situations. This may appear to be a very logical way of building on what has already been achieved, but a few words of caution may be helpful if you are contemplating this.

The first question to ask yourself is what level of transformation will be required to convert the existing materials to high quality self-study materials. Let us consider three possibilities.

At the simplest level it may be that all that is required is for the existing materials to be edited and presented in a more professional manner. If this is the case, the original author is unlikely to object, since the intent is to help the author to present his or her materials in the best possible light without changing the content in any serious manner. Unfortunately, this scenario is highly unlikely, as most existing materials will not have been designed for self-study purposes, and will at the very least need adjunct aids to be developed.

Where adjunct aids need to be developed, these may be integrated into the materials or included in a related study guide. Again, the original authors are unlikely to object to making such changes, or to having these made on their behalf, since the proposed changes do not in themselves attempt to change what the author has said. In other words, the proposed changes are not threatening. To the contrary, they are intended to clarify the purpose of the materials, to present them in the clearest possible manner, and to encourage students to become involved in the process of learning, and as such will often be welcomed by the authors concerned. Unfortunately, this is not the most likely scenario to be encountered.

In the most common scenario it is likely that there will be a desire to change some of the basic principles upon which the existing materials have been built. For example, there may be a desire to modify some of the basic aims, to modify assumptions made with regard to the target group, to present issues in a simpler and clearer manner with more real-life examples included, to restructure the way knowledge and skills are presented, to use the media in different ways, to make use of alternative teaching strategies, and so on. Unfortunately, any such modifications will have implications for the detailed content that builds on these aspects, and will inevitably require a major redrafting of the existing materials.

Since the third scenario is most likely, let us consider some of the implications, and what might be done to overcome any perceived problems. If you are the author of the original materials, you may well be willing to take on the task of transforming them in a very substantial manner, particularly if you believe that the existing materials have outlived their natural life, that you have gained appropriate recognition for your contributions, and that you are ready to move forward. However, not everyone will take this view.

Having invested a great deal of time and effort into developing their materials, you may well have colleagues who will be reluctant to put any further effort into redrafting and restructuring them when they feel quite satisfied with the results of their efforts. Likewise, they may resist any proposals to have external consultants transform their materials, seeing such a proposal as not only infringing on their ownership of the materials but also insulting the products that they have produced at such expense to themselves.

If you hope to transform materials for use in ODL you must ensure that your colleagues fully understand why this is needed, that they appreciate that the proposal in no way reflects badly on what they have achieved so far, and that they recognise there is simply a need for different types of materials designed to serve different purposes.

Where the original authors agree to either transform the materials themselves (the best option so long as appropriate guidance is provided), or agree to allow a delegated expert to transform the materials on their behalf, caution should still be exercised. If the transformation is to be undertaken by a delegated expert, authors should be provided with examples of different types of transformation before any work is undertaken on their materials, and, before proceeding towards a complete redraft, a partial redraft should be produced to ensure that the author fully appreciates the level of transformation intended.

A final option is to obtain permission from whoever holds copyright over the materials to use them as a resource in the development of new materials. This typically happens in the UK OU when a course reaches the end of its life – usually after about eight years. At this point in time the original course team and the individual authors involved have gained full recognition for the materials that they have produced, they will almost certainly recognise that the materials need to be updated to meet current needs, and they will usually be happy to see the course redeveloped or replaced with or without their involvement.

If you would like to know more about the transformation of materials, you may find it helpful to read my article (Melton, 1990) on 'Transforming text for distance learning'.

In perspective

I would hope that you now have a good idea of what I mean by frameworks within which self-study materials might be presented, and that you recognise the logic behind the various design features that have been considered. There is nothing to stop you developing your own frameworks for the presentation of self-study materials, but if you do so you should identify the logic behind the design, test out its feasibility, back up controversial features with appropriate research, and open up your design to public inspection and debate through recognised academic journals. As you will have already gathered from the examples provided, the design features discussed in this chapter have been tried and tested across a wide range of disciplines in the UK OU and in a number of other distance teaching institutions overseas.

Suggestions

This is a good point in time to sit down with some of your colleagues who are likely to be involved in the development of ODL within your own institution, and see if you can agree on the basic design features that you would like to see incorporated into your own approach to ODL.

Here are some of the questions that you might well consider. To what extent do you envisage developing materials from scratch? Do you intend to make use of existing materials, and, if so, can you identify the type of materials that you would like to use and the degree to which they would need to be transformed? Do you intend to make use of study guides to present the materials in a coherent manner, and, if so, do you plan to incorporate core learning within it? Would you like to see course teams making use of a common framework for the presentation of materials, and, if so, to what extent would you hope to adopt the design features identified within this chapter?

Do keep notes on your observations, but do remain open to further discussion of the issues. As you progress through the book I have no doubt that your thinking will become more refined.

4 The use of media in ODL

Contents

Introduction	85
4.1 Scenarios illustrating media usage	86
4.2 Traditional media	94
4.3 High technology media	99
4.4 The selection of media	104
In perspective	108
Suggestions	109

Introduction

It is recognised that most things can be taught using any given medium, but there are situations where it is recognised that one medium is likely to be much more effective than others in facilitating student learning. It is in fact quite common in ODL to move backwards and forwards from one medium to another, making use of different media at different points in time for different purposes. However, it is also recognised that a combination of media can often be much more effective than any single medium, and the intent in this chapter is to provide you with some insight into the variety of ways in which media might be exploited to facilitate student learning.

In the first section of the chapter you will find the description of a number of *scenarios illustrating media usage*. The intent is to stimulate your thinking as to how you might exploit the power of the media in your own environment.

In the next two sections of the chapter we will go on to look at the variety of media available to us and ways in which each might be exploited to advantage. However, although we will be looking at the strengths of each medium in its own right, you should not lose sight of the fact that the effectiveness of any given medium might well be increased by using it in

86 *Characteristics of ODL*

combination with other media. This does not have to be a much more expensive process, since the supporting media can at times be very cost-effective.

You will find a wide range of media to think about, and it seemed convenient to present these under two separate headings according to whether they might best be identified as the *traditional media* familiar to all of us or as the more recent *high technology media* that are evolving so rapidly. Generally speaking, the traditional forms of media are still much more widely used in ODL and much more cost-effective than their high technology counterparts, but the latter have enormous potential, and as usage spreads around the world the related costs will almost certainly decline, making them a more viable option.

Although the prime aim of this chapter is to set you thinking about the power of the media and ways in which it might be exploited, this in itself is not sufficient. When you come to thinking about the media, or combinations of media, that you would like to make use of in developing your own approach to ODL a variety of other factors need to be taken into account including such factors as the costs involved in buying and maintaining the equipment and in producing and supporting the materials required. In the last section of this chapter we will therefore take a close look at the factors that need to be taken into account when making decisions about *the selection of media*.

4.1 Scenarios illustrating media usage

In the text that follows you will find a number of scenarios illustrating some of the ways in which media may be used on their own and in combination with other media. These are included here to help stimulate your thinking about the variety of ways in which media might be used to advantage. As you consider each of the scenarios, take time to think about how you might make use of different types of media, or combinations of media, in your own situation. Make a note of your ideas. You may find reinforcement for them when you read the comments on the variety of different types of media in the next two sections of the chapter under the headings *traditional media* and *high technology media*.

Scenario 1: Exploiting the power of a single medium

Karen is a sales representative whose work takes her occasionally to Germany. She has just begun an ODL course in German during her spare time in the hope that this will help her with her work. At the moment she is driving to work and using this time to listen to an audio cassette in German. It is one of a sequence of documentary features, and although they are linked to the main themes in her course, they can be studied on their own without reference to other course materials. This particular documentary is about ways of dealing with traffic problems in the old university town of Tübingen in Germany. At the end of each documentary there are related fluency and pronunciation exercises, and she is currently practising some of these. Apart from helping her with her German, she feels that the documentaries are providing her with a useful introduction to social and cultural aspects of life in Germany.

Karen also has a cassette of a drama set in modern Germany. It is presented in a series of episodes that extend throughout the course. She has already listened to the first episode in which Bettina, Sonja and Thomas were flat hunting in Leipzig. Apart from helping her with her German, Karen found much of the information helpful, as she plans to spend some time in Germany, and feels that she now has a much better idea about how to find accommodation for herself.

She is finding the documentary features and the drama very helpful in that the pronunciation of the speakers is clearer than that of individuals in the video cassette provided with the course. This is because the video cassette introduces people in very natural settings, such as on the street, in meetings, and at the town hall, and they tend to speak less clearly than on the audio cassette. Needless to say, she recognises that this is how people actually speak, and that she needs to learn to communicate with people from all walks of life, but she finds the audio cassette valuable in that it provides her with role models for her own spoken German.

Although in this scenario a single medium (audio) is being used to facilitate learning, the course itself makes use of a variety of media. For example, it not only makes use of the audio cassettes and video already referred to, but also a study guide for language learners in general, study guides containing a great deal of core learning for each part of the course, a book of transcripts to be used in conjunction with the audio cassettes and video, a German grammar book and a German dictionary.

Scenario 2: Exploiting a combination of simple media

John is a senior science teacher, who also takes his teenage students walking and climbing in the nearby mountains. He has already picked up a great deal of knowledge about the animals, birds and flowers in the local habitat, and enjoys introducing his students to the natural environment. A short while ago he decided to take an ODL course in Earth Sciences to learn more about his local environment and how it came into being.

He has just finished reading about how different types of rocks are formed, and was very interested to see photographs of related rock formations. Among these he was able to recognise the limestone and sandstone strata that he sees regularly on his local walks, and he took note of some of the features that he planned to examine more closely when he next goes out walking. He also noted that he will be able to look more closely at other types of rock formations (found in granite and basalt) during the summer school field trip which he will be joining in the near future.

88 *Characteristics of ODL*

He has just been advised in the study guide that he should undertake a related activity concerned with the identification of rock samples. Following the advice given, he has therefore turned to the earth sciences kit accompanying the course, and is following the instructions provided on the audio cassette. He has just taken a number of rock samples from the kit and placed them on the desk in front of him. Each rock sample is polished smooth on one side. Taking the first rock sample he holds it in his hand, taking note of its relative weight, and then feels the sharp, rugged texture of the unpolished surface. He stops the tape for a moment while he makes a few notes, and then re-starts it. Following the guidance given on the audio cassette he then picks up a magnifying glass, and uses it to study the polished surface of the rock, comparing what he sees with the texture patterns illustrated in labelled diagrams within the study guide. He then goes on to repeat very much the same exercise with the various samples provided, stopping the tape periodically to make notes. You might notice that, with the guidance being provided on the tape, John's hands are free to manipulate the rock specimens, to feel their weight and texture, and to hold the magnifying glass. His eyes are also relatively free to concentrate on the texture patterns in the rocks, although he does glance from time to time at the related illustrations in the study guide. He would certainly not be as free to concentrate on the rock samples if he had to follow the detailed instructions in the study guide.

Before reading further I would suggest that you glance back through the above scenario, and make note of the senses that John used during the activity and identify the media that were exploited for this purpose.

John made use of three senses, namely those of sight (to view the rock samples and to look at the labelled illustrations in the study guide), hearing (to listen to the instructions on the audio-tape), and feeling (to take note of the weight and texture of the rock samples). The media used were the audio-tape (providing instructions), the study guide (with its related illustrations), and (according to how you define the term media) the earth sciences kit (containing the rock samples and magnifying glass). You might not have thought of a science kit as a medium for learning, but if *a medium is defined as a means of communication*, then the rock samples (just like works of art) would appear to have served such a purpose. You might prefer to describe the rock samples as a resource, but whatever term we use to describe them, they certainly had an important role to play in the above scenario.

Scenario 3: Using the media to facilitate analysis and discussion

Olga is a housewife with three children – a teenage son just starting college and two daughters at the early kindergarten stage. She used to be a nurse, but gave this up to look after the children. Although she would like to return to work once her daughters are in full-time education, she is reluctant to return to nursing because of the unsocial hours involved, and is hoping that she might find some sort of employment in the field of health and social welfare, where she would still be able to contribute to the well-being of others but with working hours that would conflict less with her role as a mother. With this in mind she is trying to obtain related qualifications, and is currently taking an ODL Foundation Course in health and social welfare.

Olga is watching one of three related video clips which include documentaries and archive footage related to the abuse of children in special care homes. Following the advice given, she watches the first video clip with a minimum of interruptions, trying to digest the main themes discussed rather than every detail. Having watched the clip Olga turns back to the study guide, and notes that, once she has viewed all three video clips, she will be required to prepare a report for assessment purposes on 'changes that would appear to be desirable in the situations reviewed' and in doing so to identify:

- the needs and rights of the children concerned;
- the extent to which these relate to age and sex;
- errors that were committed and action that needs to be taken;
- the resources that will be needed to implement change;
- ways in which change will need to be managed.

Reading on, she is interested to find that the incidents reviewed will be discussed at summer school. At that point in time students will be divided into discussion groups, with each group focusing in on one of the five issues highlighted (the needs and rights of the children, etc.). Prior to commencing their deliberations, there will be an opportunity for members of each group to refresh their memories with a quick review of the video clips. The groups will then focus discussion on the issues allocated to them. Each group will be expected take on board the views of its members and produce a joint verbal report (to the group as a whole) highlighting key errors that appear to have been committed in looking after children in care and identifying action that could have reduced the chances of the problems arising.

Before reading further, I would suggest that you glance back through the above scenario, and make a note on how the video was used to facilitate learning. Can you identify other ways in which you might exploit video to advantage?

Scenario 4: Taking advantage of computer-conferencing

Segundo is a senior education officer on a small island in the South Pacific with rather limited resources for supporting higher education. About three years ago he became involved in discussions about the possibility of taking advantage of ODL to reach out to students on neighbouring islands, and his education department agreed to provide the finances to enable him to study for an MA in ODE through open and distance learning. He has completed two of the required courses (a 'Foundation Course in ODE' and a course on the 'Applications of Information Technology in ODE') and is now taking the final course in the programme on the 'Implementation of ODE'.

Segundo is finding the final course particularly appropriate, as it is making him think very carefully about all the aspects of planning and developing ODE from a very practical point of view. The course contains the usual course guide, a study guide covering the four blocks of the course, a tutor-marked assignment related to each block of the course, the usual tutor support, and a project contributing to 25 per cent of the marks awarded on the course. In addition, the course includes on-line tutor and student support through computer-conferencing and e-mail, and includes a wide range of resources in the form of fourteen set books and a wealth of on-line materials accessed through the related on-line resources centre.

Although the course has only been under way for a few weeks, Segundo is already thinking about the project that he will need to submit as part of the course. He has been advised that this may be on some aspect of ODL learners, on course design for ODL, on learner support, on evaluation and quality assurance, on managing ODL systems – or aspects from several of these areas. The final eight weeks of the course have been set aside for writing up the final project reports, but students have been advised to start thinking about their projects from the very beginning of the course. In fact, in less than eight weeks from now Segundo will be required to submit an assignment in which he outlines his plans for his project. Although outline plan is not for credit purposes, it will be critical in ensuring that his final plans are realistic.

At this point in time Segundo is taking part in a computer conference organised by the course. He was particularly pleased to find that the conference included a Project Forum (see Figure 3.3) with specific strands (or discussion lines) to support an exchange of views on the following:

- early ideas about *appropriate topics* that might be addressed;
- *different types of projects* that might be considered appropriate (literature reviews, empirical studies, information searches, design projects, and so on);
- *factors that need to be taken into account* in planning the project (resources needed, co-operation of others required, realistic time requirements, underestimating time requirements, 100 hours set aside for project);
- *the planning and scheduling of time.*

At this point in time Segundo is clear that he wants his project to help him with the development of plans for ODL within the South Pacific, but he is not clear as to how this might be achieved in practice. He is currently participating in the first strand of the discussion which is intended to help him identify an appropriate topic for his project. He has read the general introduction by the tutor (Figure 4.1), and, in response to the tutor's suggestion, has made an initial contribution outlining his local situation and his belief that ODL could be used to open up much needed educational opportunities to students on neighbouring islands. He indicates that in order to attract international funding a full project proposal will need to be developed, and he is hoping that his course project might contribute to the project proposal that will be required. He indicates that he would like his course project to help him with his plans for the South Pacific, and indicates that he is thinking of undertaking some sort of feasibility study for the South Pacific project.

He is now reading similar contributions made by his fellow students, and is particularly interested to find that three other students (Murat from Turkey, Gustavo from Mexico, and Domani from Sri Lanka) have very similar types of interest to himself. In fact, Segundo is now in the process of sending an 'open response' to Domani identifying projects and contacts that he is aware of that seem to be closely related to the type of project that Domani is thinking about. In his response he indicates that although the projects and contacts to which he refers appear to be most relevant to Domani's project, they may also be of interest to Murat and Gustavo. He is hoping that in return he will get similar types of feedback.

Having completed his 'open response' to Domani, Segundo goes on to read a response from his tutor commenting on the contributions to date. In particular his tutor has identified a number of submissions (including Segundo's) that he feels contain great ideas but that in their present form appear to be over-ambitious to be completed within the time frame of the project. The tutor's comments are supportive and positive, and he suggests that those concerned might find it helpful to look at some of the projects that were submitted in the previous year to see how they converted their ideas into manageable projects. The projects can be accessed through the conference, and Segundo plans to look at these shortly. The tutor also suggests that when they feel reasonably confident about the topic they would like to address that they might usefully go on to think more clearly about the form that their project might take (literature review, empirical study, etc.), and points out that the next strand of the discussion will give them some ideas on what they might do, and will give them the opportunity to further develop their thinking.

At this point in time it is worthwhile reflecting back on this scenario and asking yourself what advantages Segundo might gain from participating in the computer-conferencing. As always, it is not simply the availability of a particular medium that is important but the way it is used and what can be achieved through its usage.

Msg #181 of 462 posted 3/31/00 by r.f.melton
Plenary Area |Project Forum |Project Mini-Confe... |Appropriate Topics |

Appropriate Topics

If you are one of those who already have a fairly good idea of what you would like to do for your project, I will still encourage you to remain open-minded throughout this mini-conference - testing and developing your thinking against the variety of factors that I will be introducing.

If you are one of those who are not at all sure as to what to do for your project, it might help you to think about your local environment, the educational and training needs that you perceive, and the extent to which open and distance learning (ODL) might meet those needs. What are the main assumptions that you are making about the advantages of ODL? Do you have evidence to support these assumptions? What are the main factors that you will need to be able to overcome to ensure that ODL is accepted? Does this highlight issues that need to be the subject of further study? As you think about the possible focus for your project, do make sure that it will be an issue that is within the main stream of ODL and not on its peripheral margins.

You may like to take a look at the list of projects submitted in 1999 and at some actual examples of projects that we have posted in the file area. If so, I would suggest that you start by looking at the range of topics covered by the projects. While doing this it may well help stimulate your thinking about your own project if you ask yourself the following questions:

- *Under which titles could you have submitted a meaningful project and which are way out of your range of interest?*
  Identifying broad areas of interest should not be too difficult.
- *Do any of the projects in the list appear to fall outside the mainstream of ODL?*
  One or two are close to the boundaries, and as such were at risk of not being accepted as appropriate projects. If you build your project on what you learn within this course, this should ensure that it lies within the mainstream of ODL.
- *Do any of the titles in the list fail to give you a clear insight into the purposes of the related project? If so, what clarification would you have liked to have seen?*
  Once you are clear as to what you hope to achieve through your project, producing a clear title should not be difficult.

If you would now like to take a look at the list of projects submitted in 1999, click here.

In response to earlier requests in the project forum, I approached seven top performers from last year, and asked them if they would let us post a set of their project-related documents in the mini-conference. More specifically, I asked them if they would provide us with three documents:

Figure 4.1 Computer-conference strand encouraging students to reflect on topics for projects

Source: Course H804, Implementation of ODL, Project Forum, UK OU, 2000

- a commentary providing insights into the lessons they learned from their work on their project (the things that they would do differently with the benefit of hindsight).
- the outline of their project (submitted to us in the form of TMA03), and
- the full report on their project (submitted as the examinable component).

We have had a superb response. All promised the necessary documents, and these are being posted in the file area as they come in. Look through the documents in any order you prefer. However, I must admit that I enjoyed reading the 'commentaries' first, as these gave me personal insights into how the authors felt about the work involved.

If you would like to look at any of these documents now, right click on the related cell in the table below, and from the menu that appears use the 'save target as' option to download the document on to your desktop.

Project Title	Commentary	Outline	Report
A quality assurance model for the development of distance learning courses with part reference to on-line training and evaluation	Blackwood/1	Blackwood/2	Blackwood/3
Aspects of time in the implementation of H804 and Kielipuoti	Joyce/1	Joyce/2	Joyce/3
Learning network: communication skills - and practice	McAteer/1	McAteer/2	McAteer/3
Experience into knowledge: an inquiry into the processes of reflection in open and distance education	Roberts/1	Roberts/2	Roberts/3
Tailoring support to learners' needs: improving OU pre-study guidance to Portuguese students	Trewinnard/1	Trewinnard/2	Trewinnard/3

The documents provided by Reynolds have been put in a separate table, since you need a little more information about these before you can download them. For the 'outline' you will need an Adobe Acrobat Reader, and for the 'report' you will need Winzip application. We are assuming that you already have these, but if this is not the case then please advise us as soon as possible, and we will see if there are alternative ways of making these available to you. Using these applications the downloading of these documents might take up to 3 mins for the 'outline' and 12 mins for the 'report'.

Project Title	Commentary	Outline	Report
An exploration of web CT as a tool to create a web-base learning environment within the context of an undergraduate dental programme.	Reynolds/1	Reynolds/2	Reynolds/3

You may return to these documents at any time by using the same process or by accessing the *file area* where you will find a folder labelled *projects*. Within this you will find a sub-folder labelled *project titles* and another labelled *examples of projects*. The latter is further divided into sub-folders carrying the name of the author concerned, and the project-related documents inside are labelled as *commentary, outline*, and *report* respectively.

Figure 4.1 (continued)

4.2 Traditional media

Distinguishing between traditional and high technology media is somewhat arbitrary, but under the heading of traditional media I will limit myself to discussing *printed material*, the *mass media* (radio and television), *cassettes* (both audio and video), *telephone-based links* (telephone, faxes and audio-conferencing) and *practical resources* (the natural environment and home experiment kits) – all of which continue to be used extensively in ODL.

You might prefer to think of the natural environment and home experiment kits as resources to support student learning, rather than as media. They are included in the discussion here on the grounds that they provide an important way of communicating ideas to students – in much the same way that paintings and sculptures are perceived as media for communicating the feelings and perceptions of artists. However, I have not included student–tutor interactions in the discussion of traditional media – although they are clearly a means of communication – as they will be addressed within the next chapter under the heading of *student support systems*.

Printed material

Printed material still remains the most widely used media in ODL. It is typically found in the form of study guides, self-study materials, resource materials (such as books, journals, articles), and ancillary materials (such as course brochures and assignments). It is relatively cheap to produce and simple to use in terms of skill requirements.

Mass media

In its early days the UK OU was particularly well known for its exploitation of TV and to a lesser extent radio. It continues to exploit these media, but they do have the disadvantage of being designed for continuous viewing as well as being presented at fixed points in time. To some extent the latter problem can be overcome by recording the related programmes, but where the prime concern is the support of student learning audio and video cassettes tend to be preferred.

The main value of *radio* and *television* nowadays within the UK OU is usually perceived in marketing terms in that it enables the programme makers to reach out beyond the student body to the public at large. As such, it is an opportunity to arouse the interest of members of the public and to indirectly encourage them to enrol on related programmes of study.

Radio

The most obvious topics for radio include news bulletins, documentaries, archive materials, speeches, and discussions, and these may well be presented in other languages where the intent is to exploit them for language learning purposes.

Television

TV is still an excellent medium for providing students with unique experiences. It can introduce them to remote parts of the world (jungles, frozen wastes, and remote mountainous areas) and to people from very different cultures (Hindus, Buddhists, Muslims, Christians, and Jews). It can enable students to look back in time (through archive footage), to visit facilities to which access is usually very restricted (nuclear reactors, cyclotrons, satellites in orbit, other planets), and to observe phenomena (inside the human body, inside the atom, in outer space) that cannot be seen without sophisticated equipment (such as scanning devices, electron microscopes, high powered telescopes, and so on).

Cassettes

As already indicated, *audio* and *video cassettes* have tended to replace radio and television in supporting student learning, because of their greater flexibility and the greater variety of ways in which they may be used. They also have the advantage that students are much more in control of the medium – being able to stop, start and replay at will.

Audio cassettes

Audio cassettes may also be used in a variety of ways including the following:

- They may still be used primarily as a listening experience, particularly where this is simply one of many ways of exploiting a variety of media on a course. For example, on a language course, drama and documentaries might be included on audio cassettes with activities built around the recorded events. However, an additional audio cassette might also be produced for use on its own, so that students can take advantage of any spare time they might have (such as when driving to work or when undertaking other tasks around the house) to listen to related parts of the cassette.
- However, one of the main aims of ODL is to encourage students to become actively involved in the process of learning, and one of the prime advantages of audio cassettes is that it is easy to build activities around recorded events – doing this either within the medium itself or in a study guide related to the medium. Where this is done, the activities are typically related to specified parts of the tape.
- Audio cassettes may also be used in combination with other media

and resources to provide students with aural guidance – leaving their eyes free to scrutinise the items of interest and their hands free to take notes and to manipulate related materials (such as slides, film strips, textual materials, objects, and pieces of equipment).

Audio cassettes are easy to use, and compared with videos and computer-based instruction are relatively cheap to produce. According to Bates (1982) for the UK OU 'the greatest media development during its twelve years of existence has been the humble audio cassette'.

Video cassettes

Video cassettes may be used in very much the same way as TV as a listening experience. However, in common with audio cassette usage, it is much more common to encourage students to become involved in the process of learning through activities related to the contents of the video. Although the video might be designed for continuous viewing, it is common practice to make video clips that may be viewed as entities in their own right with activities built around each clip.

For example, business language students viewing a clip of a board meeting in a German company might be encouraged to analyse the language used by board members in addressing one another. Likewise trainee teachers watching a video clip of children in a classroom might be encouraged to identify different ways in which the children respond to different types of stimuli.

Although video cassettes are easy to use and students have the same sort of control over them as with audio cassettes, they are much more expensive to produce and video recorders are much more expensive to buy than their audio counterparts.

Telephone-based links

Because of the widespread availability of telephone lines it is relatively easy to set up communication systems based on these links.

Telephone

The simplest of all of the telephone-based links is the telephone itself, and it is used extensively in ODL to provide students with a means of contacting their tutors and vice versa.

Faxes

Another very simple and well established mode of communication is by means of faxes. Transmission is cheap – and much cheaper than the telephone where international links need to be established – and it is relatively easy to gain access to the equipment required. Apart from using faxes for sending and receiving messages, in ODL they are also used for submitting student assignments.

Audio-conferencing

Audio-conferencing tends to be used in ODL to establish links between a tutor and small groups of students for conferencing purposes, rather than as a means of communicating with large numbers of students. Because of the widespread availability of telephone lines it is relatively easy to set up and relatively cheap, but the number of students who can be involved at any one time in the conferencing process is very limited. This is because it is difficult to manage more than five or six telephone links within a conference. Although the number of students involved in a conference might be increased by increasing the number of students at any of the linked locations, this in turn will reduce the extent to which any one student might be interactively involved in the process.

Practical resources

We have already highlighted the value of activities in encouraging students to become involved in the process of learning, and *the natural environment* and *home experiment kits* can provide valuable resources around which such activities may be built. They can in fact be used to help develop some very important skills, and in the text that follows we will reflect on some of these.

The natural environment

One of the most common goals of higher education courses is to encourage students to develop the skills of the 'reflective practitioner', and according to (Chown and Last, 1993) one of the best ways of achieving this is through an experiential approach to learning. The approach was pioneered by Kolb (1984) and Kolb and Fry (1975), and is essentially a problem-solving approach that progresses through four distinct stages:

- *Experiencing* – in the first stage students are exposed to something unusual, something unexpected, something that it is hoped that they will want to understand and explain. The beginning of the cycle thus depends on finding appropriate objects, phenomena, or behaviour to stimulate such feelings, and there is no better place to look for this purpose than the local environment.
- *Reflecting* – in the second stage students are encouraged to ask themselves searching questions about what they have observed and to consider the range of possible explanations.

98 Characteristics of ODL

- *Concluding* – in the third stage students are encouraged to consider a variety of possible explanations and to identify what they feel is the most plausible explanation.
- *Testing* – in the fourth stage students test out their conclusion or hypothesis through practical tests. If the evidence gathered supports the hypothesis, it adds to its validity, but, if it does not, then the whole cycle needs to be repeated.

One of the main goals of the experiential approach is to help students to perceive the links between theory and practice, and at the same time to encourage 'deep' rather than 'surface' learning.

Home experiment kits

It is very common to find home experiment kits included as important components in science and technology courses. The equipment is usually cheap and simple, but well able to carry out the tasks for which it was designed. Such equipment might be developed with a wide variety of purposes in mind, and might be used to help students to develop a deeper understanding of the phenomena discussed and to develop their scientific skills.

In terms of developing a deeper understanding of phenomena, the kits might be used to help students to do the following:

- experience phenomena described within their courses;
- gain a deeper understanding of concepts, principles and theories through the gathering of related evidence;
- develop a deeper understanding of the scientific process through experiments that demonstrate the links between observation and theory.

In terms of developing their scientific skills, the kits might be used to help students do the following:

- develop practical skills such as those of manipulating delicate instruments and making accurate measurements;
- develop basic scientific skills such as those of observing, collecting data, interpreting data, analysing results, drawing conclusions, hypothesising, and developing theories.

From the above you will have noted that home experiment kits can be used to help students develop many of the skills of the 'reflective practitioner', and that there is a close parallel between what here is described as the scientific process and what Kolb describes as an experiential approach to learning. Both are designed to help students develop problem solving skills.

Needless to say, home experiments do not replace the more complex types of experiments that can be undertaken with more sophisticated equipment at residential schools, but they do provide students with the opportunity to experience a range of phenomena and to develop a variety of valuable skills.

4.3 High technology media

Under the heading of high technology media I have included those forms of electronic communication that have been widely adopted in ODL. In order to give you some indication of the extent to which the different media are used in practice, I have included frequent references to what happens within the UK Open University, and with this in mind I thought it might be helpful to begin with a brief comment on *student computer usage within the UK OU*. We will then go on to look at the strengths and weaknesses of the main forms of electronic communication.

We will begin by taking a look at *e-mail* and *computer-conferencing*. These are similar in that they both use text as a means of communication, but they are different in that e-mail is primarily used for one-to-one contact while computer-conferencing is used to support conferencing within a group.

We will then take a look at *video-conferencing*. This is rather different from the other modes of communication discussed here in that it has not been widely adopted within the UK OU. There are good reasons for this, but I have included it here, as it has been widely adopted in North America, and is used in many other countries.

The final technologies considered are those of *CDs* and the *World Wide Web*. CDs are of particular interest, because of the extent to which they are able to make use of text, graphics, sound, and video. The World Wide Web is still some way behind in this respect, but has the advantage over CDs in that it can support interaction between individuals.

Having said this, all the modes of electronic communication considered here are evolving rapidly, and all are seeking in one way or another to make the widest possible use of the media (text, graphics, audio, and video). In the final paragraphs I will therefore add a few words about *more recent developments*.

Student computer usage within the UK OU

The UK OU has been very careful about the way it has introduced computer usage into its courses, as it did not want to deny students access to courses simply because they did not have either the equipment or the skills required. However, it appears that the vast majority of students now have access to a computer and the Internet. According to a recent survey including over 18,000 students (Student Research Centre, 1999, Qu10),

83 per cent of the students had a computer and 75 per cent of these had an Internet connection. In addition, of those with computers 85 per cent used them for study purposes within the UK OU.

As student access to, and familiarity with, computers and the Internet have increased, so has the number of courses requiring students to have access to them, and students are now making use of computers for a wide variety of purposes. According to a recent report (Melton, 2000, pp. 32–41), the purposes for which computers are being used include:

- to gain access to the World Wide Web;
- to gain access to the course website;
- to access and retrieve networked information;
- to view CD-ROMs provided by the course;
- for word processing;
- for e-mail contact with the tutor;
- for computer-conferencing with tutor and other students;
- for electronic submission of Tutor Marked Assignments;
- to run software provided as part of the course;
- for simulation activities;
- for learning about and developing specific skills such as those of group dynamics.

E-mail

After the telephone and faxes, e-mail is probably the simplest mode of electronic communication. It may be used simply and cheaply for one-to-one communication between tutors and students and also for communication between students themselves. It is the equivalent of corresponding by mail, with the possibility of copying transmissions to a group as a whole. E-mail transmissions can be delivered much more rapidly than mail, and replies can be obtained within minutes if the recipient is available and prepared to reply.

Compared with communication by telephone, there is an inevitable delay between transmission and response by e-mail, and we might describe this form of communication as being asynchronous compared with that by telephone which might be described as synchronous. However, just as with telephones (with answering facilities) messages can be left for later response.

The main advantage of e-mail is the low cost of transmission (particularly for international communication), but compared with the telephone there is no voice contact, access to related equipment (the computer) is much more restricted, and the cost of the equipment itself is much greater.

Computer-conferencing

Computer-conferencing offers an efficient means of communication between tutors and students with the tutor and students able to post messages that can be read by all the students in a group.

It is usually used to facilitate the exchange of views between tutors and relatively small groups of students. (On the MA in ODE programme in the UK OU the number of students involved in a conference might range from 12–15 in individual tutor conferences to about 40–50 in plenary, or course, sessions.)

At the simplest level, computer-conferencing may be used to provide students with rapid feedback on problems encountered, and, since all students can monitor the exchanges, it can provide a simple way of clarifying general misconceptions. It may also be used to encourage the exchange of information and ideas between students – as when developing initial ideas for projects, when learning about what has been done elsewhere, and when searching for relevant sources of information. In such situations the tutor might intervene at appropriate points in time to highlight key points emerging from the exchanges, to help clarify issues, and to identify resources that might prove to be informative.

Computer-conferencing works particularly well where students are spread around the world and would normally have negligible contact with their fellow students and very limited contact with their tutors. Since the mode of communication is asynchronous, there is an inevitable delay between transmission and response, but any significant delay in response will almost certainly be due to the recipient needing to find the time to respond in a considered manner. This means that delays in response experienced by students in different time zones are unlikely to be very different from those experienced by students within the same time zone.

Although computer-conferencing is primarily asynchronous in nature, it is possible to check who is actually on-line at the time a message is being delivered, and it is also possible for individuals to arrange to be on-line at one and the same time.

Computer-conferencing is widely used within the UK OU, but the way in which it is used varies considerably, sometimes being an essential and integral part of the course and sometimes an optional periphery. According to a recent review of related issues (Melton, 2000, pp. 32–41):

- Student participation in computer-conferencing depends on whether it is perceived as having a critical part to play in the achievement of the course objectives.
- Students particularly appreciate being able to gain access to their tutors and to a somewhat lesser extent to fellow students.
- However, they do not want to see computer-conferencing replace more traditional forms of communication with their tutors.

Video-conferencing

Video-conferencing is essentially designed to permit the transmission of lectures from a central location to students located elsewhere in schools, colleges, the place of work and other similar locations. Two-way voice communication is possible, providing the possibility for a very limited degree of interaction with students. Video-conferencing along these lines has been widely exploited in North America and has been adopted to varying degrees in many other countries, but it has not been adopted for wide-scale usage within the UK OU.

Its main advantages are that it can be used to reach out to large numbers of students, particularly with the help of satellite technology, and visual presentation enables students to identify with the speaker. However, it has two major disadvantages that need to be addressed.

First, unlike most television and video programmes developed for ODL, it is typically used to support straightforward lectures, and this does very little either to motivate students or to involve them in the process of learning.

Second, although in theory it is possible for interaction to take place between students and speaker, in practice – in common with any lecture to a large audience – meaningful interaction with individual participants is likely to be minimal. Interaction between students and speaker can be increased if student numbers are limited, but under these circumstances the medium becomes prohibitively expensive to use.

CDs

Compact disks with read-only memory (CD-ROMs) are able to store a great deal of information in the form of text, graphics, audio and video, and as such are at the forefront of technology in so far as they are able to integrate a wide variety of media. Apart from being able to store a great deal of information in a multi-media format, the main advantage of CDs is that they are easy to distribute and easy to use.

CDs have two main disadvantages. First, they are unable to support interpersonal communication, and, second, although updating of materials is very important in education, this is both difficult and expensive in the case of CDs.

Having said this, recent developments suggest that it is now technologically possible to integrate the capabilities of CDs and telecommunications, making it technically possible to build an element of interpersonal communication into the CD technology. It remains to be seen whether it will be possible to exploit this on a wide scale.

CDs are widely used on courses throughout the UK OU, and in terms of helpfulness were more highly rated than the World Wide Web in the 1999 Courses Survey (Student Research Centre, 1999, Qu1). One of the uses for which they were particularly highly rated was as a resource in helping students with literature reviews and project work (Melton, 2000, pp. 28–31).

The World Wide Web

The World Wide Web is now widely used on courses throughout the UK OU, with many courses developing their own websites, and from the data available so far (Student Research Centre, 1999, Qu1) it appears to be more appreciated by students than either e-mail or computer-conferencing.

Where students are able to use the World Wide Web as a resource to support project work and literature reviews, they make far more use of the Web than other resources such as local libraries, college libraries, the OU library, and direct contacts with individuals or companies (Melton, 2000, pp. 42–48).

As with all forms of electronic communication, we must allow time for both students and staff to find out how best to exploit the medium. It is the potential of the medium that excites most educators. This is well reflected in Mason's comments on the subject:

> The Web is the most phenomenally successful educational tool to have appeared in a long time. It combines ... text, text-based interaction, audio and video as clips, and, with somewhat less robustness, multi-way interactive audio and video. Its application in global education is unquestioned. Although access to the Internet is hardly universal ... access is growing exponentially.
>
> (1998, p. 28)

Despite this eulogy Mason (1998, p. 36) has no problem in keeping the World Wide Web in perspective. In her own words: 'Even though the Web does provide significant variety in teaching modes, there is still much to be gained from the use of print, satellite, cable, video and audio cassettes, depending on context, costs, access and flexibility.'

More recent developments

I have deliberately avoided discussing electronic forms of communication that appear to have high potential but have still not been widely adopted in ODL – either because of the cost involved or because of the limitations imposed by the existing technology. However, a great deal of research and development is going on in this field. In the words of Sir John Daniel (1996, p. 55), the Vice Chancellor of the UK OU: 'The coming together of telecommunications, television and computing is producing a media environment for distance education that is more than the sum of its component elements.'

Eisenstadt (1995) describes this environment as the knowledge media, and as director of the UK OU's Knowledge Media Institute, he is responsible for the direction of a great deal of this work within the UK OU. If you would like to learn more about some of the most recent developments in the institute you might like to read his on-line article on the KMi Stadium experiment (Eisenstadt, http://kmi.open.ac.uk/stadium/).

4.4 The selection of media

If you are hoping to develop ODL on a fairly wide scale within your own institution, it is useful to begin by getting people together within their own subject areas and asking them to discuss the type of media that they would like to have available to them to support the presentation of ODL within their own areas. In the text that follows we will take a look at the factors that need to be taken into account in developing such *a subject-based point of view*.

Those involved in these discussions will need to remain open-minded as to what will ultimately be possible, as further discussion of what is feasible will need to take place at a broader and higher institutional level. These later discussions should not only include individuals from the various subject areas but also managers from within the institution with a knowledge of the finances that might be obtained from the institution and from national and international bodies. In the text that follows we will also take a look at the additional factors that will need to be taken into account in developing an *institutional point of view*. Clarification of the latter is particularly important, as it will determine the choice of media ultimately available for the development of courses within the various subject areas.

A subject-based point of view

The easiest way to begin is for individuals from within a given subject area (science, languages, arts, etc.) to get together to consider the goals that they would like to achieve within their subject areas and the type of media, or combinations of media, that they would like to use for this purpose. This should lead to a range of suggestions highlighting the variety of media that they would like to be able to exploit in developing subsequent courses for ODL within their own areas.

The media, or combinations of media, preferred will not only depend on the *appropriateness of the media* for achieving the goals identified, but also on a number of other factors such as whether students can gain easy *access to the media*, whether students have *the skills required* to make good use of the equipment, and *the costs involved* in developing and using related materials.

Appropriateness of the media

In talking about the selection of media you might begin by considering the extent to which specific media, or combinations of media, might be used to achieve certain types of objectives. For example, within a language course you might identify some of the ways in which audio cassettes, video cassettes and print material might be used to support certain types of broad objectives.

One possibility might be to make use of audio cassettes not only for listening to the spoken language, but also for students to add their own responses in spaces immediately after the questions asked – with the added bonus of responses from role models following the related spaces. One might also consider the use of audio cassettes for the presentation of news bulletins and documentaries with student activities built around the presentations.

In doing this you would almost certainly go on to consider ways in which print material might be needed to support the type of activities you have in mind. In other words, you would clarify your thinking as to how you might make use of the media by considering very specific situations and then asking yourself how widely the media identified might be used to achieve related objectives.

You might similarly reflect on the use of other types of media or media combinations – considering in each case the strengths and weaknesses of each medium, or combination of media. For example, in discussing the pros and cons of video cassettes it might be suggested that the advantage of this medium is that it may not only be used to help students to develop skills of listening and speaking, but also to introduce them to social and cultural aspects of the country concerned in the hope that this will add to their motivation to learn the language.

You will almost certainly find a variety of ways in which each medium, or combination of media might be used, making it possible for students to learn through a variety of different types of experience. Initially you might feel lost for choice, but as you go on to consider other factors that need to be taken into consideration, you will probably feel pleased to have a wide range of choice from which to make your final selection.

Access to the media

As the discussion expands you will rapidly find yourself focusing on the type of students you are trying to help, and you will need to ask yourself where they are located and what type of media they will have access to. For example, if computers are to be used will students have access to these in their homes? If they have to travel to study centres in order to use them, this could be very off-putting for students, particularly if they can only get to the study centres one or twice a week, and if the hours when they can gain access to the equipment are very limited.

We must always ask not only where equipment will be located, but also for what purposes students will need to gain access to it and how regularly. If it is needed on a daily basis, then it should be available in the home or wherever the student expects to study on a regular basis. The day-to-day support that students need cannot be over-emphasised. If students will need to travel to study centres or residential schools in order to make use of certain types of equipment, then the related activities will need to be more loosely linked to the course, so that delays in gaining access to the equipment do not hold up their ongoing day-to-day studies.

This does not mean that equipment cannot be located to advantage at study centres and residential schools, but simply that we must consider the related implications. For example, if a decision is made to delay certain types of sophisticated experiments, field trips, and group discussions to residential schools, this should be in the knowledge that leaving the development of related skills to late in the course will not prevent students from pursuing their continuing studies in a meaningful manner.

The skills required

We have already seen (Chapter 1) that students may have strong likes and dislikes about how they learn, and it is recognised that being able to use their preferred learning styles can enhance learning. However, we also noted that students can develop new learning styles, not only increasing the variety of ways in which they learn, but also opening up wider opportunities for learning. The computer is a good example of this phenomenon. Some students may dislike the medium in itself, preferring to sit quietly with a book, or to watch a television programme rather than sitting 'glued to' a computer screen. However, many students are likely to dislike the medium, because they do not have the skills required to make good use of it, and because they do not see the advantages that it has to offer. However, given the guidance and support that is clearly required, very few students will find themselves unable to take advantage of the medium and to recognise the advantages to be gained from using it.

Having said this, do not underestimate the skills that students will require to make good use of the media provided, and assume that all students will have the skills required to make use of home experiment kits, to use e-mail, to take part in computer-conferencing, or even for such things as writing essays. In the earliest stages of course development do check out the skills that students (and staff) do and do not have, and take this into account in developing materials and systems for ODL.

The costs involved

In considering the cost of using various media we need to view it from the point of view of both the student and the institution. From a student point of view there is the cost of purchasing any required equipment and the subsequent cost of using it. Likewise, from an institutional point of view, there is the cost of developing related materials for a given medium and the subsequent cost of supporting its use.

For example, from an institutional point of view the cost of introducing computer-conferencing into a course may be relatively low (compared with that of developing a software package), so long as the system adopted (such as First Class Conferencing) has already been developed and tested on other courses, but the cost of supporting it may be high if the developers insist on making use of top academics as tutors with a maximum tutor to student ratio of about 1–15.

From a student point of view, the prime cost may be that of course fees, if these are related to the cost of developing and running the course. In addition, there is the possible cost of purchasing the computer and software required, while the cost of using the computer may be relevant if much time has to be spent on-line.

There are clearly several factors to be taken into account in talking about the cost of any given medium, and these will vary from one country to another. Having said this, it is informative to have some idea of the relative costs of using different media, and with this in mind I have included figures calculated by Bates (1995) on the cost of producing and using various media. His figures provide us with estimates of the costs of different media in terms of the average cost per student per study hour over the first eight years of using the medium, and indicate how these costs vary according to the number of students using the medium concerned. You will find the related costs (extrapolated from the data provided by Bates) for eight forms of media in Figure 4.2, according to whether 500 or 1,500 students made use of the medium.

500 students	$US	1500 students	$US
Print	1.7	Print	0.6
Computer-conferencing	2.2	Audio cassettes	1.7
Audio cassettes	2.5	Radio	1.9
Audio-conferencing	5.0	Computer-conferencing	2.2
Radio	6.4	Audio-conferencing	4.2
Video-conferencing	12.8	Computer-based learning	5.8
Computer-based learning	14.4	Video-conferencing	9.4
Broadcast television	27.2	Broadcast television	10.0

Figure 4.2 Average cost per student per study hour of various media
Source: Bates (1995)

Needless to say, the figures calculated depend on the assumptions made, and these can make a considerable difference to the costs involved. Take, for example, the case of computer-conferencing within the UK OU MA in ODE programme to which we have already referred. A large proportion of tutors on these courses are still high level central academics – in part to ensure the quality of the teaching and in part to identify the strengths and weaknesses of the new technology, ensuring that the medium is understood and exploited to the full. The student to tutor ratio is also kept relatively low with between 12–15 students per tutor. The cost of the related courses could easily be reduced by using more conventional tutors (specifically trained to support these courses) and by increasing the number of students per tutor. However, this would undoubtedly affect the quality of support on the courses. Ensuring quality does have related costs attached to it – a point made by Wagner (1977) in saying that the cost of distance teaching can be 'as expensive or as cheap as the planners wish'.

An institutional point of view

The findings that have emerged from the discussions with specific subject areas will need to be reviewed at an institutional level, and note taken of what has been said about the type of media considered desirable within each area, the extent to which it is assumed that students will have access to related equipment, the skills they will need, the training they might require, and the estimated costs involved.

In this respect, the discussions at an institutional level will reflect much of what has been said within each subject area. The main difference will be that 'the pros and cons' of different media will need to be much more carefully debated in the light of the costs involved. The simple point is that the institution will be responsible for raising the finances required.

In the discussions at this level there will inevitably be times when a particular medium, or combination of media, might be seen as the best way of helping students to achieve certain types of objectives, but it may also be seen as more expensive than the institution feels it can realistically afford. If another medium, or combination of media, can do the job almost as well as the preferred medium, but at considerably less cost, then do give serious consideration to the cheaper option. However, if there are absolutely compelling reasons for using a particular medium, or combination of media, then by all means argue the point, and make sure that those involved recognise the extent to which initial investment costs need to be set against lower recurrent costs over a number of years.

In perspective

I have attempted within this chapter to provide you with some idea of the variety of media available and the extent to which each medium might be exploited to advantage in its own right and in combination with other media. I would hope that you are now aware of the factors that need to be taken into account in selecting media, and that you have a good idea of the type of media that you would like to exploit in developing ODL within your own institution.

If you would like more information on traditional forms of media, you will find a wealth of detail in Rowntree's *Exploring Open and Distance Learning* (1992, pp. 95–122). Likewise, if you would like to learn more about how to exploit the electronic forms of communication that we have considered, you might well wish to read some, or all, of the following books: *Computer Conferencing: The Last Word* (Mason, 1995), *Networked Learning: The Pedagogy of the Internet* (Haughey and Anderson, 1998), and *Tele-Learning in a Digital World* (Collis, 1996).

Suggestions

At this stage I would suggest that you get together with two or three colleagues, preferably within a specific subject area, and discuss the types of media that you would like to be able to adopt within that area. You might also encourage colleagues within other subject areas to do the same. However, do alert those involved to the fact that further discussion will be required at a broader institutional level to determine what media the institution as a whole will be able to support.

5 Student support systems

Contents

Introduction	110
5.1 Scenarios illustrating different types of student support	111
5.2 Student support systems	116
5.3 Selection of student support systems	128
In perspective	131
Suggestions	131

Introduction

Students in ODL enjoy two quite different forms of support. There are the self-study materials produced/provided by the institution to help students to study on their own, and there are the support systems that students need to help them overcome problems that they encounter during the course of their studies.

We have already looked at the type of self-study packages that are produced/provided by the institution in discussing the pros and cons of various media. Such packages typically include such items as printed materials (study guides, books, journals and articles), mass media programmes (TV and radio programmes), cassettes (audio and video), home experiment kits, and high technology products (such as CDs, computer software, and websites). Although in designing self-study materials every attempt is made to respond to the varying needs of different types of students, it is inevitable that students will encounter problems from time to time where they will need individualised help.

Student support systems are designed to respond as far as possible to individual needs, and typically include the provision of support through tutors (or mentors), counsellors (or advisers, guidance counsellors) and centre-based staff (academics, librarians, computer specialists, and so on). In broad terms tutors (or mentors) provide students with academic support, while counsellors (or advisers) provide them with personal, or non-academic, forms of support. In practice the boundaries between tutoring and counselling are not as clearly defined as this, and you will find tutors providing non-academic support at times simply because it falls naturally within the context of the problem that they are dealing with.

In fact, student support systems can do much more than help students overcome personal problems. They can also help students to develop new skills such as those of discussion and debate, and they can provide students with opportunities to view issues from a variety of different perspectives, including viewpoints not included in the course materials. This would seem to be a valuable bonus, for, as Tait (1989) indicates, where self-study materials present only a particular perspective or limited arguments, there is always a risk of them being over authoritarian.

In the first part of this chapter we will begin by looking at a number of *scenarios illustrating different types of student support* that might be needed and ways in which the support required might be provided. It is hoped that the scenes portrayed will help you to recognise that students need different types of support at different points in time, and that what is needed is a package of support systems that is able to respond to the wide variety of needs in a coherent manner.

In the second part of the chapter we will go on to look at the variety of ways in which help may be provided through the support of tutors, counsellors and centre-based staff. However, in reflecting on the *student support systems* described, do bear in mind that you are searching for the best way of supporting your own students, and this is likely to depend on combining a number of different forms of support together.

Although in discussing various support systems we will reflect on the strengths and weaknesses of each in turn, when it comes to the *selection of student support systems* to meet the needs of students in your own local situation, you will find that other factors need to be taken into account, and we will reflect on these in the final part of this chapter.

5.1 Scenarios illustrating different types of student support

In the text that follows you will find four scenarios designed to illustrate not only the different types of support that students are likely to need, but also to highlight the fact that they need different types of support at different points in time. The scenes described are centred around the students you met in the last chapter, namely Karen, John, Olga and Segundo, but it is now a few months later. As you consider each of the scenarios, take time to think about the different types of student support you might wish to provide in your own situation, and make a note of your ideas. You may find reinforcement for them when you read the comments on the variety of forms of support in the next section of the chapter under the heading 'student support systems'.

Scenario 1: Seeking advice on courses and career

At the time you met Karen she had just begun a course in German hoping that this would help her with her work as a sales representative, particularly in Germany. The course has given her the confidence to make much better use of her German, and her work has benefited as a result. It has in fact started her thinking more seriously about her career and the benefits she might gain by improving her qualifications, but she feels that she needs to know more about the options available and the implications with regard to the further development of her career. With this in mind she arranged to see her counsellor, David, whom she first met prior to enrolling on her German course. Although she has only seen him occasionally since then, when visiting the centre for tutorials, she feels that she knows him, and that he will be able to help her to think through the options available to her.

She meets David as planned in his room at the study centre. He is very easy to talk to, and she soon finds herself bringing him up to date with events. She tells him that she is very much enjoying her course, and feels that she is making good progress. She also tells him about her work in Germany and the progress she is making, but adds that although she is happy to continue with her present line of work for another year, she feels that she could do more with her career – particularly if she adds to her present qualifications. In answer to David's query she indicates that she would welcome the opportunity to widen her experience across Europe, and would ultimately like to move on from being a sales representative, and, if she gets the right qualifications, would very much hope that she might be able to obtain a management position.

David listens carefully to what she has to say, then identifies some of the qualifications that might be of interest to her – a Diploma in German (or French or Spanish), a Diploma in European Studies, a Diploma in Management, an MBA, or a BA degree – and gives her some idea of the related course combinations that she would need to pursue for each. Karen comments on the extent to which the different options appeal and asks more questions about some of the alternatives available to her. In the discussion that follows it emerges that, regardless of the direction ultimately taken, Karen intends to take a second course in German in the next year. She still is not clear as to the direction she will take after that, but as she takes her leave she tells David that she feels well informed on the options available to her and believes that she will be able to make a well-informed decision when the time arises. David indicates that he will be interested to hear what she ultimately decides to do, and tells her to get back to him in the meantime if she wants to talk more about the options available to her.

As you reflect on this scenario do give some thought to the type of issues on which your own students might wish to seek advice from counsellors.

Scenario 2: Obtaining academic support

Remember John – the senior science teacher who enjoys taking his students walking in the mountains in his spare time. At the time you first met him he was studying rock samples as a part of his course in Earth Sciences. It is now a few months later, he has been to summer school, and he still looks back at this as the high point in the course. In particular, he feels that he got a great deal out of the field work and from the way in which he was encouraged to make wider use of computers during the laboratory sessions.

On the field trip John, in common with many of his fellow students, felt inspired by his tutor's obvious enthusiasm for the subject. He brought the subject to life with his vivid descriptions of how the rocks and fossils came to exist in their present forms, and, by pointing out the evidence to support his views, made sure that they were aware of the basis on which the related theories were based. John and his fellow students found themselves viewing a wide range of rock formations in the field, collecting rock samples and fossils, and studying them more carefully later in the laboratory with the support of their ever present tutor.

John also found the laboratory sessions particularly helpful, not only because they helped him to develop his scientific knowledge and skills, but also because he was encouraged to make use of computer-based resources that he had tended to ignore prior to summer school. In particular, he was encouraged to search for related information on the course website, and the World Wide Web, and was encouraged to share his findings with others through the course's computer-conferencing system.

In common with many of his fellow students John had tended to ignore these resources, partly because it was not an essential requirement of the course, partly because time was very limited, and partly because at first glance the technology appeared somewhat daunting. In fact, once John had been introduced to the technology, he found it so much simpler than expected and the benefits of logging on became much more apparent.

Back home John is now revising for the coming end-of-course examinations. He has just received feedback on his latest tutor-marked assignment, and is looking through this with even more care than usual. This is because the objectives for the last assignment were related to the course as a whole, and provide him with helpful insights into the nature of the end-of-course examination (which is also related to the objectives for the course as a whole).

This evening John will be attending a local tutorial, when there will be an opportunity to discuss issues arising from the latest assignment, and he is currently making notes on feedback issues on which he would like further clarification. He is expecting a fairly full turnout at this tutorial, even though some of the students have quite long journeys to get there.

In reflecting on this scenario make a note of the variety of ways in which John obtains academic support. Can you identify some forms of academic support that you would like to be given to your own students?

Scenario 3: Obtaining personal support

When we last met Olga she was watching a video documentary about children in special care homes as part of a course she was taking in the field of health and social welfare. You will remember that Olga is a housewife with three children, that she used to be a nurse, but was thinking that once the youngest children started school she would probably try to find employment in the field of health and social welfare – hence the direction of her present studies.

Since last meeting her she has been to summer school – thoroughly enjoying the experience, even though it was very hard work. As expected, one of the activities in which she took part was a group review of a number of case studies of abuse of children in special care homes. In common with other members of her group, she contributed to the discussions in a variety of ways: as a participant listening to what others had to say, as a commentator expressing her own perceptions, as a rapporteur summarising the views expressed within her group, and as a facilitator ensuring that all members of her group participated in the discussions in a meaningful manner. In undertaking these various roles she felt that she had gained valuable experience of how she would need to behave as a professional member of a team dealing with real-life care situations. In fact, the experience had given her much more confidence in her skills and abilities, and she was planning to take a course in the following year on 'management in health and social welfare' in the hope that this might help her to obtain a position as a manager in the field of health and social welfare at some point in the future.

Back home from summer school she is getting papers together in preparation for her next tutor-marked assignment. Unfortunately, she is running late with her submission. Just over a month ago her young daughters went down one after the other with chicken-pox, and not too surprisingly she fell somewhat behind with her studies. She also missed a tutorial at which the tutor gave students advice concerning the tutor-marked assignment that she still had to complete.

Fortunately, her tutor was very understanding, and agreed to her delaying the submission of the assignment she is now working on by two weeks. She will also be getting advice on what went on at the tutorial from her friends, Egmont and Irma, who are taking the same course. They will bring her up to date when she meets them tonight. She first met them at her first tutorial, when her tutor encouraged students who lived near together to form small self-help groups. Egmont, Irma and Olga discovered that they all lived within roughly half an hour of each other, and had organised themselves to meet about once a week – sometimes at a

Student support systems 115

local café and sometimes at one another's houses, depending on what they needed to discuss. Apart from being able to help each other with practical problems, they found the mutual support helped maintain their motivation and morale.

In reflecting on this scenario make a note of the variety of ways in which Olga obtains personal support (academic and social), and add a note about the immediacy or otherwise of the support obtained. Can you identify other forms of support that she might reasonably have expected to receive?

Scenario 4: Taking advantage of training and personal contacts

When we last met Segundo he was in the final year of his MA in ODE. You will remember that he was a senior education officer on a small island in the South Pacific, and was pursuing his studies with financial support from his own government. It is now twelve months later, and Segundo is sitting in his office within the education directorate, where he is the newly appointed director of the South Pacific ODL Project. He is currently preparing a proposal for submission to the World Bank. Let us look back at how he came to be in this position.

While pursuing his studies Segundo continued with his work in the education directorate, and was very much involved in discussions concerning the possibility of islands within the region joining together to produce common ODL courses for their students. He found that his MA studies were particularly helpful in that they helped him to identify the type of students they might try to help, the means by which they might reach out to these students, and the type of student support facilities that they would need to provide. His final course project proved to be equally valuable being a study of the cost-effectiveness of the proposed South Pacific project. This was well received not only as a project submission for his MA course, but also as a part of the proposed joint project for the South Pacific.

On completing his MA Segundo was made director of the South Pacific ODL project with the full backing and support of his own education department as well as that of the other island representatives. In part this was in recognition of the knowledge he had gained through his studies and in part because of the significant contributions he had made to the ODL project while studying for his MA.

Following detailed discussions with representatives from the islands in the region, he has just completed a draft proposal for financial support from the World Bank. Again, as part of his studies, he learnt a great deal about the preparation of project proposals, the most relevant bodies from which to seek funding, and the people to contact for help and advice. He has already had a great deal of help and advice from Peter, one of his former ODL tutors, who was given financial support from UNESCO to visit the project, and he is planning to include Peter's UNESCO report as an appendix to the World Bank proposal. In some ways Segundo feels that the plans for an ODL project in the South Pacific are rather like a dream, but he is aware that several such projects have gained major financial backing, and he believes that the South Pacific project has a very convincing case to present.

This scenario is somewhat different from the others in that Segundo is no longer a student. However, do reflect on the scene, and see if you can identify the different ways in which he benefited from personal support provided during the period of his studies.

5.2 Student support systems

In the text that follows you will find different types of student support considered according to who provides the support: tutors, counsellors or centre-based staff. You will in fact find the different types of support discussed under the following headings.

- *Individualised tutor support*
- *Group-based tutor support*
- *Counselling support*
- *Centre-based support.*

There are essentially two types of student support, namely academic and non-academic, and this is typically provided within the UK OU by tutors and counsellors, respectively. However, the division of responsibilities is not quite as clear-cut as this might suggest. For example, although tutors may concentrate on the provision of academic support – advising students when it is more appropriate to turn to their counsellors for help – there will inevitably be times when they find themselves giving non-academic advice, simply because this emerges naturally from the context being discussed and can be addressed immediately. Nor are tutors and counsellors the only ones to provide student support, and, as you will see in the text that follows, some forms of student support may be provided by centre-based staff.

Individualised tutor support

The majority of tutors tend to have other full-time jobs – often as teachers or trainers – and are not available on a 24-hour basis. They are typically paid on a contract basis that takes into account the number of tutorials to be provided, the number of assignments to be marked, and the number of contact hours to be spent in providing individualised support. However, although they are only available on a part-time basis, it is important that students should feel that they can gain access to their tutors without difficulty, and, that when they do, they should find them friendly and supportive in responding to their queries. Apart from choosing tutors with the desired personal qualities, it is important to ensure that they are not asked to support too many students, for, although a large student–tutor ratio may make sense from a cost point of view, it will inevitably mean that less support can be provided to students on an individualised basis.

In the text that follows you will find comments on two forms of individualised tutor support: the first is the type of *ad hoc support* offered in response to student queries, whatever these may be and whenever they might arise, and the second is the type of *more regular support* offered to students in the form of feedback on tutor-marked assignments.

Ad hoc support

The tutor may provide individualised support in a number of ways, typically making use of the telephone, mail, e-mail, faxes, and face-to-face meetings for contact purposes. Whatever medium is used for contact purposes, tutors should inform students at the beginning of their courses as to when they can normally be contacted and by what means. They should also advise their students of the extent to which they are likely to be able to respond to individual queries and the time that it will usually take to respond. Tutors should keep an eye on who makes contact and who does not, and in the first few weeks of a course make sure that if a student does not make contact with them that they contact the student. Knowing that a tutor is available and willing to help can make a considerable difference – particularly to students at risk of dropping out.

Face-to-face contact is likely to be rather limited, but where it does take place it is most likely to be arranged on a personal basis immediately prior to, or after, a tutorial session.

More regular support

One of the most important forms of communication between tutor and student centres around the regular assignments that students typically submit to their tutors during their courses. Apart from being used for grading purposes, tutor-marked assignments help tutors to identify problems being encountered and give them the opportunity to provide students with advice on what they might do to overcome such problems. The feedback may be sent by mail, e-mail, or fax according to the facilities available locally.

Computer-marked assignments may be used in a similar manner, but in this case feedback is likely to be computerised.

Group-based tutor support

Tutorials are traditionally the most common way of providing students with support on a group basis, but, where students are spread thinly over wide areas, *audio-conferencing* may be used as an alternative. In the text that follows you will find comments not only on tutorials and audio-conferencing but also on *peer group support*. Although the latter does not include regular tutor support, the tutor is usually instrumental in ensuring that it is set up.

Tutorials

Before considering the uses to which tutorials may be put, it is worth noting that they should not normally be used for presenting the basic content of instruction, as this is done through the self-study materials provided. The following are some of the purposes for which they might be used.

- To introduce students in broad terms to the course content – particularly at the beginning of a course (or block). At such points in time students may need guidance on what is expected of them, the schedules that they will need to keep to, the assignments they will be expected to submit, the resources they will require, and the forms of support that they might expect to be available.
- To respond to problems being experienced by students as a whole. These may be identified through general discussion of problems within the group or by more carefully developed strategies – such as through the analysis of feedback on tutor-marked assignments. Where problems are identified, the tutor may provide clarification of the issues, identify resources to which students might turn for further reinforcement, and provide students with the opportunity to test out their newly acquired knowledge and skills.
- To help illuminate issues through group discussion. Considerable insights can be gained by viewing issues (such as ODL) from a variety of different points of view (such as those of tutors, counsellors, subject specialists, media specialists, educational technologists, computer experts and administrators to mention but a few). Where claims from different perspectives reinforce one another, they may be accepted with increased confidence, but, where they give rise to conflicting claims, it highlights the need for more careful examination, and a deeper understanding, of the issues. Such an approach has been described as one of multi-perspective illumination (Melton and Zimmer, 1987), and is one that tutors might exploit to advantage.
- To facilitate project work. Where students are undertaking projects they may need advice on such matters as the choice of suitable topics,

the nature of the projects to be undertaken, the identification of relevant resources, the type of literature searches that may be required, the collection of data, modes of analysis, and the writing of reports, and all may be useful items for clarification and discussion at tutorials.

Audio-conferencing

Where a tutor's students are scattered thinly over a wide area, it may be extremely difficult for them to travel the distances required to attend tutorials. In such instances audio-conferencing might provide a reasonable alternative. However, these need to be carefully planned. For example, students may be asked to study related materials in preparation for the conference, they may be advised to ensure that they have certain materials available during the conference for reference purposes, they may be asked to perform specific roles during the conference, and they may be asked to undertake related follow up activities. All of these need careful consideration in advance.

Peer group support

Needless to say, tutors cannot always be available on demand, and there are times when fellow students may be able to obtain more immediate help from their fellow students. In fact, students sometimes find it easier to talk to their colleagues about problems – not wanting to look stupid in front of a tutor who will ultimately be assessing their performance. Setting up peer groups provides students with an easily accessible additional form of local support, and at the first tutorial on a course tutors typically encourage students who live near each other to form local peer groups, providing one another with a means of mutual support.

Counselling support

Whereas a great deal of tutor support can be provided at a distance, counselling usually needs to be undertaken face to face, particularly where emotional issues need to be discussed. In common with tutors, counsellors need to be open, friendly and approachable. They also need to be good listeners, able to help students clarify issues for themselves, able to point out the options available to them, and to identify the consequences of adopting any particular option. As with tutors, the duties of counsellors need to be identified as clearly as possible, and the following are simply examples of tasks that they might be asked to undertake.

- To advise students enrolling on courses about related requirements. When students are giving serious consideration to the possibility of enrolling on a particular course they are likely to need advice on such

matters as the starting date, the duration of the course, the last date on which they will be able to register, the cost of the course, any pre-requisite requirements, and the amount of time they will probably need to set aside for their studies.
- To help students in choosing courses and programmes of study. Students, particularly those planning to take an ODL course for the first time, often seek advice on whether they have the knowledge and experience to cope with a particular course or programme of study, and if not what options are available to them. They also often seek advice on the qualifications that might be relevant to their career ambitions and on the course combinations that are accepted as contributing to these qualifications.
- To advise students on problems affecting their studies. Where students encounter problems that are affecting their studies they need to be able to seek help from their counsellors. It may be that they are encountering work-related problems such as excessive pressure at work, changing jobs. They may have domestic problems such as illness in the family, moving home. They may have course-related such problems in gaining access to resources required, problems preventing them getting to tutorial sessions or residential school, or simply not coping with their studies and needing urgent advice. All these typically fall within the domain of the counsellor.
- To advise on financial issues. It may be that students have financial problems, and need advice on loans or grants and whether they qualify for such support. For example, they may be unable to afford the cost of travel to residential school or the cost of equipment (computers, etc.) that may be required for a course.

The main requirement in setting up a counselling service is to recognise the type of non-academic problems that may arise, to try to identify those where a counsellor may be able to help, and to ensure that counsellors are prepared to provide all the support that they can to help students deal with such problems.

Centre-based support

It makes sense in ODL to provide a number of support services on a centralised basis, and we will look here at those forms of support that have been traditionally provided on a centralised basis within the UK OU and then at the more high technology forms of support that have been provided on a similar basis within recent years.

Two very different forms of student support have traditionally been provided on a centralised basis within the UK OU over many years, and these are the circulation of a *student newspaper* (that keeps students up to date with events and helps them to feel part of a live student body) and the provision of *residential schools* (which have been used to help students develop a range of skills that would be difficult to develop in isolation on their own).

In more recent years the advent of high technology has seen a number of other services being provided on a centralised basis. These include *computing support* which is now available to students who are expected to use computers as an essential part of their courses. It also includes the provision of both institutional and course-related websites. *Institutional websites* have been developed to provide students with information about the institution (the courses and qualifications it offers, how students are supported in their studies, what they should do if they want to enrol, and what they should do if they would like further advice). *Course-based websites* have been developed to provide students with subject-related information, and typically include a wide range of resources to which they might refer. Similarly, *computer-conferencing* has been developed on a centralised basis to provide students with both academic and social support.

Let us look at each of these forms of centre-based support in turn.

Student newspaper

The UK OU has two newspapers that are circulated on a regular basis: one for students and one for staff. Both are highly valued as a means of bringing students and staff up to date with events, for offering individuals the opportunity to comment on events that affect them, and for providing all concerned with a feeling of belonging to a living community.

Residential schools

Within the UK OU many courses have a one-week residential school about two-thirds of the way through the course. It is referred to as summer school within the UK OU because of the time of year when it is presented. Dependent on the student numbers involved, the residential school may be offered at one or more centres, and is likely to be repeated a number of times to cope with the student numbers involved. This inevitably involves considerable expenditure with students travelling in from all parts of the country. It is therefore perceived as a one-off event on a course, but one which is much valued for the wider range of opportunities it opens to its students.

The purposes for which the schools are used depend to a large extent on the nature of the subject, but they include the following:

- To help students develop subject-related skills. In the sciences, for example, students need to learn how to manipulate sophisticated equipment with precision, make accurate observations and measurements, and collect, analyse, and interpret data.

- To help students develop interpersonal skills. Where students spend so much of their time in relative isolation, summer schools provide them with opportunities to develop their interpersonal skills through group discussions. The issues for debate may be identified at an earlier point in the course, allowing students ample time for any recommended preparatory activities. In the discussions themselves students may be invited to take on a variety of roles including those of contributors (presenting or responding to a particular point of view), rapporteurs (summarising the findings emerging from group discussions), and facilitators (ensuring that all members of any given group have a fair opportunity to present their views).
- To help students develop their confidence. We have already seen the way in which students are encouraged to develop subject-related skills in laboratories and interpersonal skills through group discussions. Similarly, on the social side, they are encouraged to exchange views with fellow participants from a wide variety of backgrounds and in the process they will usually find others with whom they share similar concerns, interests, values and aspirations. Opportunities such as these all contribute to the confidence-building process.
- To help motivate students. Residential schools open up a wide range of opportunities to students – all with the potential to stimulate interest. As one would expect, during a one-week residential school students have more time than usual in which to interact with their tutors, and as such they are able to benefit directly from the guidance and support that they can provide. They are also usually able to meet some of the people who have important roles to play in their lives – such as the authors of articles and books and the presenters of TV/video programmes, and as such have possible role models to provide them with guidance and inspiration. Finally, as already mentioned, they have the opportunity to take part in laboratory work, field trips, discussion groups and personal exchanges, all of which can enhance their confidence in themselves and their ability to succeed.

The main advantage of residential schools is that students can enjoy intense interaction with, and support from, both tutors and fellow students, and this enables them to develop skills and attitudes that would be difficult to develop in isolation as a part of their normal studies.

Computing support

Where students are required to use computers as a part of their courses, it is almost inevitable that they will run into problems from time to time. Depending on their experience they may encounter difficulties in setting up their computers, in downloading software, or in operating programs, and they will need easy access to a support service that can help sort out their problems quickly. In the case of computer support it makes a great deal of sense to provide this on a centralised basis.

Institutional websites

As far as student support services are concerned, institutional websites are usually developed to provide students with information about the courses and qualifications available, about the student support services that are provided, and about what students should do if they want to enrol.

The UK OU's website provides a useful example of the type of information that might usefully be provided. If you have access to the Internet, you might like to log on to the website at www.open.ac.uk. You will find that this provides information under six main headings, namely:

- Courses and qualifications
- The OU near you
- The OU student experience
- Open for research
- Open for business
- The OU on TV.

Entering any one of these areas will lead you in a series of steps to increasing information on the subject concerned. For example, clicking on 'Courses and qualifications' will lead you to a list of the subject areas under which courses are offered (Figure 5.1), and clicking on any given subject area will lead you to information on all the courses and qualifications offered within that particular area. Similarly, if you click on 'The OU near you', you will find information on all the OU's Regional Centres, including details of the type of student support that they provide and information on who to contact for more information about courses and how to enrol. If you do have access to the website, you might take a few minutes to take a look at some of the main components.

Course-based websites

Needless to say, every course will have its own idea of the type of website it would like to have to help students with their studies, but such websites will usually provide students with access to resource materials such as articles, books, references, and other forms of information. Although such websites will typically include materials gathered together by the course team, they will also include 'links' to related materials on websites within the institution and on the World Wide Web. In fact, it will not always be immediately obvious whether resource materials are on the actual course website or on others linked to it. The resources identified in this way may be considerable, and it needs to be remembered that students will need to

124 *Characteristics of ODL*

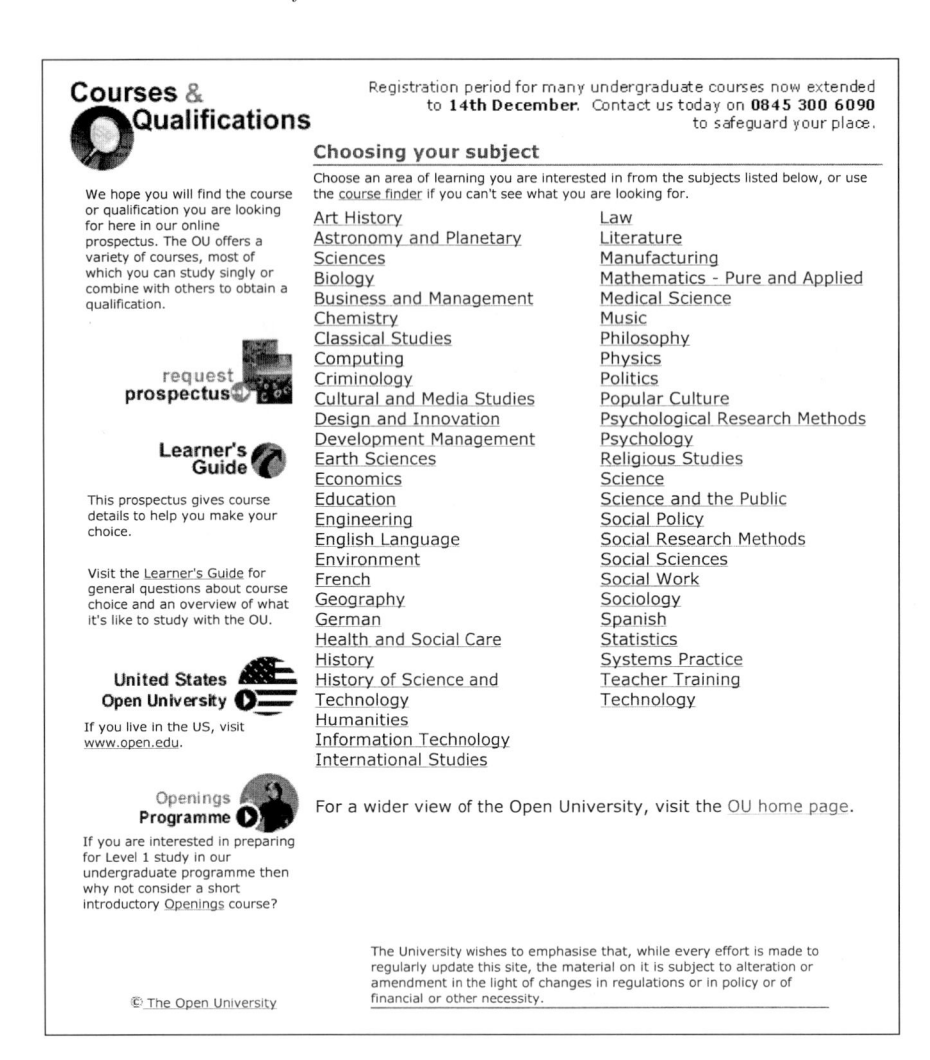

> **Courses & Qualifications**
>
> Registration period for many undergraduate courses now extended to **14th December.** Contact us today on **0845 300 6090** to safeguard your place.
>
> **Choosing your subject**
>
> We hope you will find the course or qualification you are looking for here in our online prospectus. The OU offers a variety of courses, most of which you can study singly or combine with others to obtain a qualification.
>
> Choose an area of learning you are interested in from the subjects listed below, or use the course finder if you can't see what you are looking for.
>
> | | |
> |---|---|
> | Art History | Law |
> | Astronomy and Planetary Sciences | Literature |
> | | Manufacturing |
> | Biology | Mathematics - Pure and Applied |
> | Business and Management | Medical Science |
> | Chemistry | Music |
> | Classical Studies | Philosophy |
> | Computing | Physics |
> | Criminology | Politics |
> | Cultural and Media Studies | Popular Culture |
> | Design and Innovation | Psychological Research Methods |
> | Development Management | Psychology |
> | Earth Sciences | Religious Studies |
> | Economics | Science |
> | Education | Science and the Public |
> | Engineering | Social Policy |
> | English Language | Social Research Methods |
> | Environment | Social Sciences |
> | French | Social Work |
> | Geography | Sociology |
> | German | Spanish |
> | Health and Social Care | Statistics |
> | History | Systems Practice |
> | History of Science and Technology | Teacher Training |
> | | Technology |
> | Humanities | |
> | Information Technology | |
> | International Studies | |
>
> request prospectus
>
> **Learner's Guide**
>
> This prospectus gives course details to help you make your choice.
>
> Visit the Learner's Guide for general questions about course choice and an overview of what it's like to study with the OU.
>
> **United States Open University**
>
> If you live in the US, visit www.open.edu.
>
> **Openings Programme**
>
> If you are interested in preparing for Level 1 study in our undergraduate programme then why not consider a short introductory Openings course?
>
> For a wider view of the Open University, visit the OU home page.
>
> © The Open University
>
> The University wishes to emphasise that, while every effort is made to regularly update this site, the material on it is subject to alteration or amendment in the light of changes in regulations or in policy or of financial or other necessity.

Figure 5.1 Start of search on UK OU website for information on courses and qualifications

Source: www.open.ac.uk 2001

be given guidance on how to make good use of them – just as one would with any other medium used for self-study purposes. It is in fact common practice on on-line courses within the UK OU to provide this guidance through course-based computer-conferences, where it is possible not only to advise students about web materials that might help them with their studies, but also to provide simple 'links' between the advice given and the related information on the websites used.

Computer-conferencing

Computer-conferencing within the UK OU is typically designed to provide students with *academic support* during their studies, but, as you will see, it may be also be used to provide *social support*.

The use of computer-conferencing to provide students with *academic support* is illustrated in Figure 5.2 which contains an 'Introduction to a computer conference for a course'. Let us use this example to identify some of the ways in which students might be provided with academic support through computer-conferencing.

Students on the course are assigned to one of three tutors (Barbara, Erica or Tony), and may gain access to discussions guided by them by clicking on the related buttons across the top of the screen. (The number of tutors allocated to a course depends on the number of students enrolled, but in the year of presentation illustrated there were three tutors supporting approximately forty students.)

The block buttons to the left of the screen provide students with an introduction to each block of the course, but the discussions on the contents of the block are led by the student's particular tutor. The latter may introduce the topics for discussion, provide guidance on the issues to be debated, summarise discussion threads, provide information and advice as necessary, and generally keeps things moving in a positive manner. A tutor may also encourage students to take on some of these roles in rotation.

In contrast to the discussions of block-related issues within tutor groups, a number of activities are designed for students from the course as a whole. These may be accessed through the Plenary Conference button which is located at the top left corner of the screen. Clicking on this button leads to a Notice Board, a Café and a Project Forum. The Notice Board keeps students up to date throughout the course with information on important events, such as when assignments need to be submitted, when guest speakers will be on-line and so on. The Café provides a social forum for general chat. It is well used, and typically contains all the types of exchanges that you might find in a coffee house. The Project Forum is specifically designed to support students with the development of their projects. We have already provided examples of activities within the Project Forum, and you might glance back at Figures 3.3 and 4.1 to see something of the type of discussions that were organised under this heading. Figure 4.1 is of particular interest in that it not only introduces students to relevant resources contained on the course website (in this case project reports provided by previous students), but it also indicates the relevance of these reports to the students concerned.

Beneath the Plenary Conference button you will probably have already noticed the Resources Centre button. Clicking on this button provides students with access to three types of resources. The first is a tailor-made data base of on-line resources specially prepared not just for this particular

| Plenary Conference Resources Centre | Barbara's group | Erica's group | Tony's group |

H804
Online Study Guide 2000

The Open University

The Implementation of Open and Distance Learning

- H804 home
- Block 1
- Block 2
- Block 3
- Block 4
- Block 5

TMA Office

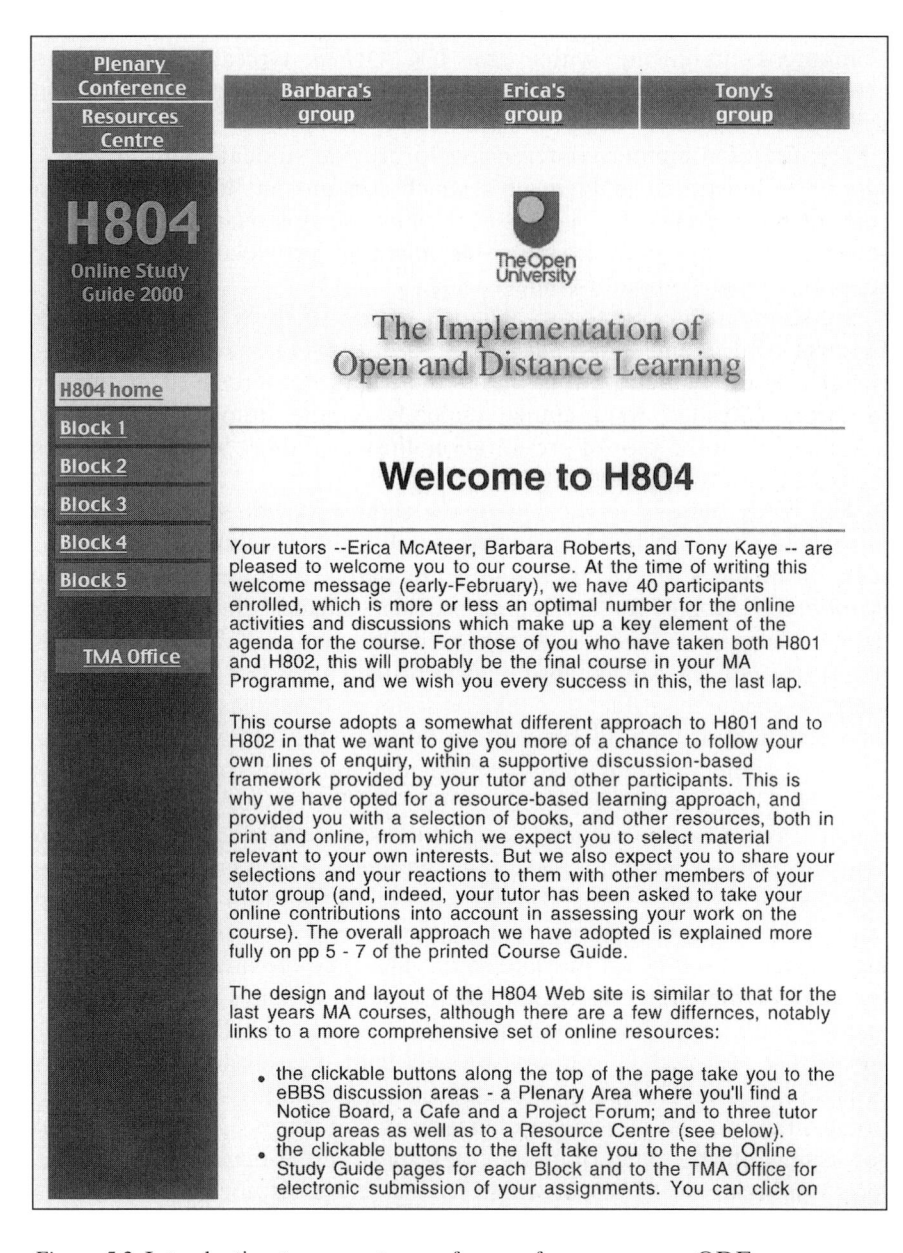

Welcome to H804

Your tutors --Erica McAteer, Barbara Roberts, and Tony Kaye -- are pleased to welcome you to our course. At the time of writing this welcome message (early-February), we have 40 participants enrolled, which is more or less an optimal number for the online activities and discussions which make up a key element of the agenda for the course. For those of you who have taken both H801 and H802, this will probably be the final course in your MA Programme, and we wish you every success in this, the last lap.

This course adopts a somewhat different approach to H801 and to H802 in that we want to give you more of a chance to follow your own lines of enquiry, within a supportive discussion-based framework provided by your tutor and other participants. This is why we have opted for a resource-based learning approach, and provided you with a selection of books, and other resources, both in print and online, from which we expect you to select material relevant to your own interests. But we also expect you to share your selections and your reactions to them with other members of your tutor group (and, indeed, your tutor has been asked to take your online contributions into account in assessing your work on the course). The overall approach we have adopted is explained more fully on pp 5 - 7 of the printed Course Guide.

The design and layout of the H804 Web site is similar to that for the last years MA courses, although there are a few differnces, notably links to a more comprehensive set of online resources:

- the clickable buttons along the top of the page take you to the eBBS discussion areas - a Plenary Area where you'll find a Notice Board, a Cafe and a Project Forum; and to three tutor group areas as well as to a Resource Centre (see below).
- the clickable buttons to the left take you to the the Online Study Guide pages for each Block and to the TMA Office for electronic submission of your assignments. You can click on

Figure 5.2 Introduction to computer-conference for a course on ODE

Source: Course H804, Implementation of ODL, Computer Conference, Home Page, UK OU, 2000

Student support systems 127

> the following phrase <u>Health & Safety Advice for VDUs</u>, to read information the OU believes is important and in your interest.
>
> The new Online **Resource Centre**, gives you direct access to a wider range of resources than we had last year:
>
> - Nazira's Web Resources: a tailor-made database on Online Resources shared with our other 'H' courses, and managed by Nazira Ismail from our International Centre for Distance Learning (iCDL)
> - the entire iCDL database for references and resources
> - a conference/eBBS (Ask iCDL) where you can ask help from Nazira and her colleague Simon Rae, on finding other course related resources
> - the main OU Library
>
> The buttons to the Online Study Guide material for **Block 1** and for **Block 5** (the Project) are active now; those for Blocks 2 - 4 will go 'live' about a fortnight before the scheduled date for the respective Block. We have made the Block 5 part active now because we think it's important that you start thinking about your plans for your Project right from the start of the course -- this is why we have also opened a discussion area for projects on the eBBS: the **Projects Forum**.
>
> We suggest that you get launched into the course by making a visit to your **tutor group** (if you've not already done so) to see if there are any messages there for you, and maybe also by calling in on the **Café** in the **Plenary Area**. Then you should go to the **Block 1** Online Study Guide pages. However, if you are new to the eBBS you may want to practice before launching into the tutor group. We have provided a <u>Practice Conference</u> and an <u>MA Tour</u> that will give you the opportunity for even more practice.

Figure 5.2 (continued)

course but for all the courses included in the MA in ODE programme. The second is the entire database of the International Centre for Distance Learning (iCDL) which is located within the UK OU. The third provides access to the resources contained within, and accessed from, the main UK OU library.

The Project Forum and the Resources Centre are also of interest in that between them they provide examples of the way in which students may gain access to course-specific materials (project reports of former students) on their own course website, to shared materials (iCDL resource materials) from a website serving the interests of a number of courses, and to even more widely shared materials (UK OU library resources) from a website serving the needs of the institution as a whole.

Finally, you will notice at the bottom, on the left-hand side of the screen, there is a button providing access to the TMA Office. This enables students to submit tutor marked assignments to their tutors and to receive detailed feedback in return.

The type of conferencing illustrated above is known as the Extended Bulletin Board System (EBBS). Other forms of computer-conferencing are used within the UK OU, and the most widely used form is that of First Class conferencing. In fact, by the time this book is published, courses within the MA ODE will almost certainly be making use of First Class instead of the EBBS system. This is not because First Class is perceived as being better than the EBBS system, but largely because using the same form of conferencing throughout the university makes it much easier to provide students and staff with centralised technical back-up. One of the main differences between the EBBS system and First Class is that the latter provides support to students on a wide range of courses, and as such is able to provide much more social support than the EBBS system. It also offers students technical computing support through an ACS (Academic Computing Service) Helpdesk. (The ACS helpdesk will presumably be renamed in the near future, since the ACS unit referred to has recently been renamed as LTS or Learning Teaching Services.)

The second type of support provided by computer-conferencing is *social support*. The use of computer-conferencing to provide students with social support might be illustrated by reference to the way in which this is achieved within First Class conferencing. Within the latter students are able to gain access to 'Study Aid Leaflets' that are relevant to a wide range of subject areas and to a 'Common Room' that provides a wide range of social environments within which to interact. The 'Common Room' is supported and run by the OU Students Association, and provides students with access to information and discussions under the headings of 'societies' (astronomy, etc.), 'interests' (books, holidays, sports, etc.), and 'social' (a bar, a steam room and a rogues gallery). The discussions within these forums range from serious to frivolous – very much reflecting the type of social interaction that one might find in the equivalent settings found in traditional institutions.

5.3 Selection of student support systems

In discussing the type of student support systems you might adopt within your own location you will need to take into account factors very similar to those considered in selecting media. These include:

- *the appropriateness of the support provided;*
- *ease of access to the support required;*
- *continuity of support;*
- *skills required to make use of the support provided;*
- *the costs involved in providing the support.*

Let us consider each of these aspects in turn.

The appropriateness of the support provided

The first question you need to ask is what type of support is needed, and within this context what type of systems are there that are likely to meet the needs you envisage. For example, if you want to help students to deal with the problems they encounter on a regular day-to-day basis, you might consider the type of support tutors might be able to provide by means of telephone contacts, faxes, e-mail and/or computer-conferencing. There is no way that tutorials or residential schools are likely to be able to provide such support on a regular day-to-day basis.

In contrast, if you want to help students to develop skills and attitudes that depend on intense interaction with, and support from, both tutors and fellow students, the obvious alternatives to consider are tutorials and residential schools.

Ease of access to the support required

When students run into problems with their day-to-day studies they are likely to want immediate support. If they have to wait for a tutorial at the end of the month to obtain answers to their questions, they are likely to feel very frustrated. This is where the telephone, e-mail and faxes come into their own right in enabling students to make rapid contact with their tutors.

Students may of course gain even more rapid access to fellow students, and there will be times when this will be appropriate, but equally well there will be times when students will prefer to make contact with their tutors – even if this involves some delay. Clearly, there needs to be a balance between the immediacy of support and the appropriateness of that support.

The same point might be made with regard to tutorials and residential schools which make much greater demands on students than support provided in the home or the place of work. In order to participate in tutorials or residential schools students have to travel further, they have to set aside more time to participate, and all at much greater cost to themselves. Such forms of support can only be justified if what they offer is highly valued and would be difficult, if not impossible, to provide by other more accessible means. In this respect it is worth noting that summer schools within the UK OU are usually only offered once (at most) during a course because of the demands that they place on both students and staff. However, they are highly valued, and I might add that in contributing to the presentation of summer schools over a period of more than twenty-five years within the UK OU, I have never heard any student or member of staff who questioned their value – in fact, the contrary has very much been the case. Clearly, the value placed on residential schools within the UK OU outweighs the problems of access associated with attendance.

Continuity of support

Continuity of basic support is important. Imagine that you need to plan student support for a course to be presented over a period of nine months, that is roughly 270 days. Within that period you might decide to provide a three-hour tutorial once per month and a seven-day residential school two-thirds way through the course. That means that students will get support from these two systems on sixteen days of the course, leaving you with the question of what type of support to provide to cover the remaining 254 days. It's a crude way of looking at the problem, but it certainly makes one think.

Skills required to make use of the support provided

We have already made the point in discussing the use of media that both students and staff should have the skills required to make good use of the media concerned, and the same point might be made with regard to the support systems being considered.

The use of computers provides a rather obvious example of the dilemma. If these are to be used to provide students with essential support (through the use of e-mails, the submission of electronic assignments with electronic feedback, and/or computer-conferencing), then it is essential that students and staff should have the skills required to make good use of the support provided, and it may be that self-study materials and/or related training will have to be provided to help students and staff develop the knowledge and skills required.

What is not always quite as obvious is the fact that students pursuing ODL courses for the first time may need to develop a range of much more basic study skills. Some of the skills required may be relevant to both ODL and FFT (face-to-face teaching) – such as those required for producing essays, for undertaking literature reviews and projects, and for producing related reports. Others might be specific to ODL, and very much concerned with ways of studying and obtaining support within an ODL environment. Within the UK OU a wide range of materials have in fact been produced to help students develop the knowledge and skills that they will require.

The costs involved in providing the support

Before adopting any particular support system you will need to determine the cost of developing and supporting that system from the point of view of the institution and the cost of using the system from a student point of view, and you will find more details on how you might go about this in Chapter 10.

The main point to note here is that if ODL is to be cost-effective, it should be designed to reach out to relatively large numbers of students, and that this is more likely to be achieved if tutor support systems are decentralised. The point is that if tutor support services are provided by central academics, they will be rapidly overwhelmed by increasing student numbers. In contrast, if a decentralised tutor support is provided by part-time tutors spread throughout the regions, and where student numbers increase rapidly, it is usually a relatively simple matter to increase the number of part-time tutors required. It is certainly much simpler and cheaper than trying to increase the number of central academics. This is an issue that has been discussed earlier in some detail, but if you would like to refresh your memory on the points made you might like to turn back to Chapter 1.

Where the courses to be presented within ODL fall within a given subject area (such as engineering, law, or nursing), you might search for part-time tutors and study centre facilities (for tutorials, resource materials, etc.) in related institutions (such as technical training colleges, local law courts, and hospitals). Where the courses to be presented cover a wide range of subject areas, you may well look for part-time tutors in the same places, but it will usually make sense to set up local study centres that are able to provide joint support facilities for a wide range of subject areas.

In perspective

The provision of high quality student support services is expensive, and where students do not always attend tutorials or consult with their tutors or counsellors on a regular basis there is always a tendency to suggest that this means that the support offered is not valued. However, this is missing the point. Students who do not make regular contact with their tutors or counsellors still value them highly as providing a safety net in much the same way that one might value having access to a doctor (Melton and Zimmer, 1987). The less we have to visit a doctor the better, but it does not mean that we do not value having access to one. In reviewing costs it is of course important to take note of the extent to which students make use of their tutors and counsellors, but sight must not be lost of the extent to which both provide an important safety net for students.

As throughout this book the intent is simply to provide a foundation on which to build, and for those of you keen to learn more about student support systems, I would recommend that you read Simpson's excellent book *Supporting Students in Open and Distance Learning* (2000).

Suggestions

At this stage I would suggest that you get together with some of your colleagues within a specific subject area to discuss the types of student support systems that you would like to be able to adopt within that area.

You might also encourage colleagues within other subject areas to do the same. The chances are that you will find a great deal of agreement between groups, but don't be surprised if groups differ to some extent in their requirements. At some stage you will need further discussion of the requirements at a broader institutional level, and it is important that the findings from the various subject areas are fed into that discussion.

Part 3

The development of materials and systems

By now you should have a good idea of the type of self-study materials and student support systems that you would like to include within any approach to ODL that you might develop in your own area, and the intent here is to help you to identify the type of development procedures you will need to adopt in order to ensure the quality of the materials and systems you envisage producing.

Within this part of the book you will in fact find a detailed description of a development process which you might adopt. However, in order to enable you to decide for yourself the type of process that is most likely to meet your needs, I will begin in Chapter 6 by highlighting typical **principles upon which development builds**. You will find that the principles discussed highlight the importance of the development process progressing in clearly defined stages from the general to the specific with feedback at each and every stage in the process, as it is this which enables quality assurance and quality control procedures to be built into the process.

In the next two chapters you will find a detailed description of a development process that builds on the principles identified. The process is typical of the type of approach adopted by course teams within the UK OU – although there is a degree of variation between the approaches adopted by different teams. **The first stage in the development process** is described in Chapter 7, and is concerned with developing an outline for a course. Although this is only the first of five stages, it will give you a good idea of the nature of the development process as a whole, as it creates the foundation upon which the subsequent stages build. **The remaining stages in the development process** are described in Chapter 8, and will take you in sequential stages from the outline for the course to the finished products. Feedback is collected at each stage in the process, providing the means by which quality assurance measures are integrated into the development process. Whether you adopt the process in its entirety or modify it to meet your own particular needs is up to you. What is important is that any development process that you adopt should be built on the principles identified.

If you plan to go ahead with the development of your own materials

The development of materials and systems

and systems you will need more detailed information on how to go about collecting data for quality assurance purposes, and in Chapter 9 you will find a review of some of the techniques that may be used in **collecting data for quality assurance and quality control**. You will in fact find that very much the same measuring instruments and data collecting techniques may be used for both purposes. The thing that makes the processes different is the way in which the data is used.

6 Principles upon which development builds

Contents

Introduction	135
6.1 Translating your vision of what students need into reality	135
6.2 Ensuring the quality of the ultimate products	136
6.3 Supporting creative thinking and a meaningful exchange of views	139
In perspective	140
Suggestions	140

Introduction

There are three important principles that need to be taken into account in designing any development process.

- The process adopted should provide you with a logical means of *translating your vision of what students need into reality*.
- The process in itself should go a long way towards *ensuring the quality of the ultimate products*.
- Within the process emphasis should be placed on *supporting creative thinking and a meaningful exchange of views*.

In the text that follows we will look at how this might be achieved.

6.1 Translating your vision of what students need into reality

In order to translate your vision of what is needed into reality you need to adopt a development process that is able to help you to progress in logical stages from your initial conception of what is required to the final details of the ultimate products. Such a process is described in some detail in

Chapters 7 and 8. It is basically designed to progress in sequential stages from initial agreement on broad principles to agreement on increasingly detailed specifics with each stage building on the preceding one.

Feedback is obtained at each and every stage in the process, and is acted upon before proceeding to the next stage in the process. The intent is to avoid individuals (or sub-groups) proceeding too far with the development of materials only to find that the foundations (the principles, broad aims, or strategies) upon which they are building are not acceptable.

If individuals proceed too far with the development of materials before obtaining feedback from related experts, they run the risk of finding that the foundations upon which they have been building are rejected in whole or part. If this happens the materials that they have developed on top of these foundations will also be rejected, and a great deal of time and effort will have been wasted unnecessarily. Individuals faced with the need to change the foundations upon which they have built are likely to experience a great deal of pressure and anxiety, and may even withdraw from the development process. Such outcomes have been reported on in some detail by Lawrence and Young (1979) and should be avoided as far as is possible. In adopting a development process that moves in stages from the general to the specific, the intent is to avoid such inefficiency and all the trauma that may accompany it.

6.2 Ensuring the quality of the ultimate products

There are two obvious ways of ensuring the quality of the end products. The first is by building *quality assurance strategies* into the development process with a view to helping course teams in a supportive manner to develop ODL to the highest possible quality. The second is by building *quality control strategies* into the development process with a view to helping the institution and its committees determine whether plans and products should be accepted.

In the text that follows we will consider how the UK Open University has made use of quality assurance and quality control in the development of its courses. Hopefully, this will help you to reflect on how you might ensure the quality of any system of ODL that you might hope to develop.

Quality assurance strategies

Experts have an important role to play in ensuring the quality of the end products. Apart from being used to provide feedback on materials produced at each and every stage in the development process, they may be used to provide guidance on what is required, and may also be involved in the actual development of materials.

Within the UK OU such specialists are invited to work together in teams on the development of course materials, and are carefully chosen because of their ability to support various aspects of the development process. A list of the type of specialists you might find in a course team is shown in Figure 6.1. Some of these (such as the course team chair, manager and authors) might be expected to be very deeply involved in all the core team work, others (such as the radio and television producer, computer expert and editor) might have co-ordinating roles with back-up support within their own areas, while others (such as the external assessor) may have more of a consultancy type of role. There are no cut and dried rules, and it is up to the chair and the core course team to decide what specialists they will need.

All members of the team will usually be invited to attend critical meetings when the products from each stage in the development process are presented for review purposes. At such points in time they will be expected to provide feedback on the materials that have been developed so far. However, the fact that individuals are recognised as members of a team does not mean that they have to attend every single meeting during the process of development. There will be times when individuals and sub-groups will work separately on agreed projects, and there will be times

Course team chair

Course team manager

Subject authors

Tutor

Educational technologist

Radio and TV specialist

Audio-visual specialist

Computer expert

Assessment specialist

Editor

Librarian

External assessor

External consultants

Figure 6.1 Some of the specialists who might be included in a course team

when inputs from particular individuals will be more important than others.

Quality assurance is seen as an ongoing part of the development process. It begins long before any development of materials takes place with such tasks as the identification of the target group and the needs to be addressed. It then continues on throughout the development process with feedback being obtained and acted upon at each stage in the process. Even after the course goes out to students, feedback continues to be collected – the intent in the short term being to identify and rectify prevailing weaknesses and in the longer term to provide guidance for the possible re-making of the course at some time in the future. At all times throughout this process the intent is to use feedback to provide guidance for the development and improvement of the materials and systems concerned.

Needless to say, as feedback is collected at the various stages in the development process, a variety of different views are likely to be expressed within the course team as to the action that will need to be taken. It is therefore important that the course team environment facilitates meaningful and constructive discussion, and we will return to this issue shortly.

Quality control strategies

There are three different points in time when quality control measures are used within the UK OU. The first point in time is during the early planning of a course when outline plans have to be submitted to related university committees for approval. Since the plans may be accepted or rejected, the process is clearly one of quality control. However, advice may be given with regard to the weaknesses in any plans, and these may be revised and re-submitted. In this respect the process might appear to be similar to that of quality assurance. The difference is that control in this case is in the hands of the institution and its respective committees.

The second point in time is during the actual development of course-related materials. Since the initial outline plans approved by university committees should have included detailed schedules identifying what might be expected at each stage in the development process, it is possible for the progress of teams to be monitored. If a team runs into serious difficulties the project may be aborted in yet another example of quality control. However, this is a last case scenario, and every effort is usually made to help a team get over its problems rather than abort the project. The reasoning is simple. A great deal of time and effort will have already been put into the development of the course, and it makes sense to do everything possible to rescue it rather than reject it outright.

The third point in time is during the actual presentation of the course to students. Within the UK OU new courses are usually monitored in the first year of presentation, and they continue to be monitored on a more sporadic basis in subsequent years. Once again courses can be removed if major problems are identified, but normally feedback is used to rectify problems rather than withdraw a course. However, the data may also be used to identify ways in which the course might be re-made at some later date, and since financing and approval would be required for this, the data collected from the continuing monitoring of the course contributes to a certain extent to further quality control.

Although in the above instances feedback may be used to improve the materials and systems being monitored, control resides in the hands of the institution and its related committees, which also have the option of rejecting the plans and products under review.

6.3 Supporting creative thinking and a meaningful exchange of views

We have already mentioned the importance of creating a supportive environment within the course team, and the reasoning behind this needs to be clarified. The main point is that if individuals involved in the development of materials and systems are to be creative and well motivated, it is important that they should find their colleagues supportive rather than judgemental, and every attempt should be made to create a supportive environment in which different points of view might be rationally discussed, rather than a critical environment where individuals are placed on the defensive.

Where individuals are working together in course teams, they will often need to be advised on how to create such an environment, and simple suggestions can make a great deal of difference. For example, members might be advised to begin any critique of materials by identifying the things that have been done well, and to ameliorate any subsequent critique by offering helpful suggestions for discussion.

The subject has in fact been well researched. Over forty years ago Thelen (1960) was emphasising the extent to which different points of view can stimulate creative thinking. However, she was aware of the need to create a supportive environment for such discussions, and this was reinforced by the findings which emerged from Rogers' (1971) work with encounter groups. There is no doubt that differences of opinion need to be handled with care if they are not to lead to unhelpful conflict. According to Smith (1980), the best way of avoiding conflict is to develop a supportive environment in a group before introducing challenges that could be perceived by some to be personally threatening. One of the ways in which you might try to achieve this is by encouraging members of your team to socialise – to see each other as friends and not simply as academic colleagues.

Needless to say, it is easier said than done, and you may well find it helpful to bring in a consultant to provide basic training in interpersonal skills and advice on actual interactions within the course team environment.

In perspective

I have made no attempt in this chapter to provide you with the detail required to undertake the development of a course. Nevertheless, the information provided is important in that it highlights the principles underlying the development process, and if you decide to modify the process (as described in the next two chapters) to take into account the conditions and constraints of your own local environment, you should attempt to ensure that this will still build on the principles highlighted here.

Suggestions

Before you sit down with your colleagues to discuss the type of development process that you might adopt to meet your own particular needs, I would suggest that you read the next two chapters, as these provide detailed information on how you might develop materials in sequential stages and on how you might build quality assurance and quality control into that process.

7 The first stage in the development process

Contents

Introduction	141
7.1 A framework for the course	142
7.2 The materials and systems to be developed	156
7.3 The assessment strategies to be adopted	156
7.4 A brief description of the development process to be followed	164
In perspective	164
Suggestions	166

Introduction

The development process described in this chapter and the next assumes that relevant experts will be working together within course teams, and that all concerned will have been introduced to the principles underlying the development process and will be aware of the type of role that they will be expected to play within the course team.

Within this chapter we will be looking at the first stage in the development process which is intended to help you with the development of an outline for your course. Bearing in mind that your plans will almost certainly need to be approved by the powers that be in your institution, your outline should include four key requirements.

First, you will need to identify the logic behind the proposed course: the nature of the target group, the perceived needs of members of the group, the way in which a course might be designed to meet some of the perceived needs, the content that might be included in such a course, the teaching strategies that might be adopted, and the actual structure of the proposed course. In other words what is needed is *a framework for the course* and the logic behind it.

Once you have a basic framework you will need to think about the media to be used, the student support systems to be developed, and the resources that will need to be made available to students. In other words your next task will be that of identifying *the materials and systems to be developed*.

You will need to include details of *the assessment strategies to be adopted*, and these should clarify your position with regard to issues such as the following. Will assessment be on a continuous basis, at the end of the course, or a combination of both? Will students be awarded credit and, if so, on what basis? What measures have you taken to ensure that the awards system will stand up to the scrutiny of external examiners? Do you intend to make use of computer-marked assignments, tutor-marked assignments, tutor-marked projects, a combination of these, or some other strategy? Who will be responsible for preparing the assessment papers and for marking them? To what extent will assessment be used for credit purposes and to what extent will it be used to help students overcome perceived problems? Systems will need to be set up to support the assessment strategies planned, and it is important to clarify them at this stage, so that the necessary action can be taken in good time.

Finally, your outline should include *a brief description of the development process to be followed* indicating how this is designed to ensure the quality of the ultimate products. The outline should include details of what is expected at each stage in the development process, and should include deadlines for the review of the products emerging from each stage in the process. You will also need to identify those who have agreed to become members of the course team, and you will need to include details of the roles that they will be expected to play in the development process.

7.1 A framework for the course

Three logically related tasks can do a great deal to help you with the development of a framework for a course. The tasks are concerned with the following:

- *Identifying the characteristics of the target group and its perceived needs.*
- *Clarifying the aims and objectives of the proposed course.*
- *Deciding on the structure of the course.*

Although the findings from each of these tasks provides a logical basis on which the next might build, in practice you will find that discussion related to the tasks tends to move backwards and forwards with the findings emerging from later tasks often providing insights into findings emerging from earlier ones.

Identifying the characteristics of the target group and its perceived needs

Before talking about the type of course that you hope to develop, you need to be quite clear about the nature of the target group and the needs to be addressed. You might begin by trying to describe the typical characteristics of members of the target group including such aspects as the spread of ages, the knowledge and skills possessed, where members of the group are located, whether or not they are in full-time education or employment, and so on. You will also need to talk about the needs of members of the target group in terms of employment prospects, health requirements, societal needs, personal development, and so on. As these needs are clarified, you should try to identify the needs that have already been addressed through the provision of related courses, and you will need to ask yourself what is different and special about the course you are proposing to develop.

The ultimate aim of the discussion is to identify the broad aims of your proposed course and the logic behind it. In discussing these do give consideration to the full range of skills that students might need to develop, including those identified in Figure 7.1.

In discussing the broad aims of the course you will inevitably make assumptions about the knowledge and skills that individuals already possess. Do keep a record of these, as they will be taken into account in

---

Subject-Related
  Knowledge and Understanding

Subject-Related Skills
  (e.g. skills of scientific enquiry)

Professional Competences

Generic Skills
  Problem Solving
  Communication
  Inter-Personal Skills
  Numeracy
  Information Technology
  Language Skills

Study Skills

Figure 7.1 Some of the different types of aims to be considered

developing self-study materials for the course. Similarly, once your aims become clearer, try to estimate the number of students likely to enrol on the course in its early years of presentation. This is an item of particular importance if the course is to be cost-effective, and is one on which you will need to obtain supporting statistics.

Clarifying the aims and objectives of the proposed course

Hopefully, discussion along the lines indicated will help you to identify the broad aims of the course you are contemplating. However, these are likely to be expressed in somewhat general terms and you will need to translate them into more specific statements indicating what students should be able to do on completion of the course. A number of strategies might be used for this purpose, but two are particularly useful in that they are simple to use and widely applicable. The strategies referred to are those of *functional analysis* and *hierarchical analysis*, so let us look at examples of each.

Functional analysis

In the early 1990s an initiative was undertaken to identify the skills that 'middle managers' require (Management Charter Initiative, 1992), and these were expressed in terms of what such managers should be able to do. It was argued that middle managers should be able to do four things:

- Manage operations.
- Manage finance.
- Manage people.
- Manage information.

However, these are very broad statements of skills, and the Management Charter Initiative (MCI) made use of functional analysis (as illustrated in Figure 7.2) to provide a clearer indication of what managers would need to be able to do under these headings. Starting from each of the four general skills identified, the MCI experts asked themselves what managers would need to be able do in order to demonstrate that they had the broad skills required. For example, in order to demonstrate that they had the skills required to 'manage operations' it was rationalised that managers would need to be able to do two things, namely 'Initiate and implement change and improvement in services, products and systems' and 'Monitor, maintain and improve service and product delivery'.

Accepting that each of these statements also needed clarification, the analysis went on to identify in more specific terms what managers would need to be able to do in order to demonstrate that they had these particular skills. Such an analysis can continue to ever increasing levels of specificity, and in the case of the analysis carried out by the Management

Managers should be able to →

Manage operations	1 Initiate and implement change and improvement in services, products and systems	1.1 Identify opportunities for improvement in services, products and systems 1.2 Evaluate proposed changes for benefits and disadvantages 1.3 Negotiate and agree the introduction of change 1.4 Implement and evaluate changes to services, products and systems 1.5 Introduce, develop and evaluate quality assurance systems
	2 Monitor, maintain and improve service and product delivery	2.1 Establish and maintain the supply of resources into the organisation/department 2.2 Establish and agree customer requirements 2.3 Maintain and improve operations against quality and functional specifications 2.4 Create and maintain the necessary conditions for productive work activity
Manage finance	3 Monitor and control the use of resources	3.1 Control costs and enhance value 3.2 Monitor and control activities against budgets
	4 Secure effective resource allocation for activities and projects	4.1 Justify proposals for expenditure on projects 4.2 Negotiate and agree budgets
Manage people	5 Recruit and select personnel	5.1 Define future personnel requirements 5.2 Determine specifications to secure quality people 5.3 Assess and select candidates against team and organisational requirements
	6 Develop teams, individuals and self to enhance performance	6.1 Develop and improve teams through planning and activities 6.2 Identify, review and improve development activities for individuals 6.3 Develop oneself within the job role 6.4 Evaluate and improve the development processes used
	7 Plan, allocate and evaluate work carried out by teams, individuals and self	7.1 Set and update work objectives for teams and individuals 7.2 Plan activities and determine work methods to achieve objectives 7.3 Allocate work and evaluate teams, individuals and self against objectives 7.4 Provide feedback to teams and individuals on their performance
	8 Create, maintain and enhance effective working relationships	8.1 Establish and maintain the trust and support of one's subordinates 8.2 Establish and maintain the trust and support of one's immediate manager 8.3 Establish and maintain relationships with colleagues 8.4 Identify and minimise interpersonal conflict 8.5 Implement disciplinary and grievance procedures 8.6 Counsel staff
Manage information	9 Seek, evaluate and organise information for action	9.1 Obtain and evaluate information to aid decision making 9.2 Forecast trends and developments which affect objectives 9.3 Record and store information
	10 Exchange information to solve problems and make decisions	10.1 Lead meetings and group discussions to solve problems and make decisions 10.2 Contribute to discussions to solve problems and make decisions 10.3 Advise and inform others

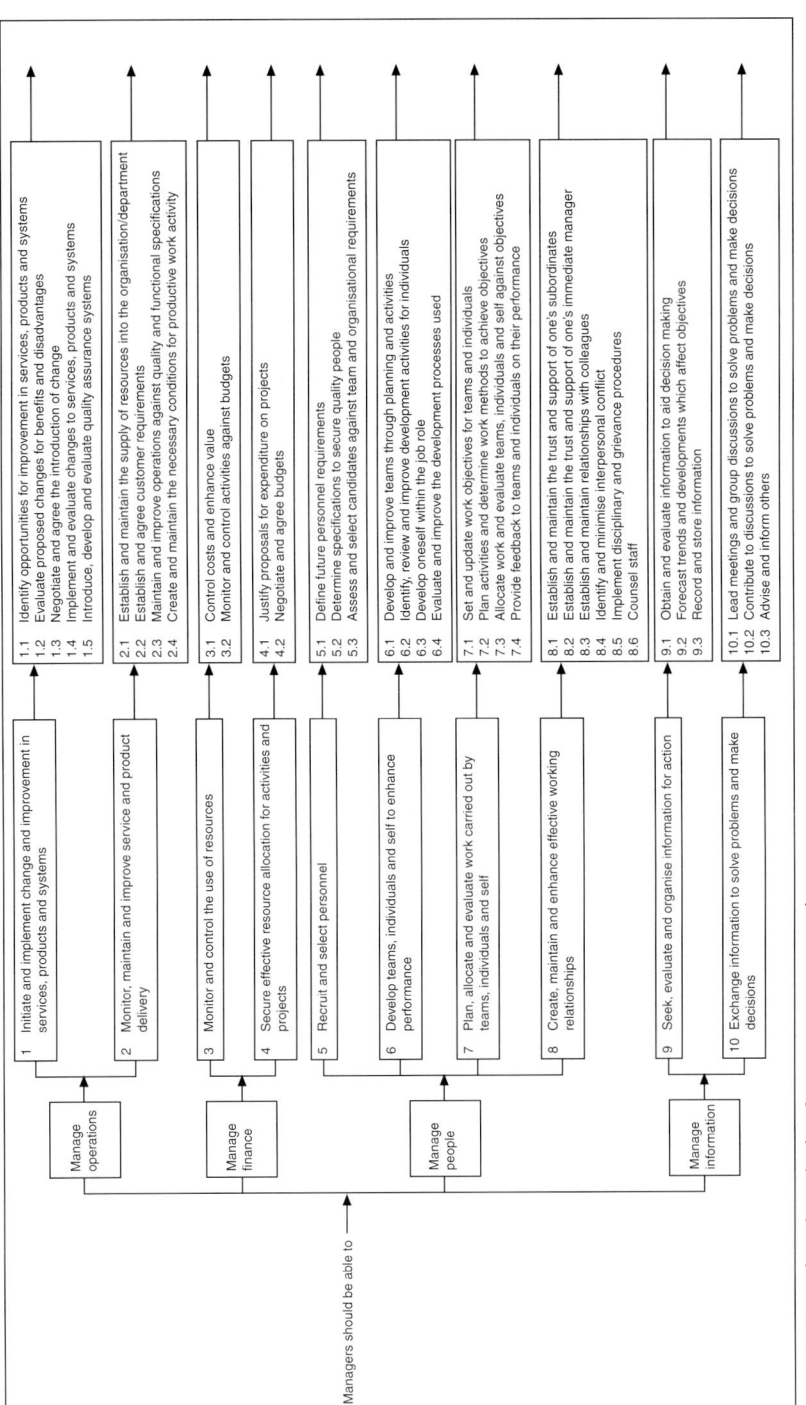

Figure 7.2 Functional analysis of management requirements

Source: Management Charter Initiative (1992)

Charter Initiative it went on to a fourth level of specificity that is not included in Figure 7.2.

The value of this process lies in the way in which it helps clarify your thinking about the aims and objectives to be achieved and the way in which it opens this up to public inspection and rational debate. If you adopt this process you will soon find that different individuals (or groups) starting from the same initial statements of intent are quite likely to come to somewhat different conclusions as to precisely what students should ultimately be able to do. This is not a problem, as it will help to illuminate issues that have been overlooked, and as such should help provide further clarification of what is required. However, once you have had an open debate on the issues, it should be possible to present your conclusions in a format similar to that illustrated in Figure 7.2.

Hierarchical analysis

Although you should ultimately express your objectives for a course in terms of what you hope students will be able to do on completing it, the whole of the analysis does not have to be expressed in functional terms. For example, it is quite possible that you will prefer to express some of your broad aims in terms of knowledge and understanding required, and this is acceptable so long as your analysis continues on to identify what is meant by this in terms of what students should ultimately be able to do.

In Figure 7.3 you will find an example of this type of analysis. It was undertaken by a team developing plans for a new undergraduate course on 'Man and Energy'. The members of the team were agreed that the broad aim of the course should be to help students to 'Understand the way in which energy may contribute to survival in a changing habitat' and they used the process of hierarchical analysis, as illustrated in the figure, to clarify what they meant by this.

In both Figures 7.2 and 7.3 only the first three levels of the analysis undertaken are included in the diagrams. Needless to say, the analysis could be pursued to more specific levels, and where this is done it can provide useful guidance on how students might ultimately be assessed. However, during this first stage in the development process the analysis is only intended to help clarify the main aims of the course and its overall structure (in terms of the units, and other major components, to be developed), and it will be up to individual authors in the next stage of the process to come up with proposals for the structuring of the content within individual units based on similar analysis. It follows that the process of analysis will continue to more detailed levels, but this will be at the next stage in the development when initial responsibility for this will lie in the hands of individual authors.

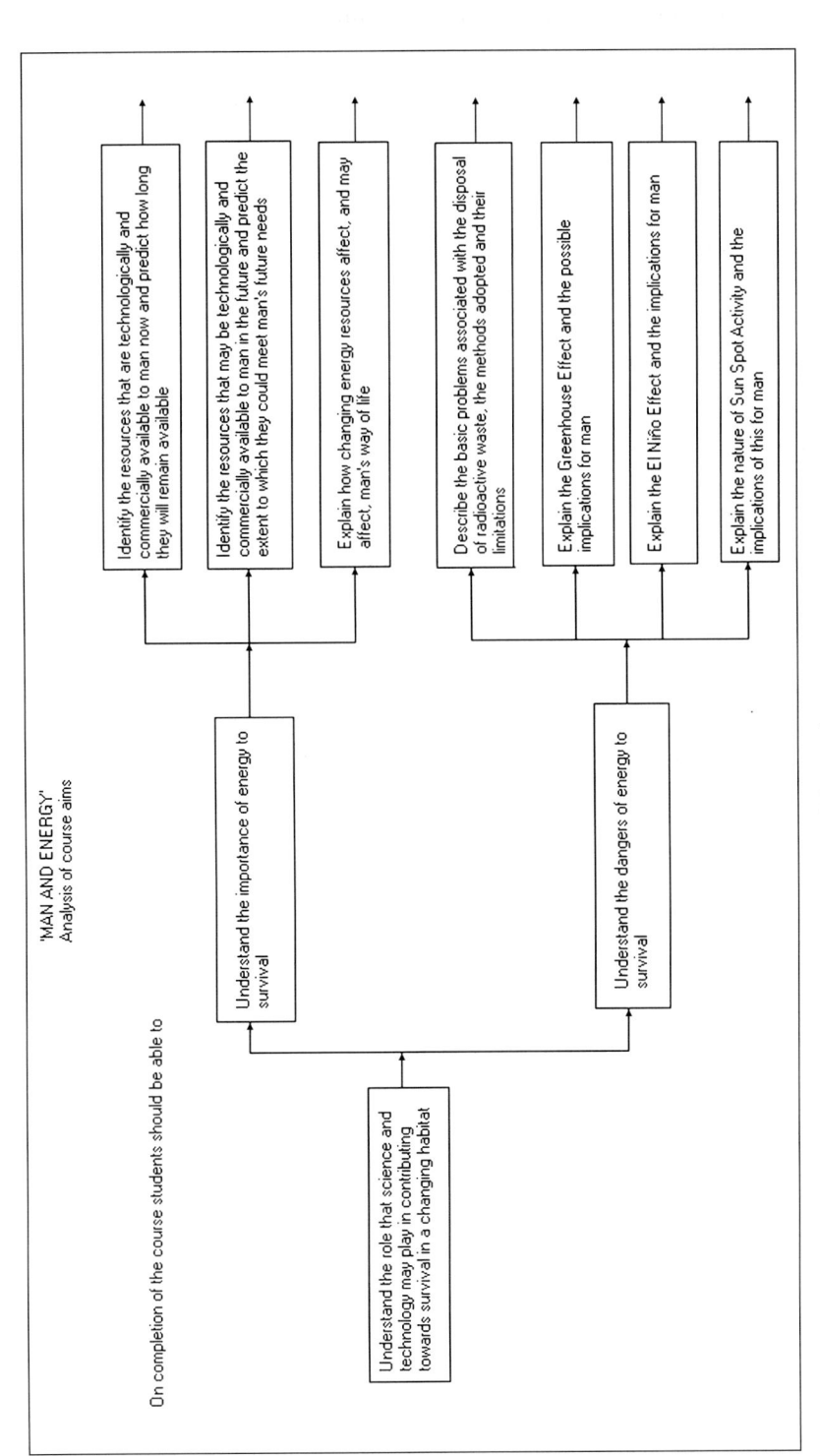

Figure 7.3 Hierarchical analysis of aims of course on 'Man and Energy'

Deciding on the structure of the course

Once the aims for a course have been identified in broad terms, the next step is to determine how these are to be achieved through the course being planned. The course structure will usually indicate how the course is to be broken down into units. However, it will also identify other components that may be outside the unit structure. These might include such components as radio and television programmes designed to run in parallel to the units and residential schools with their own specific objectives. In developing a structure for a course the main requirement is to ensure that it is clear how the various components will contribute to the achievement of the course objectives. A variety of alternative approaches might be adopted for this purpose, but here I will focus on three in particular, namely

- *a functional approach;*
- *a scenario-based approach;*
- *a project-based approach.*

Although these highlight the key issues that need to be addressed, they are not the only approaches that can be adopted, and I will conclude with brief comments on a number of *other approaches*.

A functional approach

We have already seen how functional analysis may be used to help clarify the aims of a course, and in turn this may be used to determine the structure of a course – with units specifically designed to achieve related objectives. The approach might be illustrated by reference to the aims and objectives identified in Figure 7.2 for a course in management. In the analysis illustrated you will note that the four course aims were broken down into ten objectives and thereafter to thirty-six sub-objectives.

Within a functional approach it would be quite logical to develop a course presented within ten units, with each of these concerned with the achievement of one of the ten main objectives. This option is illustrated in Figure 7.4. You will see that following this approach the unit headings provide students with a clear indication of what they might hope to be able to do on completion of the related units of study.

The same analysis of the aims and objectives (Figure 7.2) might be used to suggest how the units might be grouped together within four main blocks. From the analysis can you identify appropriate titles for the blocks and the aims to be achieved within each?

In the case illustrated you will see that most of the objectives for the course will be achieved through activities closely integrated into the course units. However, the achievement of some of the objectives will also depend on student participation in the residential school.

First stage in the development process 149

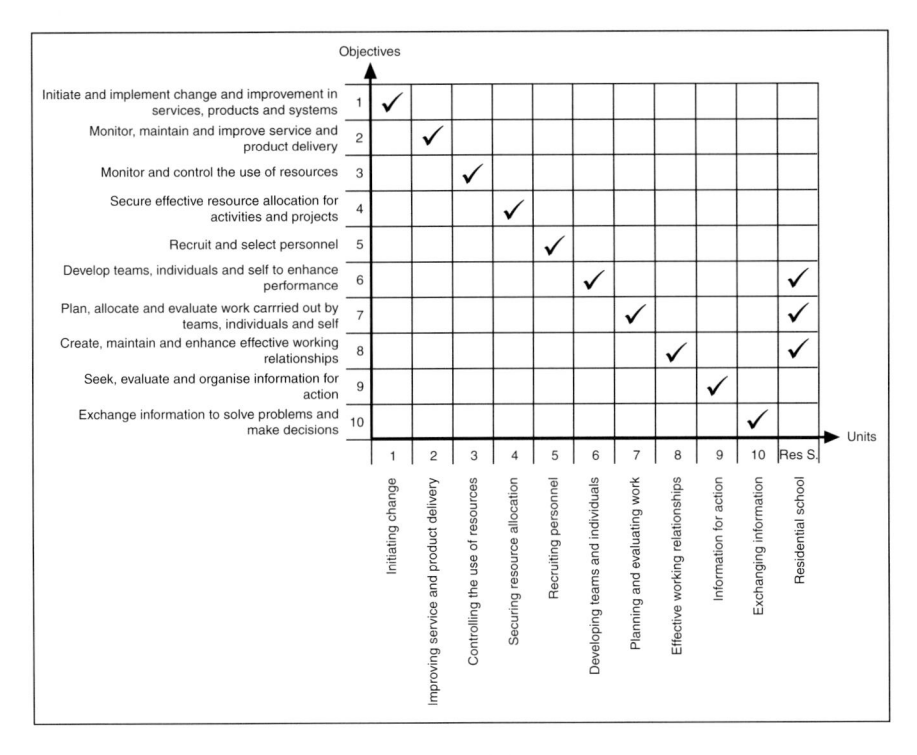

Figure 7.4 A 'functional approach' used to link course structure to course objectives

A scenario-based approach

In adopting a functional approach to decide on the structure of a course there is always a risk that the presentation will appear to be dull and boring. For example, in a language course the analysis of the aims for a course might lead to long lists of objectives grouped together under headings such as the following:

The article (masculine, feminine, neuter)
The plural
Personal pronouns (I, you...)
Possessive pronouns (my, your...)
Verbs (to be, to have, to talk...)
Prepositions (at, on, with...)
Negatives
etc.

You do not have to go very far back in time to find courses broken down into components under such headings. However, although the approach might have appeared highly logical to teachers, to children unable to see its relevance it more often than not proved to be very uninspiring. Although students may strive to achieve very much the same objectives within more up-to-date courses, study materials for young students are much more likely to be developed around scenarios such as:

Meeting people
Travelling to your destination
Obtaining overnight accommodation
Eating out
Visiting the tourist information centre
Changing money
Shopping

while materials for business people might be developed around scenarios such as:

Seeking advice from the town hall
Exchanging views in the boardroom
Making a presentation at the trade fair
Negotiating contracts

In following such an approach the intent is to introduce students to situations that they perceive to be relevant in the hope that this will encourage them to learn more about the people, their society and culture, and the language itself. In developing self-study materials around these scenarios, every attempt will be made to ensure that language learning emerges in a natural way from these settings. However, the self-study materials will also be developed with clear learning objectives in mind, and this is illustrated in Figure 7.5 which identifies some of the objectives to be achieved on a language course and the units within which each of the objectives will be addressed for the first time.

As you will have noticed, there is nothing to stop you using as many charts as you wish to identify the links between course objectives and units of study. (In practice, language courses often adopt a 'spiral approach' to the development of language skills, returning repeatedly to the same type of broad objectives – such as the 'use of the present tense' – but at a more sophisticated level, and this approach usually becomes much more apparent as one moves on to the more detailed analysis that typically takes place during the next stage in the course development process.)

Although the above example of a 'scenario-based approach' relates to the teaching of languages, the same approach can be used to good effect within a wide variety of subject areas. For example, in a 'materials science' course concerned with helping students to understand such concepts as elasticity, plasticity, stress, strain, breaking force, and so on, the teaching might be centred around such scenarios as

> farm tools (forks, scythes, ploughs...)
> farm machinery (milking machines, escalator belts...)
> forms of transport (bicycles, rickshaws, car components...)
> factory machinery (storage racks, basic machinery...)
> and so on.

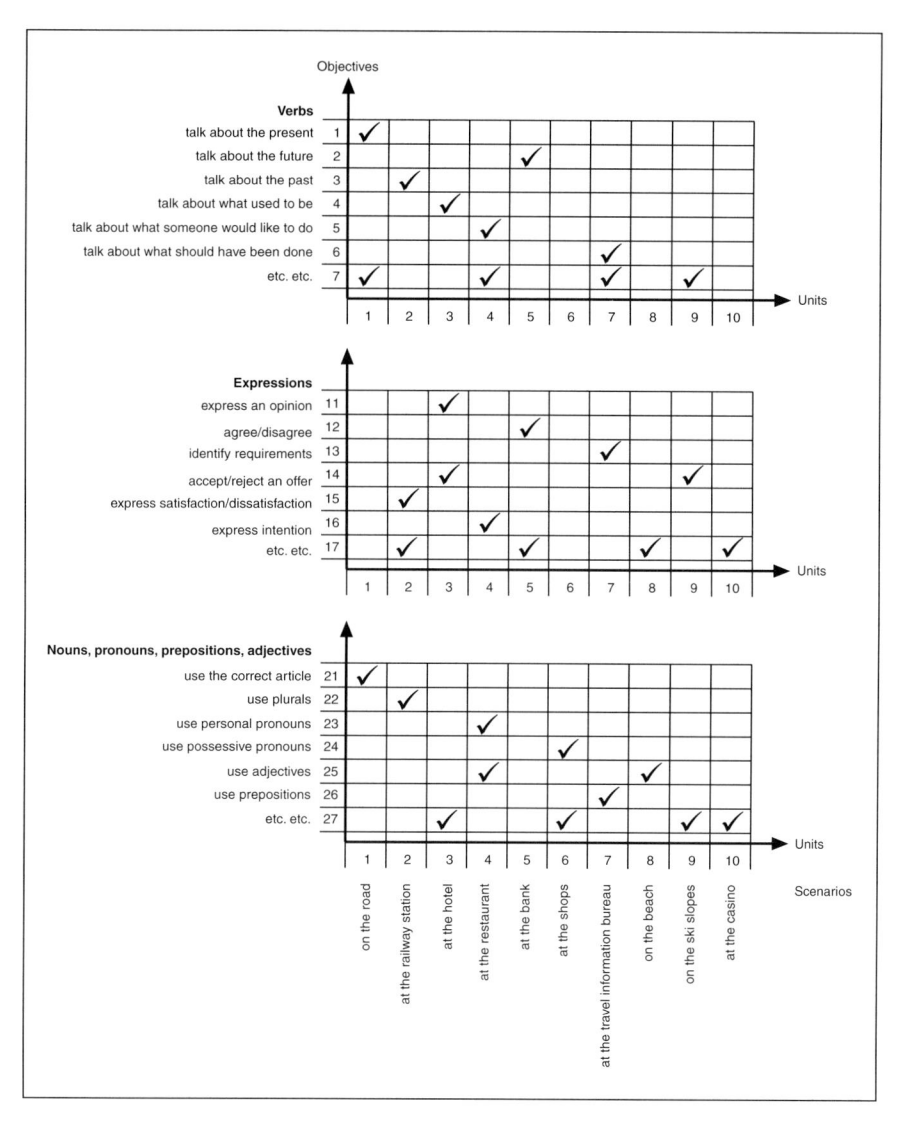

Figure 7.5 A 'scenario-based approach' used to link course structure to course objectives

152 *The development of materials and systems*

In a unit centred around the bicycle, the strengths and weaknesses of cranks might be used to introduce students to the concepts of stress and strain. Similarly, the subject of tyres might be used to introduce the notions of elasticity and plasticity and the characteristics of materials that might be used for this purpose. Interesting comparisons might be made between the materials used in bicycles for touring, cross-country riding, and professional racing – highlighting in the process the characteristics of different materials and why they are preferred for different purposes.

Whatever scenarios are chosen, it is important to indicate how these will be used to help students achieve the related course objectives, and the use of charts along the lines illustrated in Figures 7.4 and 7.5 are a useful way of doing this.

A project-based approach

In a project-based approach some, or all, of the main components of the course are linked to an important project with a view to helping students to perceive more clearly the relevance of the various components.

To illustrate the approach let us take a look at how it was used during the early planning of a course intended to help students to improve the quality of care provided in the community. Following initial discussion of the broad aims and objectives of the course the following objectives were identified:

> Students should be able to
> Describe the nature of community care and the care relationship
> (The Nature of Community Care)
> Describe community care policies, practices and services
> (Policies, Practices and Services)
> Describe the needs, rights and demands of users of care
> (Needs, Rights and Demands)
> Identify the extent to which types of care are related to demographic factors such as age
> (Demographic Factors)
> Identify the financial resources that are needed and available to support care
> (Financial Resources)
> Illustrate how the development of care is dependent on changing factors
> (The Changing Nature of Care)
> Describe ways of managing change
> (Managing Change)

Following what was essentially a functional approach, the team identified the titles of the units (indicated in parentheses) that would need to be developed to meet these objectives. In drawing up the list of objectives it was also agreed that students should be able to apply their newly acquired knowledge and skills to real-life situations, and that one of the best ways of achieving this would be by helping students to carry out a project in their own communities. A further objective was therefore added to the list, namely that of helping students to

> Improve the quality of care in the community
> (Student Project)

At this point in time the project was perceived as simply one more element in the course. However, in drawing up proposals for discussion purposes one of the options proposed was for the project to be a key element around which the course might be built, and this is illustrated in Figure 7.6. Although a chart could have been used to illustrate the links between the project, the units to be developed and the course objectives, a flow diagram is preferred in this particular case. There are in fact many ways of illustrating such linkages, and it is a matter of choosing the ones that illustrate the links to best effect. Let us look at what this flow diagram illustrates.

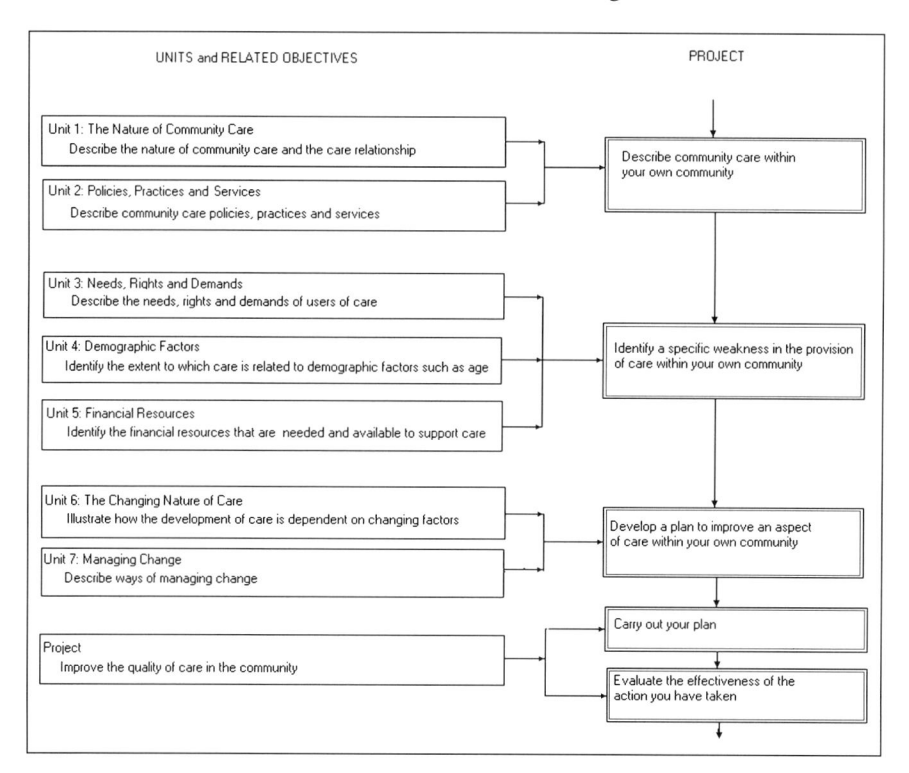

Figure 7.6 A 'project-based approach' used to link course structure to course objectives

One of the prime aims of the course was to help students to develop the knowledge and skills that would enable them to improve the quality of care within their own communities. With this in mind, the option presented for discussion suggested that students should be required to undertake a project to improve an aspect of the quality of care within their own community. The project was perceived as progressing through five stages with related units providing the knowledge and skills that students would require at each stage in the process. The flow diagram provided was intended to help clarify the logic behind the proposal and to open this up to debate. Before reading further do study the diagram carefully, and identify what you perceive as the strengths and weaknesses of the proposed approach.

Other approaches

There are numerous other ways of deciding on a structure for a course, and we will look briefly at what might be described as

- a case study approach;
- a chronological approach;
- a sequential approach;
- a forward chaining approach;
- a backward chaining approach;
- a modular approach.

Most of the approaches to be discussed in the text that follows have a great deal in common with the approaches that we have already considered, and the 'case study approach' illustrates the point. Case studies might be used in very much the same way as scenarios, with the aims of the course being achieved through the study of various aspects of the case study presented. Case studies may also be used in much the same way as projects, with the course being built around the procedures followed during an investigation.

One might use 'a chronological approach' to help decide on the structure for a course with events being presented in the order in which they occurred, and such an approach is typically adopted for the teaching history. However, there is much more to learning about history than simply memorising dates and events. It is always claimed that many lessons can be learnt from a study of history, and these need to be expressed in terms of course objectives. It is important to identify how these objectives are to be achieved through a study of a series of historical events (scenarios), and, if these objectives can be achieved through the study of a limited number of historical events, we might then ask to what extent students need a knowledge of all the events in the period under consideration.

There is a fine dividing line between a 'chronological approach' and the 'sequential approach' considered here. In a sequential approach a course is designed to follow a logical sequence of events (such as those found in a typical ecosystem) where one event leads on to another in a cause and effect type of relationship. Once again the question to be addressed is 'What are students expected to achieve as a result of their study of the events described?'. Will it be sufficient for students to simply understand how the events are linked one to another, or will there be other objectives to be achieved at the same time? The objectives for the course need to be clearly identified, and there needs to be a clear indication of how the study of the sequence of events will contribute to the achievement of the objectives identified.

Technical training is often related to a logical sequence of events such as that found on a typical production line, and where it focuses on each stage in the process in turn it is often described as 'a forward chaining approach'. The disadvantage of such an approach is that it is very easy for trainees to lose sight of the purpose of detailed tasks that they might be required to perform in the very early stages of the approach, since it is difficult for them to see the relevance of these tasks to the production of the ultimate end product. A well recognised alternative to this approach is to start by teaching trainees about the last stage in the process, making use of products emerging from the previous stage in the process. Once trainees have seen the ultimate product and the way in which products emerging from the previous stage contribute to this, they are then ready to learn about the previous stage in the process. In this manner they might repeat the process, learning about each stage in the process in reverse order in what is usually described as 'a backward chaining process'. The advantage of such an approach is that trainees can see the relevance of what they are trying to produce at each and every stage in the process. Again, the important question that needs to be addressed is 'What objectives are to be achieved in following such an approach?'. Bearing in mind that the trainees could be preparing themselves for a variety of roles, such as line operators, technical support personnel, or line managers, it follows that the objectives for the course will depend very much on the roles that the trainees are subsequently expected to undertake.

One final approach is worth mentioning and that is that of 'a modular approach'. In this type of approach the idea is to ensure that individual modules (or units) can be studied separately in their own right without oppressive requirements of prior knowledge. However, within each module objectives still need to be identified in just the same way as for a course. The idea behind a modular approach is to provide students with greater freedom of choice in determining their lines of study, and to avoid situations where a module can only be studied if students have already studied a range of other prerequisites. To a certain extent it is possible to adopt such an approach within an institution, and in fact the UK OU

156 *The development of materials and systems*

makes a deliberate attempt to avoid producing courses with unnecessary prerequisites. However, the degree to which freedom of choice is possible within such institutions is usually limited by qualification requirements. Within the UK OU, for example, where students are seeking professional recognition for the studies they have undertaken, freedom of choice is limited by the extent to which the award of specific qualifications is dependent on students successfully completing the study of particular combinations of courses at certain prescribed levels.

Whatever approach is adopted to help decide on a structure for a course, it is important to ensure that the relationship between the aims of the course and the structure developed is made clear.

7.2 The materials and systems to be developed

Once you have produced a basic framework for your course you will need to think about the media that you intend to exploit, the student support systems you hope to provide, and the resources to be made available to students. In other words, you will need to think about the issues that were addressed in Chapters 4 and 5 in particular. Each of the issues should be discussed separately, and members of the course team should make sure that they are familiar with the contents of the related chapters before participating in the discussions. Although this requirement can be expressed in a few words, each of the issues needs to be given careful consideration and is likely to involve a great deal of thoughtful discussion.

The media that you will be able to use, the student support systems that you will be able to provide, and the resources that you will be able to make available will depend to a large extent on the support you can expect to obtain from your institution. It is therefore important not only to discuss these issues within your own course team but also within the wider institutional context, as you will need specialist support not only in developing the materials and systems required, but also in providing related supporting services during the presentation of the course.

The importance of institutional support cannot be underestimated, and we will be looking in greater detail at the type of support that might be provided in Part 4 of the book.

7.3 The assessment strategies to be adopted

It is tempting to leave discussion of assessment until later in the development process when subject specialists will be much clearer about what it is they want to test. Although this might make sense as far as the development of actual tests is concerned, it is important to discuss the broad assessment strategies now – during this first stage in the development process – as the development of appropriate support systems can take time.

First stage in the development process 157

You have already seen examples of comments describing assessment strategies (see examples in Figures 3.14, 3.16 and 3.17), and you will need to produce a similar statement describing the approach to assessment you intend to adopt on your own course. Needless to say, this should reflect your own philosophies. Starting from scratch is always rather difficult, so here are four commonly discussed issues that might help stimulate your thinking.

Is your prime concern to determine whether or not students have achieved the objectives specified for the course, or are you more interested in ranking students relative to one another in terms of some particular ability (such as intelligence)? In other words which is more relevant to your needs: *a criterion-referenced or a norm-referenced approach to assessment* or something in between the two?

Do you have a preference for *continuous assessment or end-of-course examinations* or some combination of both? Many courses finish up with a combination of both, but it is easy to do this without thinking through how scores related to various assignments should be accumulated for credit purposes.

Do you envisage assessment being used solely for summative purposes (for the award of credits) or do you hope that it will be possible to use it for formative purposes (to provide students with feedback and to help them overcome related problems). If you are thinking of making use of both *formative and summative assessment* you will need to think through how one might affect the other.

In the text that follows we will be simply reflecting on the merits of the options referred to above, although in practice you will also need to think carefully about the level of institutional support that you will need to carry your plans through to completion. However, we will be considering this aspect in its own right in Part 4 of the book. In the meantime let us consider the merits of the assessment strategies referred to.

A *criterion-referenced or norm-referenced approach to assessment*

There are two classic forms of assessment, namely *norm-referenced* and *criterion-referenced assessment*, with a wide range of often ill-defined variations in between. However, *graded assessment* is one of the more interesting variants that is well worth a second look.

Norm-referenced assessment

Norm-referenced assessment is primarily concerned with ranking students relative to one another in terms of the extent to which they appear to possess a particular form of knowledge, skill, or ability (such as intelligence), and test items are specifically designed to discriminate between students on the scale concerned. Test items that can be answered correctly by all students or by none at all have no part to play in norm-referenced tests, as they are unable to discriminate between the students being tested. The items most likely to discriminate well between students are likely to have a 'facility index' in the range 40–60 per cent. (This means that if the items simply require yes/no type answers, then 40–60 per cent of students will be able to respond to them correctly. If the answers are more complex, then the mean score achieved on each item expressed as a percentage of the maximum possible score will lie roughly between 40–60 per cent.)

Criterion-referenced assessment

Criterion-referenced assessment is concerned with determining whether students have achieved specified objectives, and most curriculum developers would be delighted if related test items indicated that all students have achieved certain objectives, even though such items would do nothing to discriminate between students in terms of their ability. Nevertheless, criterion-referenced assessment was very much popularised in the 1960s when a great deal of emphasis was placed on the specification of objectives in very precise terms (by those such as Tyler, 1934, Mager, 1962 and Popham, 1969) in the belief that this would enable examiners to determine with a considerable degree of precision whether students had achieved the objectives specified. The approach at the time was over simplistic, for the best that one might hope to achieve is an estimate of the probability of students having achieved the objectives specified. An example might usefully illustrate the point. Consider the following objective, namely that 'Students should be able to calculate the product of any pair of two-digit numbers (23×79, 58×43, etc.)'. Although this might appear to be a very simple objective that can be measured with ease, in practice there are 8,100 possible combinations of pairs of two-digit numbers, and a test consisting of, say, ten items would only provide an estimate of the probability of students being able to calculate the product of all the possible combinations. A test consisting of twenty items would be somewhat more reliable in providing an estimate, but it would still be no more than that. Providing students with examples of how they might be assessed against specified objectives is one of the simplest ways of providing clarification of what is required.

One of the problems with the most simple form of criterion-referenced testing is that students have very different abilities and will progress at very different rates. If a common set of objectives is identified, it is possible that weaker students will need all the time available to them to master the objectives, while more able students will master them quickly and be ready to move on. The question then is how to respond to the needs of the more able students. One of the simplest options is to identify a core of objectives to be mastered by the vast majority of students and to identify additional objectives for those able to progress beyond the core in the time available. Where such options are considered it is likely to have implications for the design of related self-study materials, and, if you are seriously considering the possibility of adopting a criterion-referenced approach, you might find it helpful to read more about the options available in my book *Objectives, Competences and Learning Outcomes* (Melton, 1997, pp. 77–89).

Graded assessment

Attempting to assess students according to whether they have achieved/not achieved particular objectives might be described as 'a binary approach' to assessment, and for many educators the approach is over-simplistic. The obvious alternative is to adopt some form of graded approach to assessment. Graded assessment may adopt a number of forms. At one extreme it may be related to actual performance criteria and at the other extreme to purely numerical scores, but it may well be a combination of both. Let us therefore look at two examples of how graded assessment may be used in practice.

The first example is provided by Dreyfus and Dreyfus (1984) who developed a range of criteria for identifying the levels of performance against specific skills. As such, they identified students as 'novices' in the first instance and as progressing from there in sequential stages to become 'advanced beginners', then 'competent' performers, 'proficient' performers, and ultimately 'experts'.

The second example is provided by the UK OU's Centre for Modern Languages which adopted a graded approach to the assessment of interactive communication skills in its early courses (L120, L130, etc.). For example, on the French language course 'Ouverture' (L120, 1999), prior to the end-of-course examination, students were sent an information pack which included the description of a number of rambles selected from 'Le Guide de la Randonée Pédestre'. Students were advised to imagine that they had been assigned a summer job helping groups of tourists and to prepare themselves to describe the rambles to their clients and answer questions concerning them. This scenario was then re-enacted within the end-of-course examination as a means of assessing students' interactive communication skills. At the time of the examination students were typically divided into groups of four – each group with a tutor acting as an assessor. Each student in turn was provided with a description of one of the rambles which he/she had previously studied, and was asked to talk about the nature of the ramble: the highlights and what was involved. The students not presenting were asked to make notes on the points made during each presentation, while the tutor assessed the content of the presentation. In the next phase students were required to discuss the selection of rambles presented, and were asked to come to a joint decision

160 *The development of materials and systems*

as to which choice they would prefer. During this phase the tutor was required to assess the ability of each student to communicate interactively in French. The criteria against which the tutor assessed each student are indicated in Figure 7.7. You will see that these are not only graded, but

Assessment criteria for ECA 2

Presentation Phase

Presentation content

5	(a)	Presentation incorporates fully the content of the information handout.
	(b)	Material very well organized and presented.
4–3	(a)	Presentation incorporates most of the content of the information handout.
	(b)	Material well organized and presented.
2	(a)	Presentation incorporates half of the content of the information handout.
	(b)	Material adequately organized.
1	(a)	Presentation incorporates less than half of the content of the information handout.
	(b)	Material not very well organized.
0	(a)	Virtually no information conveyed, or the information conveyed is not based on the handout.
	(b)	No evidence of organization of the material.

Presentation Phase

Quality of language: accuracy and range of expression

5	(a)	Can nearly always handle quite complex language with few errors.
	(b)	Very good range and variety of vocabulary, sentence structure and links.
4–3	(a)	Simple structures usually accurate. More complex structures, e.g. past tenses, often accurate.
	(b)	Good knowledge of vocabulary relevant to topic. Uses a variety of more complex linguistic structures. Successful linking of sentences.
2	(a)	Fair command of simple structures, but with some inaccuracies (e.g. verb forms and gender) which do not generally impede comprehension of the message.
	(b)	Vocabulary usually adequate for the task, though some mother-tongue interference. Satisfactory use of some more complex structures and linking of sentences.
1	(a)	Frequent basic errors (e.g. in verb forms, gender of commonly known words) which may impede comprehension of message.
	(b)	Severely limited vocabulary. Uses only simple structures. Sentences mostly not linked.
0	(a)	Minimum production of language or language so inaccurate that it is difficult to understand.
	(b)	Minimum production of language or use of inappropriate vocabulary. Language generally unstructured.

Figure 7.7 Assessment criteria for an interactive speaking test

Source: Course L120: Ouverture, Notes on end-of-course assessments, UK OU, 1999, pp. 10–11

	Presentation and Discussion Phases
	Pronunciation and fluency
5	Very good pronunciation and intonation. The communication of the message is clear and unimpeded, except for minor errors. Flows very well.
4–3	Generally good pronunciation and intonation. Errors only occasionally cause difficulty with comprehension. Reasonable flow.
2	Pronunciation at times impedes communication. Some success in producing appropriate intonation. Slow delivery.
1	Poor pronunciation with errors which frequently impede communication. Little success at appropriate intonation.
0	Not enough language produced to assess pronunciation and fluency, or pronunciation so poor that it is (almost) impossible to understand.

Discussion Phase
Quality of discussion

5	Able to exchange opinions effectively and to react to others' questions and statements with ease. Participates in the discussion with confidence. Displays conversational skills such as the ability to agree/disagree, to interject and to move the discussion forward.
4–3	Able to exchange opinions competently and to follow and participate in the discussion with some confidence. Able to maintain fair share of the conversation. Displays conversational skills such as the ability to clarify and maintain own point of view in the face of objections from others.
2	Able to exchange some opinions and to follow and participate in the discussion adequately, but has difficulty in maintaining fair share of the conversation. Displays some conversational skills, but does not react very effectively to the pressure of debate.
1	Takes part in the discussion, but only intermittently. Has difficulty in following the arguments and only occasionally able to interject own point of view, raise objections or support another's point of view.
0	Participation in the discussion rarely goes beyond an occasional *oui/non*. Largely unable to follow or contribute to the discussion.

Figure 7.7 (continued)

that scores are allocated to each grade, so that a numerical value can be assigned to the overall performance of each student. As such, this provides an interesting example of the way in which levels of performance may be graded and related to numerical scores. However, it also worth noting that once grades are converted into numbers that are subsequently added together, it is all too easy to lose sight of the actual criteria achieved.

Continuous assessment or end-of-course examinations

At first glance the most logical way of assessing students against the ultimate objectives specified for a course would appear to be through end-of-course assessment, since this gives students the time and opportunity to achieve the objectives concerned. Unfortunately, 'one-off' assessment at the end of a course tends to place a great deal of stress on students, and there is a strong tendency to prefer to use continuous assessment or a combination of continuous assessment and end-of-course assessment. The problem with these alternatives is that continuous assessment is often more concerned with determining whether students have achieved 'enabling objectives' – that is objectives that combine together to enable students to achieve the ultimate objectives for the course as a whole – and there is no guarantee that achievement of 'enabling objectives' will lead to students achieving the ultimate objectives. There is therefore a degree of risk in using 'continuous assessment scores' to measure student overall achievement on a course. Having said this, continuous assessment is often combined with end-of-course assessment, and it is interesting to look at an example of how this might be justified.

On the UK OU's French language course 'Ouverture' (L120, 1999) it was agreed that the most obvious point in time to measure the skills achieved by students on the course would be at the end of the course, and we have already seen how graded assessment was used for measuring various language skills. However, it was also recognised that it was important from the point of view of both students and staff to monitor student progress throughout the course, and it was felt that students might well ignore assignments if these did not contribute to the ultimate grades awarded on the course. It was therefore suggested that the continuous assessment should be combined with the end-of-course examination to determine the ultimate grades awarded on the course, but two safety measures were built into the process.

First, all the assignments (both continuous and end-of-course) were designed to measure the same basic skills of reading, writing, listening and speaking, although these were measured at increasing levels of sophistication as the course progressed. Second, when all the assignment scores were added together, much more weight was attributed to the scores achieved in the end-of-course examination. This was a sensible precaution at the time, as the course team did not know to what extent the scores on the two forms of assessment would correlate. In fact, a more equitable weighting might have reasonably been contemplated, as it transpired that there was a high degree of correlation between scores on the continuous assessment and the end-of-course examination.

Where scores are added together for grading purposes, it is very easy for scores from any given assignment, or group of assignments, to have an undesirable influence on the ultimate scores, and this is best avoided by thinking carefully through the logic behind the accumulation of scores.

Formative and summative assessment

In the discussion so far the emphasis has been on the use of assessment for 'summative' purposes, that is to determine what students have achieved in terms of knowledge and skills. However, assessment may also be used for 'formative' purposes, that is to provide students with feedback on how they are performing and to give them guidance on what they need to do to remedy apparent weaknesses.

Formative assessment is primarily concerned with the monitoring of student progress with a view to helping students identify and overcome existing weaknesses, and there are good reasons for trying to keep this separate from summative assessment. This is because students are more likely to be open with their tutors in discussing their problems if the prime aim is to help them (in a formative manner) to overcome their weaknesses, but they are much less likely to be so open if the knowledge provided is likely to be used (in a summative manner) to make judgements regarding their knowledge and skills. However, students need to be convinced of the value of formative assessment, they need to see a very clear link between what they learn from the assignments and what they are ultimately able to achieve, otherwise they will not invest the time and effort required to participate in a meaningful manner in the process. This explains why low scores are often awarded to students for undertaking formative assignments, even though this may detract to some extent from the logic on which summative assessment is based.

Having said this, there are situations where assessment might be used primarily for formative purposes and yet where there is a very strong logic for awarding related scores for summative purposes. Such an approach is often adopted within the UK OU for project work where students are expected to submit plans for their projects before carrying them through to completion. Although tutors are happy to provide students with help in drawing up their plans, they are also able to recognise the extent to which the plans reflect the inputs of the students concerned, and they are therefore able to award marks for the plans submitted. This has two main advantages. First, it ensures that students do not waste time and effort on misdirected efforts, as their plans are carefully checked before they invest considerable time and effort in implementing the plans. Second, it ensures that students gain appropriate recognition in the form of scores for the extent to which they contribute to the development of their plans. The ultimate score achieved on the project is thus an indication of the extent to which students were able to produce their own plans and the extent to which they were able to carry these through to completion.

If you would like to read more about assessment you will find that Rowntree (1987) provides a broad coverage of the issues in his book on *Assessing Students*.

7.4 A brief description of the development process to be followed

You should include a reasonable summary of the development process within your outline plans, including if necessary reference to other documents describing the process in greater depth. Your description should indicate how the process moves forward in stages from the general to the specific and should include the logic behind this. It should highlight the importance of obtaining feedback at each and every stage in the process and of ensuring that this is acted upon. It should include details of what is expected at each stage in the process, and should provide a schedule identifying key dates in the development process – in particular the deadlines by which the products from each stage in the development process should be available for review purposes.

You will be able to complete this task much more effectively once you have read the next chapter, as by then you will be familiar with what is involved in each and every stage in the development process. With this in mind I have also left the discussion of actual scheduling to the end of the next chapter, as by then you will be more able to deal with the variety of activities that need to be integrated into the schedule.

In perspective

All that now remains to be done is to collect all your plans together to produce a written outline for your course. The full range of issues that needs to be included within an outline is summarised in Figure 7.8.

There are three good reasons for producing an outline in writing. First, individual course team members, and individuals recruited to undertake tasks on behalf of the course team, will need to be aware not only of the framework for the course, but they will also need to be fully conversant with the nature of the development process and their roles within it.

Second, in most institutions concerned with developing courses for ODL, it is normal to submit outline plans to an appropriate committee for approval and funding.

And finally, and very importantly, you will find that relevant parts of the outline plan that you have developed can easily be converted into an actual 'introduction to the course' for students. The last point is particularly important, as it will get you started with the actual development of materials for student consumption. With this in mind you might find it helpful to look back at Figures 3.12–3.14 and 3.18 to remind yourself of the issues that need to be addressed within 'an introduction to the course'. Among other things the introduction will need to identify the framework within which the content of the course is to be presented, and this is also the framework within which you will be developing materials for student consumption.

STAGE 1: OUTLINE FOR THE COURSE

The outline for the course should include details of the following

Course Title

Students Targeted
(estimate future enrolment figures)

Needs of Target Group

Course Aims and Objectives
(identify assumed knowledge and skills)

Course Structure
(course units and other components)

Media to be used

Student Support Systems to be developed

Resources Required

Assessment Strategies

Development Process to be adopted

Course Team Members and Their Roles

Schedule for Development Process

Figure 7.8 Items to be included in the outline for a course

Suggestions

One of the best ways of gaining a good understanding of the development process is to get together with some of your colleagues to develop an outline for a course. However, I would suggest that you wait until you have looked carefully at what is involved in the remaining stages in the development process (Chapter 8) before undertaking such an activity, as you will then have a more comprehensive picture of what is required.

8 The remaining stages in the development process

Contents

Introduction	167
Stage 1: Developing an outline for the course	168
Stage 2: Developing unit outlines	169
Stage 3: Developing the core content for unit study guides	171
Stage 4: Developing the self-study materials in full	173
Stage 5: Editing and layout	178
In perspective	178
Suggestions	181

Introduction

By the end of the first stage in the development process (Chapter 7) individual subject specialists (whom I will refer to as 'authors') will usually have agreed to take on responsibility for the development of specific units within the course, and as such will be responsible for the development of unit study guides and for ensuring that all related resources are developed and integrated into the units for which they are responsible.

In describing the remaining stages of the development process particular emphasis will therefore be placed on what authors need to do at each stage in the process. One of the advantages of such an approach is that it will provide a clear picture of the basic development process and help identify key deadlines that need to be built into the core schedule. Inevitably there will almost certainly be some activities (such as the development of audio-visual materials, computer software, and so on) that will need to run in parallel to the basic process, and related schedules will need to be integrated with the core schedule. The way in which this might be achieved is illustrated in the final part of the chapter (under the heading 'In perspective').

The five stages in the development process might be briefly described as

168   *The development of materials and systems*

follows. During the *first stage* the course team as a whole is involved in the *development of an outline for the course*. During the next three stages subject specialists have a key role to play in the development of the materials, but the process should remain very much a team approach.

During *the second stage* individual authors will be responsible for *developing unit outlines* following strategies very similar to those used in developing the course outline. In *the third stage* the authors will be responsible for *developing the core content for unit study guides* in whatever medium is to be used for this purpose. Within this core content authors will indicate where such items as examples, case studies and activities are to be included in their units, but they will not develop these items in full until the basic ideas have been discussed in the formal review at the end of the stage. During *the fourth stage* authors will be responsible for *developing the self-study materials in full* – ensuring that both the study guides and related materials are fully developed.

It follows that in Stages 2–4 unit authors will be responsible for taking their units through three sequential drafts from unit outlines (draft 1) to core materials (draft 2) and then on to fully developed materials (draft 3). Although the stages in the process are clearly identified and sequentially related, you will find that thinking about earlier issues will often be clarified as you move on to later stages. There will therefore be times when earlier ideas will need to be refined. This is not a problem if the only person affected by the refinements is the unit author, so long as the course team agrees that the refinements are logical. However, problems can arise if proposed refinements have implications for other members of the course team.

Although emphasis is placed on the role that the authors have to play during these stages, it does not mean that they will be working in isolation – quite the converse. Towards the end of each stage in the development process there will be full course team meetings at which authors (and other specialists involved) will present the materials developed during that stage, and they will receive feedback on how these might be improved prior to moving on to the next stage in the process. In addition to these formal meetings there is likely to be a great deal of informal interaction between course team members during each stage in the process, and the materials presented for review purposes are likely to be familiar to key members of the course team prior to the formal meetings that take place at the end of each stage.

Once the course team has reviewed and approved the final drafts, these will be handed over for *editing and layout* in *the fifth and final stage* in the process.

Stage 1: Developing an outline for the course

This stage in the development process has already been described in detail in Chapter 7. It is the most creative stage in the development process, and it is important that members of the team should be able to exchange ideas freely in a relaxed and supportive environment. If you are able to manage it, during this stage you might consider arranging for 'a retreat' away from campus pressures where the team can concentrate in peace and quiet on the issues in hand without the interference of day-to-day affairs.

By the end of this stage you should know who is to be responsible for the development of each unit within the course, and you should also have agreed a schedule identifying the dates on which the products from each stage in the process will be reviewed.

Stage 2: Developing unit outlines

If you are one of the authors given responsibility for the development of the self-study materials for a particular unit, you will need to develop an outline for your unit. You will need to have contact with other specialists about the development of related materials (audio cassettes, home experiment kits, computer-conferencing, and so on), and you should have regular discussions with your fellow authors not only about your own unit but also about theirs. The outline that you develop for your unit should in fact be a joint effort undertaken in co-operation with all the relevant parties involved.

In developing the outline you might usefully adopt the same strategies as those used in developing the course outline. As such, it is logical to begin by identifying and analysing the broad aims and objectives for the unit, and then indicating how the unit components might be developed to help students achieve the related objectives. You will need to indicate how the unit is to be broken down into sections/study sessions and how these will contribute to the objectives to be achieved.

You will need to identify the teaching strategies to be adopted and the logic behind them, and as a part of this process you will almost certainly want to reflect on the type of activities/projects that might be built into the various parts of the unit and how you might make best use of the media available for these purposes. You will also want to think about the type of support that students will need, the resources that will need to be made available to them, and the way in which you might monitor and assess student progress. In other words you will need to think about all the issues discussed in Chapters 2–5, and you might like to refer back to these to refresh your memory. The full range of items to be included in the outline is summarised in Figure 8.1.

Whether you break your unit down into 'sections' or 'study sessions' will be a matter of policy decided by the course team as a whole, but in debating this issue do take into account the fact that the motivation of students to achieve the objectives specified for 'a study session' or 'a section of a unit' will depend on their perception of the achievability (and relevance) of the related objectives (Stotland, 1969). Breaking a unit down

---

STAGE 2: OUTLINE FOR A UNIT

The outline for a unit should include details of the following

Unit title

Aims and objectives
(identify assumed knowledge and skills)

Structure of unit
(breakdown of unit into sections/study sessions)

Teaching strategies to be adopted

Media to be used

Student support systems required

Resources required

Assessment strategy

Figure 8.1 Items to be included in the outline for a unit

into 'study sessions' is intended to make the related objectives appear more achievable. If students can achieve the objectives for 'a study session' within the time they set aside for it, this will increase their confidence in their ability to make progress. In contrast, where students need to sit down on several occasions to achieve the objectives specified for 'a section of a unit', the perceived achievability of the objectives may begin to diminish, particularly if students have little to indicate that they are making good progress.

Once you have produced an outline for your unit, and this has been approved by the course team, you should convert it (or a copy of it) into an introduction to the unit for the students who will be studying it.

Stage 3: Developing the core content for unit study guides

Before reviewing what you will need to do at this stage in the process, I will begin with a few comments on *the principles underlying the approach adopted*. This is because other options are possible, and the present one needs to be justified. So let us look first at the logic underlying the approach, and then we will move on to *the tasks to be undertaken at this stage* in the development process.

The principles underlying the approach adopted

In developing the outline for the course and then for your unit you will have noticed the role played by advance organisers in helping to identify the structure of first the course and then the unit. You can in fact use precisely the same procedures to produce advance organisers for each section/study session within a unit and for any further subdivisions of these parts. In other words, the advance organiser may be used progressively to help clarify the structure of the materials being developed. If you want to see an example of how this works you might like to turn the pages of this book, and see how I use the same process to identify the structure of the book in terms of the parts, chapters, sections and, at times, even subsections. The process only stops making sense when the advance organiser is only required to look forward a very short distance into the content. If you glance through the book again you will probably find that where a section of the text covers two or three pages the chances are that I will have used an advance organiser (and related content structure) to add clarity to the content, but where a section covers less than a page the chances are I will not have used one, since the structure of the content is likely to be self-evident without the need for an advance organiser.

In practice the process may not be quite as clear-cut as is implied here. As you progress with the development of the materials your thinking is likely to be clarified, and you are quite likely to want to modify the advance organisers in certain ways to reflect your new perceptions. However, in doing this you need to be aware that if the structure of an advance organiser is modified, then the structure of the related self-study materials will also need to be modified.

Using advance organisers in the way described has a number of advantages. From an author's point of view they provide a logical link in the development process. We have already seen how an analysis of aims can help us identify the type of structure within which these might be achieved, and a logical way of expressing this structure is through the use of advance organisers. As such, the advance organiser is able to provide a framework within which the development of more detailed materials might take place. Used in this manner the advance organiser ultimately becomes a part of the self-study materials presented to the student –

providing a framework for the assimilation of the more detailed learning to follow in the manner prescribed by Ausubel (1968) in his original formulation of the concept.

Some will argue that the approach described leads to over-structuring of the content, and that students should be given much more freedom – as prescribed by Rogers (1969) – to determine their own goals and the means of achieving them. However, it is in fact possible to provide students with a great deal of freedom to pursue their own interests within the approach described, if courses are structured around the skills to be developed. For example, within a given discipline area a course might be designed to help students to do the following:

- Search the literature.
- Make judgements on the quality of related studies.
- Apply newly acquired knowledge and skills to new situations.
- Test hypotheses through related studies/experiments.
- Collect, analyse and interpret data.
- Draw appropriate conclusions from studies/experiments.

One of the great advantages of project-based courses is that they can concentrate on the development of such skills leaving students free to determine the issues to be addressed within their projects. If you turn back to Figure 3.17 you will find a list of criteria to be used on an MA course in ODE for assessing related project work. You will find that the criteria listed identify the skills that students will need to demonstrate through their work and make no reference to the issues to be explored within the projects.

The tasks to be undertaken at this stage

How is this all going to help you to get started with your writing? Well, you already have an advance organiser for your unit which identifies the sections/study sessions to be contained within it, and you might get started by producing an advance organiser for the first of these sections/study sessions. To do this you will need to have analysed the aims and objectives for the section/study session and thought carefully about the best way of helping students to achieve them. This process should lead you to identifying a structure for the section/study session in the same way as it did previously for the course and for the unit.

Once you have identified the structure of the section/study session, all that you now need to do is to present your ideas within the structure identified. In doing this do remember that the material you are developing should be the core of what is to be presented to your students, so do write in the 'one-to-one' style of tutor conversing with student, addressing the student as 'you'. Where you intend to include diagrams, photographs, examples, case studies, activities, and so on, simply insert notes at appropriate points indicating what you have in mind. Similarly, add notes about the media you intend to use and indicate the logic behind your ideas. The main point is not to develop these items in detail at this stage in the process, but to discuss them with the course team before taking the detailed development further. Figure 8.2 contains an example of the type of core content you might produce. As you will see, it looks in some respects like the content of a book from which all examples, diagrams, photographs, activities and so on have been removed. The idea is that if you need to make any changes to the core content, this can be done relatively easily without the necessity of having to change a whole range of items that have built on top of the foundation provided by the core content. The same process will need to be repeated for each of the sections/study sessions to be included within the unit.

In following the process described you will automatically be developing the core content of your unit within a clearly defined framework, and it is worth looking back at Figures 3.11 and 3.18 to remind yourself of the type of framework we have in mind for the presentation of the sections/study sessions and unit that you are developing. Although at this stage you may not be able to include all the information included within these figures, you should present the core content of your unit within the type of framework illustrated.

In Figure 8.3 you will find a summary of all the items you should include in your draft at this stage in the process. You will see that you will need to produce a checklist at the end of each section/study session and the unit as a whole indicating what students should be able to do on completing their study of the related components. You will also need to indicate how students might assess their progress against the objectives identified and how this progress might be assessed for credit purposes through related assessment procedures.

In developing the core text for your unit you might find it helpful to look back at Chapter 3 where you will find examples of advance organisers, checklists, summaries, assessment strategies and other features that you might wish to incorporate within your draft.

When you have completed the core content, you will need to present it to the course team for approval, and you may well need to revise certain aspects of it before moving on to the next stage in the development process.

1.2 Coping with pressure

Most people would agree that a certain amount of pressure is tolerable, even enjoyable. A lot of us feel that we are at our best when the adrenalin is flowing and when we are working under pressure to achieve good results within a limited time.

The problems start to arise when the pressure becomes too great or continues unabated for long periods. It then becomes stress. It ceases to be enjoyable. It becomes detrimental, even dangerous and, if you suffer from it, it can impair your effectiveness as a manager.

Different people, of course, react in different ways. Some people, it is said, become addicted to adrenalin and, like any other addict, they suffer very stressful withdrawal symptoms when they are not under pressure. There is not a simple dividing line, with pressure on one side and stress on the other. The one merges into the other, almost imperceptibly. The important thing is that managers should be able to distinguish between them, so that they can avoid stress while making the best use of pressure. Let us therefore look at ways of *recognising stress*, then at some of the *causes of stress*, and finally at ways of *alleviating stress*.

Recognising stress

A simple way to differentiate between pressure and stress is by the effects that they have. Most high achievers (and a lot of managers would fall into this category) find pressure to be positively motivating. They are able to respond to it energetically. Stress, on the other hand, does not produce a positive, energetic response. It is debilitating. It deprives people of their strength, their vitality and their judgement. Its effects are negative. This, as you will recognise, is a rather gross polarisation. Between these two extremes is a large intermediate area in which pressure merges into stress, and this is the danger area. This is where one needs constantly to be on the look out for tell-tale signs.

Activity 5
I propose to ask our trainee managers to view the video clip of managers performing tasks under considerable pressure. This will help them to recognise typical signs of stress. The activity should not take more than about 10 minutes.

The medical effects are well known. Ask most managers about the possible outcomes of stress, and you will probably be told about ulcers, high blood pressure, heart disease, strokes and early death. On the face of it, the managers themselves are the victims, but under excessive pressure their families may also suffer. Managers experiencing stress may have little time to spend with their families, and, when they do find time, they may be irritable, unable to relax, and far from congenial company. When stress leads to medical problems the State is also affected by having to supply medical facilities, treatment and drugs.

Figure 8.2 Example of core text for part of a study session
Source: 'Core text' produced by the author for a course in management

News cuttings
Attached you will find cuttings from 2 articles providing data on the effects of stress on health. I suggest that we include one of these in a box around here as one of the series of news reports that we plan to include in the units.

Causes of stress

So serious are the effects of stress that it is worth spending a little time considering the causes.

Activity 6
Here trainees will be asked to view the video once again, but this time to identify factors that appear to be contributing to stress.

Activity 7
I will then ask the trainees to identify 3 or 4 colleagues at work who appear to be under too much pressure, and will ask them to identify the apparent causes of stress in each case. I will provide them with a comprehensive checklist to facilitate this task.

Alleviating stress

The next thing to consider is what can be done to assist in the reduction of stress levels, either in yourself or in those you manage. The latter is less within your control, but you can often do quite a lot to assist or, at least, to make your organisation aware of the problem.

Activity 8
I have several very good articles on ways of alleviating stress and would like students to read at least two of these. I will include these for you to read and for comment as to which appear to be most appropriate. They all include ways of alleviating stress, but differ in the extent to which they back up their proposals with well founded studies. I would expect the reading of two articles to take about 20 minutes.

Activity 9
Having read these articles I propose to ask trainees to choose one person from those considered in Activity 7, and to identify practical suggestions as to how some of the stress might be alleviated. I would expect this activity to take about 10 minutes.

Summary

This study session has highlighted some of the things you will need to think about as a manager, and it is of interest to reflect on these from a converse point of view. When we experience pressure which is not excessive, we are left feeling in control: we know that through extra effort we can meet the deadline. When pressure is excessive and we feel under stress, there is a feeling of having lost control: there is too much to deal with, it is too complex, we cannot see our way clear to the goal, or we are not even sure what the goal is. Maintaining control depends on doing all the things that we summarised in Activity 9. If you don't do these things, you are likely to find it extremely difficult to cope with the mounting pressures.

Figure 8.2 (continued)

176 *The development of materials and systems*

STAGE 3: CORE TEXT FOR A UNIT

The core text for a unit should include the following

Advance organisers
(for each section/study session and for unit as a whole)

Statement of aims
(for each section/study session and for unit as a whole)

Core text
(for each section/study session)

Comments for colleagues
(indicating plans for examples, case studies, activities, media usage, student support needed, resources required, photographs, indexes, etc.)

Summary
(for unit as a whole)

Objectives in form of a checklist
(for each section/study session and for unit as a whole)

Figure 8.3 Items to be included in the core text for a unit

Stage 4: Developing the self-study materials in full

Within the core text that you have produced you will already have notes identifying all the things that you need to do during this stage in the process, and it will be up to you, with the support of your colleagues, to ensure that they are carried through to completion. Much of your time at this stage in the process is likely to be taken up with such things as finding, or producing, examples, case studies, and activities. A great deal of time is likely to be required for the latter, as this is the point in time when you will need to integrate resource materials (articles, audio-vision, audio and video clips, computer-based materials, etc.) into the unit through the development of related activities and appropriate referencing. As your materials come to fruition you are also likely to spend some time searching for interesting quotes and photographs to help highlight the relevance of your materials.

The full range of items to be included in your fully developed materials is summarised in Figure 8.4, and it should lead to a final package of self-study materials for your unit that reflects many of the characteristics identified in Chapters 2–5.

STAGE 4: FULLY DEVELOPED MATERIALS FOR A UNIT

The fully developed materials for a unit should include the following

INTRODUCTION

Advance organiser
(for each section/study session and for unit as a whole)

Statement of aims
(for each section/study session and for unit as a whole)

Study Time, Resources, Study strategies, Student Support
(for unit as a whole and as appropriate for each section/study session)

CONTENT

All self-study material fully developed
(including examples, case studies, activities, media usage, resource materials, photographs, indexes, signalling devices, etc.)

CONCLUSION

Summary

Objectives in form of checklist
(for each section/study session and for unit as a whole)

Assessment materials for credit purposes
(may be produced later)

Figure 8.4 Items to be included in fully developed materials for a unit

178 *The development of materials and systems*

Stage 5: Editing and layout

The final stage in the process is that of editing and layout in whatever media are being used, and is usually handled by related professionals. However, before handing over all your materials for design work and editing do have a final discussion about the form in which you want the materials to be packaged. For example:

- Do you want to include all the guidance students need (the introduction to the course, detailed guidance for students throughout the course, and details of assessment) together within a Study Guide?
- Would you prefer to include the 'Introduction to the Course' in a separate brochure that can be circulated in advance to students? If so, will you also like to include details of assessment in a separate 'Assessment Booklet' that can be referred to at appropriate times during the course?
- Alternatively, would you prefer to include the introduction to the course and details of assessment in a separate 'Course Guide' with students being referred to it at appropriate points in time during their studies?

In perspective

Now that you know what is involved at each and every stage in the development process you should be in a position to begin thinking about producing a schedule for the development of any course you are planning. The main schedule will need to include dates indicating when the products from each stage in the process will be made available to course team members for review purposes and the dates on which the materials will be discussed within the course team as a whole.

In practice, the schedule developed is likely to be somewhat more complex than this, since work on a number of tasks is likely to run for periods of time in parallel to the main schedule. For example, in developing a language course it might be agreed during the first stage of the development process that video clips of particular scenes should be professionally produced on location, and that these should be made available for authors to use as a resource in developing activities for their particular units. Such work will need to be carefully scheduled so that it is made available to the authors at an agreed point in time. Similar schedules may be needed for the development of such items as audio cassettes, home experiment kits, CD-ROMs and for the 'developmental testing' of the products by typical students.

In Figure 8.5 you will find an example of a main schedule that has been modified to include developmental testing of the materials by typical students. There are many ways in which developmental testing can be carried

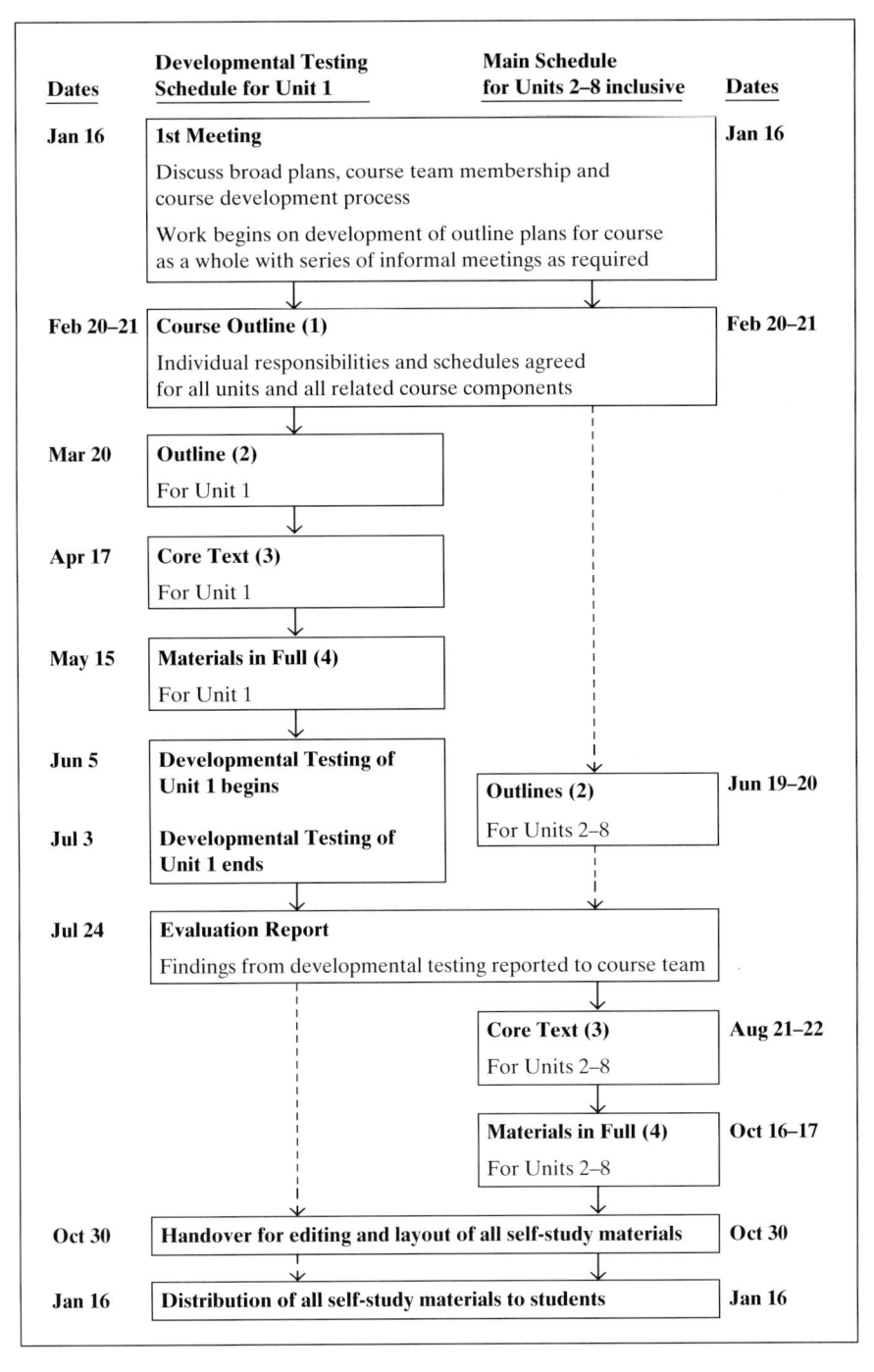

Dates	Developmental Testing Schedule for Unit 1	Main Schedule for Units 2–8 inclusive	Dates
Jan 16	**1st Meeting** Discuss broad plans, course team membership and course development process Work begins on development of outline plans for course as a whole with series of informal meetings as required		Jan 16
Feb 20–21	**Course Outline (1)** Individual responsibilities and schedules agreed for all units and all related course components		Feb 20–21
Mar 20	**Outline (2)** For Unit 1		
Apr 17	**Core Text (3)** For Unit 1		
May 15	**Materials in Full (4)** For Unit 1		
Jun 5	**Developmental Testing of Unit 1 begins**	**Outlines (2)** For Units 2–8	Jun 19–20
Jul 3	**Developmental Testing of Unit 1 ends**		
Jul 24	**Evaluation Report** Findings from developmental testing reported to course team		
		Core Text (3) For Units 2–8	Aug 21–22
		Materials in Full (4) For Units 2–8	Oct 16–17
Oct 30	Handover for editing and layout of all self-study materials		Oct 30
Jan 16	Distribution of all self-study materials to students		Jan 16

Figure 8.5 Example of a course development schedule including developmental testing

180   *The development of materials and systems*

out, but in this case the approach illustrated depends on accelerating the development of the first unit of the course. The idea is ensure that the findings from developmental testing of the accelerated unit are taken into account in the further development of the remaining units.

In the case illustrated the course is scheduled for completion within a period of 12 months. This is a relatively short period of time. Within the UK OU two years is not a long period of time to set aside for the development of a course, and new teams often struggle to produce high quality products within such a time span. However, in this case although the time set aside for the development process is relatively short, so too is the course itself. The basic idea in the schedule illustrated is for the course team to join forces in developing the first unit with individual authors taking responsibility for the development of each study session contained within the unit. This means that related materials can be developed quickly. Once the unit has been fully developed, the idea is for students to study it under conditions as similar as possible to those under which future students will actually study the course. As part of the agreement to take part in the study they will be asked to take part in interviews and respond to questionnaires. The evaluation as such will focus on strategies that are common to all units rather than on the specifics that are applicable only to the unit concerned. In this way the findings that emerge should be relevant to the course as a whole. The whole point of the developmental testing is to provide authors with insights into how well the various strategies are working and to ensure that the findings can be taken into account in completing the development of the remaining units a well as the one tested. In this case responsibility for the development of the remaining units will be placed in the hands of individual authors in the usual way.

In providing the above example the intent is simply to illustrate the way in which the schedules for various processes need to be integrated with the main schedule. The schedule itself should not be used as a model for the development of your own courses. The reason for this is that any schedule will depend on a wide variety of circumstances that are specific to your own situation. Thus the complexity of the schedule and the timing of the various stages within it will depend very much on such factors as the length of the course, the extent to which use is made of various media, the support systems that need to be developed, the number of individuals actively involved in the course team and whether they are able to give full-time or only part-time commitments to the development of the course. It will therefore be up to you and your colleagues to develop your own schedule for the various stages in the development process taking into account the constraints under which you have to operate.

Suggestions

At this point in time I would strongly recommend that you join together with a group of colleagues within a specific subject area to produce an 'outline for a course'. This will only take you through the first of the five stages in the development process, but you will find it will give you considerable insights into the nature of the development process as a whole.

If in doing this you would like to see more examples of materials development, you might refer to Rowntree's book *Preparing Materials for Open, Distance and Flexible Learning* (1994). Similarly, if you would like to gain greater insights into specific aspects such as team selection, how to assess student workload, desktop publishing and so on, you will find some thoughtful articles in the book *Materials Production in Open and Distance Learning*, edited by Lockwood (1994).

9 Collecting data for quality assurance and quality control

Contents

Introduction	182
9.1 During the first stage in the development process	183
9.2 During subsequent stages in the development process	185
9.3 During the presentation of the course	189
In perspective	199
Suggestions	199

Introduction

The aim in this chapter is to identify the variety of ways in which quality assurance and quality control might be integrated into the development process. In doing this, particular emphasis will be placed on the way in which data might be collected at three distinct points in time, namely:

- *during the first stage in the development process;*
- *during subsequent stages in the development process;*
- *during the presentation of the course.*

You will find that the same techniques and instruments (questionnaires, tests, etc.) may often be used for the collection of data for both quality assurance and quality control. However, although the same data may be used by different individuals and groups for a variety of different purposes, it is useful to try to keep some space between the two processes. This is because there will be occasions when overlap between them could lead to problems, and you should be alert to the type of situation where this might occur.

The first type of situation you should look out for relates to the collection of data where there is a possibility of it being used for either quality assurance or quality control purposes. Although individuals might be very open in *providing* feedback for quality assurance purposes, they are likely to be much less open if they believe that the data collected might be used for quality control purposes that could affect them personally. Since an individual can be affected as a member of an identified group, confidentiality of data can only go part way towards protecting individuals.

The second type of situation you should look out for is where critical data could be used in a supportive manner to help improve the quality of a product and in a critical manner to pass judgement on an individual or group. Although critical feedback might be *accepted* by individuals within a supportive course team environment where the prime concern is to improve the quality of the products, if such feedback is used to pass critical judgements on individuals, or the group as a whole, not only is it is likely to be rejected, but there is every possibility that it could destroy the supportive environment that is so essential to course team work.

It does not follow that an overlap between the two processes will lead to the type of problems that are referred to here, but you should consider the possibility of such conflicts, and develop procedures that will help to avoid them.

9.1 During the first stage in the development process

As a member of a course team your prime concern during the first stage in the development process will be the development of an outline plan for your course. Your outline will depend very much on the nature of the target group, and you will need to collect data on the characteristics and needs of this group. You may well include some of this data in your outline plan to justify the type of course you are proposing, and it follows that some of the data initially collected for *quality assurance* purposes may ultimately be used by an approval committee for *quality control* purposes. However, because of the nature of the data collected and the way in which it is used this should not give rise to problems. You will be aware from the start of the type of data that will be required by any approval committee, and, although you will need to collect that data, you will have a strong say in determining the full range of information and data that will ultimately be included in your outline plan.

Quality assurance

Before you can begin developing an outline for a course, one of the first things that you will need to discuss, and collect data on, will be *the nature of the target group and its perceived needs*. Once you have a good knowledge of what members of the target group need, you will be ready to move on to discuss the type of course that might be developed, and it will help clarify the discussion if you have *data on what has been done before*, including examples of good and bad practice. Once you have a fairly clear idea of the type of course you hope to develop you should try to obtain reasonable *estimates of possible enrolment figures*, as these will need to be included in your outline proposal.

The nature of the target group and its perceived needs

You might begin by discussing the characteristics of the target group with other members of the course team. What is it that draws your attention to this particular group? Between you, can you describe the type of individuals that might be included within the target group, and can you begin to identify their particular needs? By taking a variety of examples can you begin to identify typical group characteristics? What data do you already have on the type of individuals you are describing? Do you have any information on such things as the spread of ages of members of the group, where such individuals are located, whether or not they are in full time education or employment? Can you identify the type of knowledge and skills they are likely to possess? Do collect together any information that is readily available, and discuss it with members of your team.

As your perception of the nature of the target group begins to clarify, do make a point of talking with members of the target group about their concerns and the extent to which your institution might be able to respond to their needs. The discussions should begin on a very open-ended basis – providing members of the target group with the opportunity to identify their own concerns and their own perceptions of what is needed. They may well highlight many things that your institution is unable to address, so do have a follow-up agenda to determine the extent to which they are interested in the things that your institution might be able to do. The information you ultimately collect will be more reliable if you develop follow-up questionnaires to determine the extent to which the views expressed during open-ended interviews reflect those of the target group as a whole.

Data on what has been done before

As you become clearer about the needs of the target group and the way in which your institution might respond to these needs, you will inevitably move on to talk about the type of course you might be able to produce. In doing this you will want to talk about such things as the knowledge and skills that students will need to develop, the type of teaching strategies and media that might be used for this purpose, and the student support systems that will be needed, so do make a point of gathering together data that demonstrates what does and does not work well with the type of students you have in mind. Hopefully, this will ensure that as you move on to develop an outline for your course that you will be able to do this on a well-informed basis.

Estimates of possible enrolment figures

As your thinking about the course clarifies, do make a conscious effort to obtain an estimate of the number of individuals who are likely to enrol on it – even if it means bringing in professionals to collect this data for you. The potential enrolment figures will be important in predicting the cost-effectiveness of any course you might produce, and will need to be estimated and backed up with convincing evidence. The credibility of such data may be critical in determining whether you will be able to obtain the support you are likely to need from your own institution.

Quality control

Where outline plans need to be submitted to related committees for approval, the course team will need to demonstrate not only the obvious needs of the target group, but also the ability of the team to produce a course that will clearly meet the perceived needs. The outline plan will be a crucial document in that it should demonstrate not only the logic behind the proposal, but also the ability of the team to produce a high quality product within a reasonable time frame at an acceptable cost. In setting out its case the course team is quite likely to draw on a great deal of the data it collected in the first place for quality assurance purposes.

9.2 During subsequent stages in the development process

A great deal of time and effort usually goes into the development of an outline plan for a course, and, once this has been approved, it makes a great deal of sense to place prime emphasis on collecting data for *quality assurance* purposes within the course team with a view to improving the quality of the products being developed. However, most institutions involved in the development of ODL materials and systems will want to keep an eye on the process of development, and will usually have some form of monitoring committee or project control unit to monitor the progress of individual course teams. Although such a committee or unit is likely to place prime emphasis on overcoming any problems that may arise, it will usually have the power to delay or abort a project if this is absolutely essential. In other words, the role of the committee or unit concerned will be one of *quality control*.

Quality assurance

In describing the basic development process (Chapter 6) particular emphasis was placed on the way in which feedback should be obtained at each and every stage in the process from related experts in the field (usually within the course team), and it was stressed that this should be acted upon before proceeding to the next stage in the process. However, being assured by experts that the materials produced are of the highest possible quality does not guarantee that students will find the materials equally acceptable. It follows that feedback should also be obtained from typical students, and this is usually obtained through some form of *developmental testing*, and we will consider here the different forms that this might take. You will find that open-ended interviews and questionnaires are used extensively in developmental testing, and I will add a few words on the *types of questionnaires* that might be used for this purpose.

Developmental testing

'Developmental testing' typically involves students in the testing of parts of a course under conditions that simulate as near as possible those under which the course will ultimately be presented. However, it needs to be carefully integrated into the development process (as illustrated in Figure 8.5) in order to ensure that the findings can be acted upon in the further development of the course, and this places clear limitations on what can actually be achieved. So let us take a look at what might be achieved in practice.

Although developmental testing could be designed to provide feedback on the whole of a course, this is likely to be an unlikely proposition where the study time alone for a course involves several months of study. With this in mind, developmental testing is usually designed around specific parts of a course rather than the course as a whole.

Where a specific course component is a matter of particular concern it is possible for this to be subjected to testing on its own. However, where the testing is exploratory in nature, it is logical to test all the components used within one or two units of study, since this can provide feedback on all aspects of the course: the media used, the student support systems provided, study conditions, and so on. In fact, every effort should be made to obtain feedback on the distance teaching systems developed as well as on the self-study materials used.

Where one or two units are subjected to developmental testing as suggested, it is logical to focus on the strengths and weaknesses of broad strategies, rather than on specific detail, since it is important to be able to generalise the findings obtained to the course as a whole.

The number of students involved in the testing process may vary from around six to sixty or more, and the number involved will determine the type of feedback that can be obtained.

For example, with a random sample of only six students, once they have studied the materials, you might limit yourself to interviewing each in turn to determine their major concerns and their thinking about what might be done to improve the materials.

If you have about thirty students you might again interview a random

Quality assurance and quality control 187

sample of six on an individualised basis and then use follow-up questionnaires to determine the extent to which the views expressed in the interviews represent those of the group as a whole.

If you have about sixty students involved, you could divide them into an 'upper group' and 'lower group' according to their qualifications, and determine how this affects their reactions to the materials studied. In such a scenario you might interview about twelve students (six from each group) following the completion of their studies, and you might again use follow-up questionnaires to determine the extent to which the views expressed in the interviews represent those of students in the upper and lower groups.

Bearing in mind the time limitations likely to be imposed on the developmental testing process, follow-up questionnaires will need to be produced with the minimum of delay. However, there is no reason why questionnaires on a range of pre-determined issues (such as study time, achievement of specified objectives, related study problems) should not be presented to all the students involved in the developmental testing process at the same time as the interviews. Such questionnaires will need to focus on broad issues that can be generalised to the course as a whole. The characteristics of questionnaires are discussed in the next section, and you will find an example of the type of broad questionnaire required in Figure 9.2.

In describing the type of developmental testing that might be undertaken, emphasis has been placed on the importance of obtaining feedback from students. However, it also makes a great deal of sense to collect data from others involved in the testing process such as tutors and administrators, thus obtaining feedback from a variety of different perspectives.

Types of questionnaires

In designing questionnaires it is important to recognise that the percentage of students giving a particular response to a question will depend very much on the way a question is asked and on the number and type of alternative keys provided for the response. It therefore makes sense in developing questionnaires on various aspects of ODL to design the questions in a manner that will enable easy comparison between different aspects.

In Figure 9.1 you will find two examples of how this might be achieved. Using the Q1 format it is possible to compare the relative difficulty of various objectives by comparing the percentage of students indicating that they have achieved each objective either 'only in part' or 'not at all'. Using the Q2 format you can do very much the same thing simply by comparing the percentage of students placing a tick against each objective. The advantage of the latter format is that it is economical in the use of space, it provides a very simple format for student responses, and the fluctuations

Q1 Objectives for Unit 1
Identify the extent to which you feel you have achieved the objectives listed below.
(Against each objective ring <u>one</u> number only)

	Completely	Mostly	In Part Only	Not At All
Objective 1	1	2	3	4
Objective 2	1	2	3	4
Objective 3	1	2	3	4
Objective 4	1	2	3	4
Objective 5	1	2	3	4
Objective 6	1	2	3	4

Q2 Objectives for Unit 1
Identify below any objective which you feel you have achieved 'in part only' or 'not at all'.
(Place a tick in the box against each objective that you felt you achieved 'in part only' or 'not at all')

- **Objective 1** ☐
- **Objective 2** ☐
- **Objective 3** ☐
- **Objective 4** ☐
- **Objective 5** ☐
- **Objective 6** ☐

Figure 9.1 Alternative question formats for making comparisons between student responses

in student responses are immediately apparent. The advantage of the Q1 format is that there are more ways of comparing the difficulty of objectives, and it is quite possible that one approach will prove to be more sensitive than the others. For example, you might compare the relative difficulty of the objectives by comparing the percentage of students indicating that they have 'completely' achieved each objective or by comparing the percentage indicating their degree of achievement as being 'not at all'. In the examples that I will include in this book I will use the shorter, simpler format.

Quality control

Any monitoring committee will need to have a system for checking on the progress of individual course teams, and this is one of the reasons for insisting that any outline plan (produced at Stage 1) should include a schedule identifying deadlines for key events in the development process. However, this should not be a one-way process, and individual course team chairs should accept that any major problem should be reported to the committee without delay. There may be good reasons why a course team might fall behind schedule or why some of the products emerging at a particular stage are not up to the standard required, and it is in everyone's interests that this should be reported as soon as possible. Whatever the problem, the sooner action is taken, the more likely it will be that it can be resolved. Bearing in mind the time and effort that will already have been invested in the development process up to this point in time, the first reaction of any monitoring body should be to do all in its powers to help overcome the problem and to get the course back on schedule. Permitting a course team more time to complete a course has to be viewed as an extreme measure, as it will inevitably result in the first presentation of the course being delayed beyond the date promised/advertised. Even more extreme is the idea of withdrawing permission for the continuing development of a course at this stage in the process, and this must be viewed as a measure of last resort.

9.3 During the presentation of the course

Following the launch of a course one might hope that it will run for a number of years without substantial modification and that in the first year of presentation the main requirement will be to identify and rectify matters of detail. However, although you may collect data with this in mind during the first year of presentation, you will almost certainly find that although the data collected will highlight some problems that can, and should, be rectified immediately, it will also highlight some issues that might be better acted upon at a later point in time. In thinking about the data that might be collected during the first year of presentation it therefore makes sense to think about how the data collected will be used in both the short and long term.

What is required is an institutional policy with regard to course presentation: how courses will be maintained and improved during the period of presentation, and what will happen to them at the end of this period. Needless to say, every course has a natural life span. Knowledge evolves over time, new technologies become available, teaching methods change, and the knowledge and skills that students need to develop inevitably change with the times. Institutions therefore need to develop policies to cope with such change: courses will need to be constantly updated, they will need to be re-made in whole or in part at regular intervals, and at times some will be dropped and replaced in response to perceived needs. The continual updating of courses is important, and might be perceived as an important principle upon which to build.

Institutions need to decide how long they expect courses to run on average before they need to be re-made or replaced. According to the resources available it might well be somewhere between six to eight years, but for some it could be longer or shorter. Within such an approach numerous alternatives might be permitted. For example, an institution might permit the allocated re-make budget to be spread evenly over a number of years, so that, instead of completely re-making a course after a period of, say, six years, it might permit one-sixth of the course to be re-made each year over the six-year period. Budgeting along these lines has the advantage of allowing individual course teams some flexibility in developing policies of maintenance and re-make to suit their particular needs. Within the UK OU, once a course is presented to students, a small 'maintenance team' is established to ensure the smooth running of the course, to collect feedback from various sources, to make urgent changes as required, and to collect other data together with a view to facilitating the subsequent re-making of the course in part or whole. In this way the collection of data can be related to the way in which it is to be used.

In the text that follows we will begin by reflecting on the variety of ways in which data might be collected for *quality assurance* purposes, focusing attention on the ways in which the data might be used to help improve the course being presented. However, as we have already noted, every course has a natural life span, and your institution will also need to reflect on how long courses should be presented, when they will need to be re-made, and when they might best be replaced, and we will also consider the type of data that will need to be collected for *quality control* purposes.

Quality assurance

In collecting data for quality assurance purposes the strategies described here tend to identify problem areas in the first instance in rather broad terms, and there is often a need for follow-up studies to illuminate related issues in much greater depth. Such follow-up studies may be undertaken immediately or at a later point in time depending on the urgency with which the problem needs to be resolved.

With this in mind it makes sense during the first year of presentation to start collecting data with both short-term and long-term usage in mind, and in the paragraphs that follow we will consider four distinct ways in which data might be collected. They include the following:

- *the collection of data by the course maintenance team;*
- *the use of open-ended interviews;*
- *the use of questionnaires;*
- *the analysis of assessment data.*

Let us consider each of these in turn.

The collection of data by the course maintenance team

When a course is first presented it is important to have a simple system in place to ensure that feedback from any source (tutors, counsellors, course team members, and various forms of data collection) can be processed and acted upon without delay. One of the simplest ways of doing this is to appoint an appropriate individual who will be responsible for processing feedback and ensuring that appropriate action is taken. Within the UK OU the appropriate person would be the chair of the course maintenance team with the backing of the course manager.

The use of open-ended interviews

Open-ended interviews are valuable in that they often highlight issues that have not been contemplated, and should be undertaken as a matter of routine as soon as possible during the first year of presentation. The interviews should not only include discussions with students, but also with others who are involved with the teaching process such as tutors, counsellors, and administrators.

An example might usefully illustrate their value. In 1992 I was asked to advise on the setting up of an evaluation system for the Indonesian Open Junior High School (OJHS) system prior to its rapid expansion throughout the country. (You will remember, from Chapter 1, that the OJHS system was established to meet the needs of Junior High School students in Indonesia, that it depended on the setting up of 'Learning Centres' in local communities that were often located in very remote areas, and that clusters of Learning Centres were each linked to, and supported by, a central Mother School.)

Not surprisingly, the staff were keen to set up a system that would provide them with feedback on the self-study materials that they had developed, but one of the first things we did together was to undertake open-ended interviews of students and other personnel involved with the system. Some of the insights gained were predictable in that they related to such matters as the quality of the self-study materials, and would probably have surfaced through questionnaires addressing pre-determined issues. However, other insights that emerged were less predictable. For example, it emerged that:

- It could not be assumed that self-study materials would always arrive at the Learning Centres in time for scheduled studies.
- It could not be assumed that the equipment required by the Mother Schools (such as televisions and videos) would always be in operational order.
- Although students were normally only expected to attend the Mother School once a week, getting there could be problematical because of distance, difficult tracks, lack of transport, costs, and so on.
- It also appeared that attendance at local centres was sometimes affected by the need for students to help their families with work at home and in the fields, particularly during the planting and harvesting seasons.

The data collected through such interviews may in some cases be sufficiently explicit to highlight action that needs to be taken immediately. In other cases the issues highlighted may need to be studied more carefully with the help of follow-up questionnaires to determine the extent to which the views expressed are representative of students on the course.

The use of questionnaires

During the first year of presentation it makes sense to use questionnaires to monitor all aspects of a course with a view to initially identifying problem areas in fairly general terms. The questions included in such questionnaires are likely to be expressed in relatively broad terms along the lines illustrated in Figure 9.2.

The questionnaires may address a wide range of topics including such issues as the extent to which students have achieved the objectives specified, difficulties they may have encountered in striving to achieve the objectives, and problems they may have encountered in making use of various media, resources, and related support systems. Needless to say, the issues covered will depend very much on the contents of the course, the media used, and the student support systems provided, and the questionnaires developed will have a strong local orientation. For example, in developing questionnaires for the Open Junior High School system to which we have just referred, it was clear that the questionnaires needed to cover not only the quality of the self-study materials provided, but also

Quality assurance and quality control 193

Q3 Forms of support

In answering the questions below please reflect on the way in which you have made use of the forms of support listed below during your study of Unit 1

(a) Which forms of support have you *used to good effect* in studying Unit 1?
(Ring <u>all</u> that apply in column (a) of the table below)

(b) Which forms of support, if any, would you describe as being of little help?
(Ring <u>all</u> that apply in column (b) of the table)

Forms of support	(a) Used to good effect	(b) Of little help
Study guide	1	1
Reference articles	1	1
Activities using audio clips	1	1
Activities using video clips	1	1
Tutor feedback on assignments	1	1
E-mail contacts with tutor	1	1
Computer-conferencing	1	1
Self-help group	1	1

(c) Do you wish to comment further on any of the above materials?
(If yes, ring the code, and comment below) 1

Figure 9.2 A question format for identifying broad problem areas

such issues as the timely delivery of materials, the quality of support provided by Mother Schools, travel conditions between home and Mother Schools, the effectiveness of the support provided in Learning Centres, and the effect of conflicting demands of work at home and in the fields.

Although the feedback from such questionnaires may identify broad

194 *The development of materials and systems*

problem areas, it is often not sufficiently specific to determine what needs to be done to rectify the problems identified, and follow-up interviews and/or follow-up questionnaires may be needed to look more closely at the issues involved. Two examples might usefully illustrate the type of follow-up activity that might take place.

The first example relates to a new language course where the broad data collected indicates that students are finding activities built around video clips are much less helpful than those built around audio-tapes, but the reasons are far from obvious. In such circumstances it would make sense to interview students and others involved with the development process to see what light they can throw on the problem. Where students may well be able to identify the nature of the problems, it is quite possible that course team members may well be more able to identify possible solutions.

The second example refers to a new science course where it transpires that students are encountering unusual difficulties in understanding the concepts presented in a particular unit. In this case it is felt that a follow-up questionnaire could provide clearer insights by focusing in more sharply on the issues addressed within the unit. You will find an example of the type of question that might be used for this purpose in Figure 9.3.

You might wonder why detailed questionnaires covering all aspects of a course are not produced in the first instance instead of producing broad questionnaires followed by more specific follow-up ones. The reason is simple. If questionnaires were designed to cover every aspect of a course in great detail they would be extremely long and detailed, and as such would be an impractical proposition. Apart from the time, energy and resources that would be needed to produce such questionnaires, the demands placed on students in terms of time and patience in responding to them would be considerable, and this would undoubtedly affect the response rates and the ultimate credibility of the data collected.

The analysis of assessment data

We usually think of assessment as a way of monitoring student progress – on the one hand for accreditation purposes and on the other hand to provide students with feedback on the progress they are making and with advice on how they might overcome related problems. It may also be used to help highlight weaknesses in related self-study materials with the help of item analysis.

I will not try to summarise here the variety of ways in which item analysis might be used, but instead will provide an example of the type of data that might be collected, indicating at the same time how it might be used to identify weaknesses in related self-study materials.

In Figure 9.4 you will find an example of the type of data that may be collected on a test item. Although the data collected here refers to a mul-

---

Q4 Concepts discussed in Unit 1

Do you have difficulty in understanding any of the following phenomena as discussed in Unit 1?

(Place ticks in the boxes below against all the phenomena which you find difficult to understand)

Biogeochemical cycle (carbon) ☐
Biological cycle (carbon) ☐
Carbon cycle ☐
Chemical cycle ☐
Climate model ☐
Geo-chemical cycle ☐
Greenhouse effect ☐
Photosynthesis ☐
Respiration ☐
Solar radiation ☐
Transpiration ☐
Water cycle ☐

Figure 9.3 A question format for identifying specific problem areas

tiple choice test item, very similar data may be collected on the various parts of a tutor-marked assignment. In the example illustrated there are eight possible responses (A–F, don't know and technical error), and 56 per cent of students have identified the correct answer (E). What is rather disturbing is that not only have 28 per cent of students identified one of the incorrect answers (C), but the students concerned are among the most able of those tested, with average mean test scores of 84 per cent compared with that of 72 per cent for those identifying the answer presumed to be correct. This suggests one of two things. Either the alternative response (C) is in some way misleading, or the related self-study materials have led students to believe that this is the best response to the question. Given these indicators, it is up to the subject specialists concerned to examine the test item and the related self-study materials to try to find an explanation.

Item	Facility Index (f)	Disc Index (r)	Cell Statistics	Alternatives A B C D E F	Don't Know	Tech Error
Q5	57%	0.13	Status	N N N N B N		
			Response %	0 2 28 11 56 1	1	1
			Mean Score on Test	39 67 84 70 72 61	67	64

B = correct/best response
N = incorrect response

Figure 9.4 Example of item and cell statistics for a multiple-choice test item

You will have noticed that the example also includes a facility index and a discrimination index. These are the indices that alert you to related problems. The facility index is simply the mean score achieved by students on the item expressed as a percentage of the maximum score that is possible. An index of 100 per cent means that all students responded correctly, while an index of 0 per cent indicates that no student provided a correct response. (The term 'difficulty index' was originally used to describe this index, but the term 'facility index' is used here and in the UK OU, since it does in fact provide a measure of the 'facility' of an item.) The facility index for the item in the example is 57 per cent, and this could be a matter for concern if high levels of achievement are expected of students and particularly if the facility indices for most other items in the test are much higher. However, before jumping to this conclusion other factors need to be taken into account (including the discrimination index).

The discrimination index for an item is a measure of the correlation between student scores on the item compared with those on the test as a whole. Where a test is perceived as homogeneous in nature, one might expect students who perform well on the test to perform well on the test item and vice versa. In other words, one might expect a high correlation between the way in which students perform on the test item and on the test as a whole, and where this occurs the discrimination index for the item could approach +1. In theory the discrimination index can vary from -1 to +1, although one would not expect a negative discrimination index unless an incorrect answer has been mistakenly identified as the correct one. A low discrimination index (close to zero) might suggest a rather poor test item or some misleading factor in the self-study materials, but this is not always the case as the relationship between facility indices and discrimination indices needs to be taken into account in interpreting the data.

Quality assurance and quality control 197

There is in fact a close relationship between the two indices. For example, if a test item is answered correctly by all students, it cannot discriminate between them. Likewise, if no student is able to respond correctly to a test item, it too cannot discriminate between the students concerned. It follows that if a test item has a facility index of either 100 per cent or 0 per cent, the related discrimination index will be zero. A test item is more likely to have a high discrimination index when the facility index lies somewhere between 40 per cent and 60 per cent. The actual relationship between facility and discrimination indices (for a norm-referenced test) is illustrated in graphical form in Figure 9.5, and is based on a mathematical analysis of the relationship between the indices undertaken by Moss (1974). In the sample test item that we have been examining, the discrimination index of 0.13 would alert you to the existence of a problem, since the facility index of 57 per cent for the item lies in the region where one would expect high discrimination indices.

If you would like to know more about item analysis, and in particular the way in which it is used within the UK OU, then you might like to read

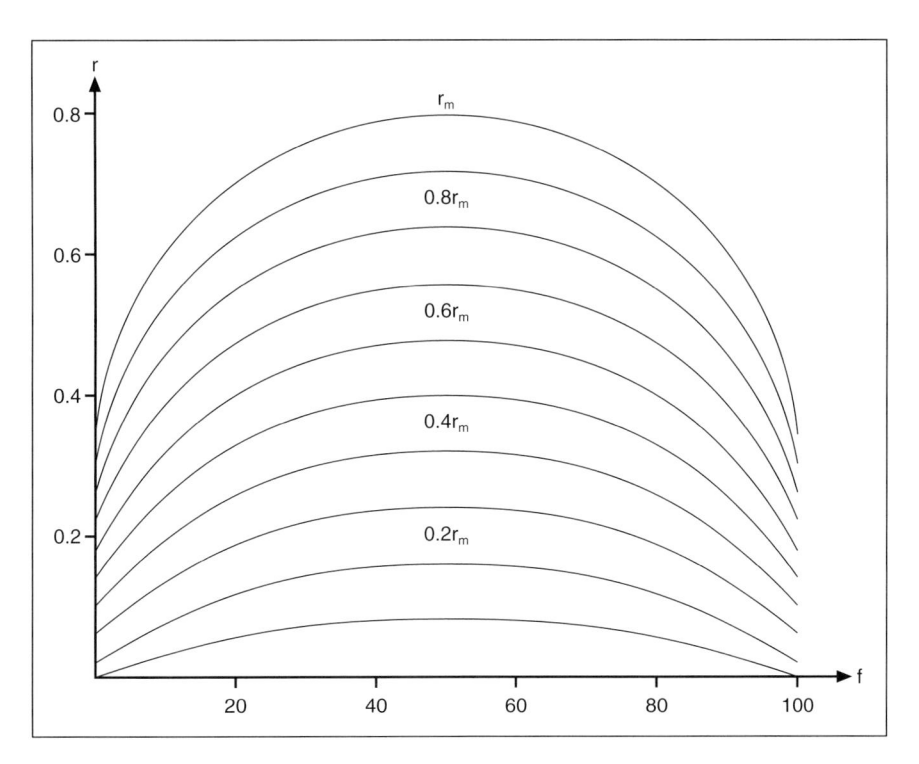

r_m = maximum value of discrimination index (r) for given values of facility index (f)

Figure 9.5 Theoretical variation of discrimination index (r) with facility index (f)
Source: Moss (1974)

my article 'Item analysis at the Open University: a case study' (Melton, 1978b).

Quality control

Once you have a number of courses up and running within your own institution you will need to reflect on how long courses should be presented, when they will need to be re-made, and when they might best be replaced, and you will need appropriate committees to address these issues. Needless to say, such committees will need to draw up their own criteria for decision-making, taking into account local conditions and requirements, but the following are some of the issues that they may address and on which they may well wish to obtain data:

- The number of students enrolling on courses – possibly with a special emphasis on enrolment from specific social groups.
- The percentage of students successfully completing their courses.
- The percentage of students progressing on to related higher level courses.
- The percentage of students obtaining related employment on completion of their studies.

In addition, you will almost certainly have external government agencies who will have a legitimate interest in the quality of teaching within your institution. Such agencies may collect some of their own data, but are quite likely to ask your institution to provide some of the data required. It is up to such agencies to identify the type of data that they require, but they are quite likely to ask for information not only on the issues already highlighted, but also on such items as the following:

- the standards set for accreditation purposes (e.g. for certificates, diplomas and degrees);
- the standards set for individual courses;
- the performance of students against the objectives specified for each course;
- factors affecting student performance, and evidence of the action taken to overcome any problems identified.

Such external agencies (particularly those involved in quality audits) may also have a strong interest in the quality assurance and quality control procedures operating within your institution, and may well ask for information not only on the procedures that have been put in place but also for evidence of their efficacy.

In perspective

If you would like more information on the variety of ways in which data might be collected for quality assurance and quality control purposes, you will find a very good review of the main ideas, approaches and practices in Calder's book *Programme Evaluation and Quality* (1997, pp. 81–100).

Suggestions

This is a good point in time to sit down with your colleagues to discuss the whole development process, to consider to what extent you can accept it as it stands, and to what extent you will need to modify it to take into account the conditions and constraints under which you have to operate. However, in doing this do keep in mind the basic principles underlying the approach and the importance of building quality assurance and quality control into the process.

Part 4
Institutional support

If you hope to develop self-study materials and related student support systems for open and distance learning you will need institutional support, and if you have not already done so, you will need to convince key members of your institution of the advantages of ODL: its cost-effectiveness, how it can reach out to students regardless of where they might be located, how it can provide effective support for student learning, and how the quality of the products and student support systems can be assured.

In turn, your institution will want to know more about the scale of your plans (what you hope to achieve and how) and the level of institutional support that this will require in terms of personnel, training, equipment, facilities, and costs. With this in mind the aim in this part of the book is to help you with the task of determining **the level of institutional support required**.

10 The level of institutional support required

Contents

Introduction	203
10.1 The main advantage of ODL	204
10.2 Key issues that need to be addressed	204
10.3 The level of institutional support required	206
In perspective	212
Suggestions	212

Introduction

By now you will be more than aware that, if you are to develop a system of open and distance learning in your own local environment, you will need the support of your institution. In turn, your institution will need to be convinced of the advantages of ODL, and will need to have a clear understanding of what is involved in developing and supporting a system of ODL. This chapter is intended to help you and your institution to reflect on the key issues involved.

If your institution is not already aware of the advantages of ODL, I would suggest that you introduce key members to the nature of ODL, and give them time to reflect on its advantages and its potential in your own local environment. You will find a summary of *the main advantages of ODL* in the first section of this chapter, and it will help your case if you can relate these to the actual benefits that might be gained in your local environment.

If there is a broad interest in what ODL can offer, your institution will want to know in fairly broad terms what is likely to be involved in the development and maintenance of ODL, and you will find a summary of *key issues that need to be addressed* in the second section of the chapter. Having read the book, these should all be familiar, and you may be able to expand on these for those who wish to have greater insights into what is likely to be involved.

If your institution is impressed by the broad arguments for the development of ODL, it will undoubtedly want more detailed information about the implications if such a venture is to be supported, and at this point it would make a great deal of sense to draw up a project proposal identifying what you hope to achieve through the adoption of ODL, how you propose to go about it, the costs involved, and the financial support that would be required. The proposal is likely to be better received if it is perceived as a joint institutional project with inputs from specialists both inside and outside the institution. In particular, the institution will want detailed information on *the level of institutional support required*, and you will find a summary of related issues that will need to be addressed in the final part of the chapter.

10.1 The main advantages of ODL

As you will have already gathered, it is possible to develop a wide variety of different approaches to ODL, and the advantages of any particular approach will depend on the principles upon which it builds. However, any approach to ODL should aim to do the following:

- reach out to students wherever they might be located;
- provide students with high quality self-study materials and related support systems;
- be highly cost-effective where large number of students are involved.

Depending on the goals of the designers concerned, ODL may also be designed:

- to increase access to education by removing unnecessary barriers;
- to help students to realise their potential;
- to encourage lifelong learning.

Self-study materials may also be designed in a manner that will help:

- to motivate students by allowing them as much freedom as possible to determine their own goals and the means of achieving them;
- to motivate students by highlighting the relevance and importance of the issues addressed;
- to encourage deep rather than superficial thinking through related activities and projects.

10.2 Key issues that need to be addressed

If your institution is to become involved in the development of ODL, serious consideration will need to be given to all the issues addressed within this book. However, two issues are of critical importance, and are worth expanding upon. First, many institutions and governments are particularly impressed by the claim that ODL is much more cost-effective than traditional face-to-face teaching. However, ODL will only be more cost-effective if careful attention is paid to the *factors upon which cost-effectiveness depends*, and these are reviewed in the paragraphs that follow. These are particularly important as they require the designers of ODL to think in very different ways from the designers of more traditional face-to-face teaching. Second, institutions and governments are often both surprised and impressed to learn about the high quality of teaching and learning that can be supported in ODL. However, the development of high quality materials and systems does not happen of its own volition. Careful consideration must be given to ways of *ensuring the quality of the materials and systems to be developed*, and these are summarised in the following text. Having read the book, the issues should all be familiar, but you may be called upon to expand on some of these by others who may not have read the book.

Factors upon which cost-effectiveness depends

In discussing the cost-effectiveness of ODL compared with traditional face-to-face teaching (FFT) the following points need to be emphasised:

- The recurrent costs of ODL tend to be much lower than those of FFT so long as the student numbers involved are relatively high. However, it needs to be recognised that the initial costs of ODL (such as those involved in developing courses and related support facilities) tend to be much higher than those of FFT.
- If cost-effectiveness is to be achieved, the system must be flexible enough to permit easy expansion of student numbers without overloading central academics. This suggests that central academic staff should not be used to provide ongoing support for students on a permanent basis (tutor support, tutorials, continuing assessment, etc.), since any expansion of student numbers will directly increase their load, and will dramatically reduce the time they have available for course development.
- It makes more sense to employ part-time staff as tutors. They are cheaper to employ than central academics, and it is usually relatively easy to expand the number of tutors required to cope with increasing student numbers. Using part-time tutors in this manner leaves central academics unaffected by increased student enrolments, and as such makes rapid expansion of student numbers much easier.
- In the above type of scenario it needs to be recognised that whereas most of the teaching time of academics in FFT is spent on face-to-face teaching, most of the teaching time of central academics in ODL is usually spent on the development of new courses.

Ensuring the quality of the materials and systems to be developed

The quality of the self-study materials and student support systems developed will very much depend on the choices made by the course teams and the institution in designing them, and those involved in developing ODL need to be very familiar with the options available to them (see Parts 1 and 2).

However, there is no guarantee that we will make the right choices, or that our choices will lead to the high quality products that we anticipate. What is needed is the building of quality assurance mechanisms into the development process, ensuring that problems are identified at an early stage in the development process at a point in time when they can be readily rectified.

The type of development process typically adopted for this purpose depends on the use of appropriate specialists working together in course teams over a substantial period of time. The specialists have a variety of roles to play including those of advising on the design and development of materials and systems, contributing to their development, and providing feedback on the materials developed. The process typically moves forward in clearly defined stages – progressing from agreement on broad issues to agreement on more specific issues. Within this approach, feedback is obtained at each and every stage in the process, and action is taken at each stage to rectify problems before moving on to the next stage (see Parts 3 and 4).

10.3 The level of institutional support required

Whether you are planning a small or large-scale project you will need to draw up plans identifying the level of institutional support required. Your requirements will depend on a range of factors such as the number of courses you hope to develop, the number of students you expect to enrol, the student support facilities to be provided, the equipment and facilities that will be needed, the number of personnel that will need to be trained, and the amount of finance that you will need to raise for this purpose.

If you are planning a system of ODL that will offer a wide range of courses reaching out to a large number of students, you will need to break your plans down into sequential stages, differentiating clearly between what you hope to achieve in the short and long term. Such an approach should help you to balance the practicalities of what can be achieved in the short term (with the limited resources that may be currently available) against the ideals of what you might hope to achieve in the longer term (with the possibility of support from national and international agencies).

If, in contrast, you are limiting yourself to the development of a single course, you may be able to limit the extent to which you will need institutional support, particularly if you are able to persuade academics and other specialists to take on a range of tasks way beyond their usual remit for a short period of time. However, you should still draw up plans identifying the level of institutional support required, bearing in mind that at the end of the day you want a high quality, cost-effective course.

In order to determine the level of institutional support that will be required you will need to identify in broad terms *what is to be achieved at each stage in the project* in terms of course development and presentation, and then you will need to provide *details of the tasks to be undertaken and the support required* within each stage of the project.

What is to be achieved at each stage in the project

If you are planning to develop a system of ODL offering a wide range of courses, during the first stage you might well decide to limit yourself to the development of a very limited number of courses (or even a single course). You might also initially limit the number of students involved – being more concerned about improving what is being offered than with ensuring cost-effectiveness at this stage.

In subsequent stages you will almost certainly want to move rapidly towards involving larger numbers of students with a view to achieving cost-effectiveness, and you will probably want to increase the number of courses on offer in order to provide students with a range of choice. In fact, the number of students enrolling on the initial courses may well depend on the promise of other courses becoming available in the near future. As the number of courses on offer increases, the potential for cost-effectiveness should also increase, since many of the support systems developed may be shared across a wider range of courses.

If you intend to develop a wide range of courses, this will place considerable demands on those involved in the development process, and the rate of expansion from one stage to another will need to be planned with great care. In fact, you will almost certainly need to consider a variety of possible scenarios with differing rates of expansion, determining the costs and implications of each in turn before drawing up a firm plan.

Details of the tasks to be undertaken and the support required

Once you have a specific scenario identifying what is to be achieved (in terms of courses to be developed and presented) at each stage in the project, you will then need to identify the tasks to be undertaken at each stage and the support that will be required to carry out the individual tasks. This will involve analysis of a wide range of tasks (ranging from the development of multi-media materials to the development of varying forms of student support), and is best undertaken by a group whose members have a comprehensive knowledge of the issues to be addressed.

208 *Institutional support*

The group will need to undertake two forms of analysis: identifying the level of support that will be required for *the initial development of the courses required* and then for *the subsequent presentation of the courses that have been developed.*

The initial development of the courses required

Once the group has identified the number of courses to be developed during the first stage of the project, it will need to identify the specific tasks involved in the development of the self-study materials and student support systems required. These may include such tasks as the setting up and running of appropriate course teams, the development of audio-visual materials, and the development of various forms of computer support. A more comprehensive range of tasks is included in Figure 10.1, but it will be up to the group to determine for itself the actual tasks to be undertaken in your own situation.

Once the full range of tasks has been identified, the group need to focus in on each of the tasks concerned, identifying the level of support that will be required to ensure that the task can be carried through to completion. As such, the group will need to reflect on such aspects as the personnel required, the related training that may be needed, the equipment and facilities required, and the costs involved in providing all of these.

The issues to be addressed might be presented in the form of a framework as illustrated in Figure 10.1, ensuring that all the relevant issues are addressed. The same type of framework may also be used to present a summary of the findings that emerge from the related discussions. The following examples are intended to illustrate how the framework might be used to guide related discussion.

The first group of tasks identified in the framework relates to 'the course team activities' and the role that course teams play in developing self-study materials and student support systems. If, say, three courses are to be developed during the first stage of the project, it should not be too difficult for the group to identify the different types of specialists required for each team and hence to determine the total number of specialists that will be needed. Having done this, it should be possible to identify the type of facilities the specialists will require (such as desk space and rooms for meetings), the type of equipment they will need (such as computers, photocopiers, library facilities, laboratories, and so on), the amount of training they will require before they can go ahead with the course development required, and the cost of all these aspects.

The second group of tasks relates to the development of audio-visual materials for the courses, and includes the development of such items as audio-tapes, video-tapes, and radio and television programmes. Thus the tasks to be undertaken may include not only the development of materials and programmes, but also ensuring that appropriate equipment and

Course Development Tasks related to development of courses during first stage of project	Support Required to ensure tasks can be completed				Costs
	Personnel	Training	Equipment	Facilities	
Course team activities development of self-study materials and student support systems					
Audio-visual support development of audio-tapes, video-tapes, radio and TV programmes and systems of delivery					
Computer support development of CD-ROMs, computer software, computer-conferencing, etc.					
Assessment materials and systems development of assessment materials and monitoring and marking systems					
Home experiment kits development of kits					
Editing, layout and publication of textual, audio-visual, and computerised forms of presentation					
Tutor support systems development of systems of tutor support					
Residential schools development of residential schools					
Evaluation activities monitoring and evaluation of materials and systems developed					
Distribution distribution of all types of materials to students					

Figure 10.1 A framework for determining the support required for development of courses

systems of delivery are available. For example, the receipt of television programmes in remote areas of a country could well be dependent on ensuring that appropriate equipment and satellite links are made available for this purpose. Once the group has identified the tasks to be undertaken, it will need to consider the type of personnel that will be required to carry out these tasks, the facilities and equipment that they will require, the training they will need, and the finance that will be required to support their work.

The third group of tasks relates to the development of computer support which may be in the form of CD-ROMs, computer software programmes, computer-conferencing, and so on, and again the group will need to consider the support that will be required (in terms of personnel, equipment, facilities, training and finance) in order to support the development of the materials and systems required.

Hopefully, the remaining groups of tasks identified in Figure 10.1 will be self-explanatory, but, if you have any doubt as to what is required, do refer back to Parts 2 and 3 where you will find a full discussion of the type of materials and systems that might be developed.

The subsequent presentation of the courses that have been developed

Assuming that the newly developed courses are to be presented to students as part of the first stage of the project, the group will need to identify the tasks that will need to be undertaken and the level of institutional support that will be required for this purpose.

Again, the tasks to be undertaken and the related support requirements might usefully be presented within a framework, and an example of the approach is shown in Figure 10.2. Although the detailed tasks are somewhat different from those concerned with course development, the framework has much in common with that produced for the development of courses. Once again, it is up to the group to identify the actual tasks to be undertaken in your own situation.

Having provided several examples of how the first framework might be used, I trust that one more example will be sufficient to illustrate how the present framework might be used to guide the discussion of related issues.

You will have noted that the first group of tasks identified within the framework relates to 'the course team activities' and the role that the maintenance course team plays in supporting the course being presented. The tasks undertaken by a 'maintenance course team' are usually much less onerous than those involved in course development, and are likely to be limited to such tasks as collecting feedback on the course, rectifying problems that may arise, and, in general, ensuring the smooth running of the course. The actual tasks to be undertaken will need to be determined by the group, and this in turn will determine the number of individuals

Course Presentation Tasks to support presentation of courses during first stage of project	Support Required to ensure tasks can be completed				Costs
	Personnel	Training	Equipment	Facilities	
Course team activities monitoring of course, rectification of problems, student assessment etc.					
Audio-visual support presentation of radio and TV programmes, technical support for audio-visual users					
Computer support computer-conferencing, technical support for computer users, etc.					
Assessment materials and systems development of assessment materials, monitoring and marking assignments					
Home experiment kits technical support					
Tutor support systems support of students by telephone, e-mail, through tutorials, by providing feedback on assignments, supporting project work, etc.					
Residential schools development and presentation of residential schools					
Evaluation activities ongoing monitoring and upgrading of materials and systems					
Distribution ongoing distribution and collection of all types of materials					

Figure 10.2 A framework for determining the support required for presentation of courses

required to support the work of the maintenance team. It may be that no more than two or three people will be required (a maintenance team chair, a course manager, and a secretary) with periodic additional support (e.g. for examination boards). Once the personnel requirements have been determined, the group will need to reflect on the facilities that will be needed (such as desk space), the type of equipment that may be required (such as computers), any training requirements (for monitoring techniques, item analysis feedback on assignments, etc.), and the costs of these requirements.

I hope that the above is sufficient to illustrate how the two frameworks might be used to help determine the level of support required during the first stage of a project. The same approach may also be used to determine the level of support required in subsequent stages – taking into account that the number of courses to be developed and presented will vary from stage to stage.

In perspective

You will by now be very aware that the quality of any materials and systems that you might develop will depend to a large extent on the institutional support that you are able to obtain and not just on the building of quality assurance and quality control mechanisms into the development process. Within this book I have focused attention on key factors that need to be addressed if you are to produce high quality materials and systems, but the quality of the products developed could be affected by other factors. You will find a comprehensive list of the factors that need to be taken into account in Robinson (1994, pp. 185–194) checklist which is reproduced in Figure 10.3. As Robinson so aptly states, 'quality lies in the totality of products, delivery, services and general ethos', and in developing your own approach to ODL you should be alert to the full range of factors that could affect the quality of the products being developed.

Suggestions

If you have reached this stage of the book, I think there is a very high probability of your going on to produce a project proposal leading to the development of ODL in your own area.

In drawing up your plans do not hesitate to seek advice from experts in the field. ODL is offered in many regions of the world, and you may find appropriate experts within your own area. If you cannot find the help you are looking for within your own area, you might find it helpful to contact the Open University Worldwide (OUW) which is an integral part of the UK OU. OUW offers a full range of consultancy services, and is able to enter into various forms of partnership to help institutions involved in developing or improving their own systems of ODL. The range of services

Quality policy and plan
  Has your organisation developed a policy on quality which all staff are familiar with?
  Has this been translated into a practical plan?

Specification of standards
  Are there specified and clearly defined standards in place?
  Have they been communicated to all concerned?
  Are they specified for key activities?
  Are they achievable, reasonable and measurable?

Identifying critical functions
  Have the critical functions for achieving the standards been identified?
  Have they taken the learner as the starting point for some of these?
  Have the procedures to achieve them been analysed?

Documentation
  Are the procedures to be followed clearly documented?
  Are they explicit?
  Do they represent fact (practice as it happens) or fiction (an idealised version)?
  Are they consistent in different documents?
  Are they concentrated on essential procedures?
  Are they in a readable and user friendly form?
  Do all those who need them have access to copies?

Staff involvement
  Have all staff been involved in the development of quality-assurance systems in your organisation?
  Have their suggestions been built in?
  Has enough time been given to this process?

Monitoring
  Are there systematic monitoring mechanisms for critical functions?
  Do they check whether standards are being met and procedures followed?
  How do you know? (What is their product and impact?)
  Are the findings disseminated?
  Are they harnessed to appropriate action?
  Do they result in improved performance or a review of practice, or a reappraisal of standards?
  Do they provide effective feedback loops between providers of products and services and learners or clients?

Involvement of users
  Have learners and clients and staff been involved in setting and monitoring standards?
  Have staff made an input as 'internal customers' or 'clients'?

Training
  Is there adequate provision of training and staff development?
  Is this linked to the achievement of standards?
  Are there effective mechanisms for assessing training needs?
  Are these reviewed regularly?
  Are there resources allocated to meet them?

Costs
  Is there a strategy for monitoring the costs of implementing and maintaining quality assurance activities?
  Does this take account of human and financial costs?
  Are the costs greater than the benefits?
  Is there a review process to find out?

Figure 10.3 Checking the effectiveness of quality assurance procedures
Source: Robinson (1994)

214 *Institutional support*

available is described in a brochure entitled *Educational Partnerships with the Open University*, which is produced by the Open University Worldwide (2001). You may also find it of interest to take a look at the UK OU's website http://www.open.ac.uk which contains a wide range of information about the UK Open University.

All that remains for me now is to wish you well with your project and the ventures that lie ahead.

Bibliography

Ausubel, D.P. (1968) *The Psychology of Meaningful Verbal Learning*. New York: Grune and Stratton.

Bargar, R.R. and Hoover, R.L. (1984) Psychological type and the matching of cognitive styles. *Theory into Practice*, 1, 56–63.

Bates, A.W. (1982) Trends in the use of audio-visual media in distance teaching systems. In J.S. Daniel, M.A. Stroud and J.R. Thompson (eds) *Learning at a Distance: A World Perspective*. Athabasca University and International Council for Correspondence Education, pp. 8–14.

Bates, A.W. (1995) *Technology, Open Learning and Distance Education*. London: Routledge.

Calder, J. (1997) *Programme Evaluation and Quality: A Comprehensive Guide to Setting up an Evaluation System*. London: Kogan Page.

Chown, A. and Last, J. (1993) Can the NCVQ model be used for teacher training? *Journal of Further and Higher Education*, 17(2), 15–26.

Collis, B. (1996) *Tele-Learning in a Digital World*. London: International Thomson Computer Press.

Daniel, J.S. (1996) *Mega-Universities and Knowledge Media*. London: Kogan Page.

Dreyfus, H.L. and Dreyfus, S.E. (1984) Putting computers in their proper place: analysis versus intuition in the classroom. In D. Sloan (ed.) *The Computer in Education: A Critical Perspective*. Columbia, New York: Teachers' College Press.

Dunn, R. (1984) Learning style: state of the science. *Theory into Practice*, 1, 10–19.

Eisenstadt, M. (1995) Overt strategy for global learning. *Times Higher Education Supplement*, Multimedia Section, 7 April, vi–vii.

Haughey, M. and Anderson, T. (1998) *Networked Learning: The Pedagogy of the Internet*. Montreal, Canada: Chenelière/McGraw-Hill.

Henry, J. (1994) *Teaching through Projects*. London: Kogan Page.

Hilgard, E.R. and Bower, G.H. (1975) *Theories of Learning*. Englewood Cliffs, NJ: Prentice-Hall Inc, pp. 608–609.

Hunt, D.E. (1971) *Matching Models in Education*. Toronto, Ontario: Institute for Studies in Education.

Hyman, R. and Rosoff, B. (1984) Matching learning and teaching styles: the jug and what's in it. *Theory into Practice*, 1, 35–43.

Joyce, B.R. (1984) Dynamic disequilibrium: the intelligence of growth. *Theory into Practice*, 1, 26–34.

Keegan, D. (1996) *Foundations of Distance Education*. London: Routledge.

Kolb, D.A. (1984) *Experiential Learning: Experience as the Source of Learning and Development*. Englewood Cliffs, NJ: Prentice-Hall.

Kolb, D.A. and Fry, R. (1975) Towards an applied theory of experiential learning. In C.L. Cooper (ed.) *Theories of Group Processes*. Chichester: John Wiley.

Laidlaw, B. and Layard, R. (1974) Traditional versus OU teaching methods: a cost comparison. *Higher Education*, 3, 237–261.

Lawrence, W.G. and Young, I. (1979) *The Open University, TIHR Document No. 2T-271*. London: The Tavistock Institute for Human Relations.

Lockwood, F. (1992) *Activities in Self-Instructional Texts*. London: Kogan Page.

Lockwood, F. (ed.) (1994) *Materials Production in Open and Distance Learning*. London: Paul Chapman Publishing.

McIntosh, N. and Woodley, A. (1980) *The Door Stood Open: An Evaluation of the Open University Younger Students Pilot Scheme*. Milton Keynes: Institute of Educational Technology and the Open University.

Mager, R.F. (1962) *Preparing Instructional Objectives*. Palo Alto, CA: Fearon.

Management Charter Initiative (1992) *Middle Management Standards*. London: National Forum for Management Education and Development, pp. 8–9.

Marton, F. and Saljo, R. (1976) On qualitative differences, outcomes and process, I and II. *British Journal of Educational Psychology*, 46, 4–11, 115–127.

Mason, R. (ed.) (1995) *Computer Conferencing: The Last Word*. Victoria, British Columbia: Beach Home Publishers Ltd.

Mason, R. (1998) *Globalising Education: Trends and Applications*. London: Routledge.

Melton, R.F. (1978a) Resolution of conflicting claims concerning the effect of behavioural objectives on student learning. *Review of Educational Research*, 48, 291–302.

Melton, R.F. (1978b) Item analysis at the Open University: a case study. *British Journal of Educational Technology*, 9, 111–130.

Melton, R.F. (1990) Transforming text for distance learning. *British Journal of Educational Technology*, 21, 3, 183–195.

Melton, R.F. (1997) *Objectives, Competences and Learning Outcomes*. London: Kogan Page.

Melton, R.F. (2000) *Feedback on High Tech Issues (II)*. Milton Keynes: Student Research Centre, IET, Open University.

Melton, R.F. and Zimmer, R. (1987) Multi-perspective illumination. *British Journal of Educational Technology*, 2, 111–120.

Moore, M.G. and Kearsley, G. (1996) *Distance Education: A Systems View*. New York: Wadsworth Publishing Company.

Moss, A.G. (1974) *A Method of Decoupling Item Discrimination Index from Facility Index*. Milton Keynes: Institute of Educational Technology, Open University.

Open University (1993) *Course B601: Managing Health Services, Book 2*. Milton Keynes: Open University.

Open University (1996) *Course L130: Auftakt, Get by in German, Book 1*. Milton Keynes: Open University.

Open University (1998) *Course L120: Ouverture, Valeurs 2*. Milton Keynes: Open University.

Open University (1998) *Course S103: Discovering Science, Block 2*. Milton Keynes: Open University.

Open University (1999) *Course L120: Ouverture, Notes on end-of-course assessments*. Milton Keynes: Open University.

Open University (2000) *Course H801: Foundations of ODE, Block 1*. Milton Keynes: Open University.
Open University (2000) *Course H801: Foundations of ODE, Course Guide*. Milton Keynes: Open University.
Open University (2000) *Course H804: Implementation of ODL, Assignment Guide*. Milton Keynes: Open University.
Open University (2000) *Course H804: Implementation of ODL, Block 1*. Milton Keynes: Open University.
Open University (2000) *Course H804: Implementation of ODL, Block 5*. Milton Keynes: Open University.
Open University (2000) *Course H804: Implementation of ODL, Computer Conference*. Milton Keynes: Open University.
Open University Worldwide (2001) *Educational Partnerships with the Open University*. Milton Keynes: Open University.
Popham, W.J. (1969) Objectives and instruction. In Stake *et al.* (eds) *Instructional Objectives*. American Educational Research Association Monograph Series on Curriculum Evaluation. Chicago, Illinois: Rand McNally.
Robinson, B. (1994) Assuring quality in open and distance learning. In F. Lockwood (ed.) *Materials Production in Open and Distance Learning*. London: Paul Chapman Publishing, pp. 185–194.
Rogers, C.R. (1969) *Freedom to Learn*. Columbus, OH: Charles E. Merrill.
Rogers, C.R. (1971) *Encounter Groups*. Harmondsworth: Penguin.
Rowntree, D. (1974) *Educational Technology in Curriculum Development*. London: Harper and Row.
Rowntree, D. (1987) *Assessing Students: How Shall we Know Them?* London: Kogan Page.
Rowntree, D. (1992) *Exploring Open and Distance Learning*. London: Kogan Page.
Rowntree, D. (1994) *Preparing Materials for Open, Distance and Flexible Learning*. London: Kogan Page.
Rumble, G. (1987) Why distance education can be cheaper than conventional education. *Distance Education*, 8(1), 72–94.
Simpson, O. (2000) *Supporting Students in Open and Distance Learning*. London: Kogan Page.
Smith, P.B. (1980) *Group Processes and Personal Change*. London: Harper and Row.
Stotland, E. (1969) *The Psychology of Hope*. San Francisco, CA: Jossey-Bass.
Student Research Centre, Open University (1999) *Courses Annual Survey, 1999*. Milton Keynes: IET, Open University.
Tait, A. (1989) The politics of open learning. *Adult Education*, 61, 4.
Thelen, H. (1960) *Education and the Human Quest*. New York: Harper and Row.
Tyler, R.W. (1934) *Constructing Achievement Tests*. Columbus, OH: Ohio State University.
Tyler, R.W. (1949) *Basic Principles of Curriculum and Instruction*. Chicago: University of Chicago Press.
Wagner, L. (1977) The economics of the Open University revisited. *Higher Education*, 6, 359–381.

Index

Aims of ODL   3–20
   Achievement of student potential   9
   Cost effectiveness   15–18
   Decentralisation of student support systems   17–18
   Deep v Superficial Learning   12–13
   Design of self-study materials   10–13
   Freedom to determine own goals   8–9
   Lifelong learning   9–10
   Multi-media approach   11
   Open access to education   6–8
   Removal of barriers to education   7–9
   Responding to student needs   8–10
   Structuring of study materials   10–11
   Student numbers, optimisation of   15–17
   Student support   13–15

Assessment   156–163, 194–198
   Analysis of assessment data   194–198
   Assessment strategies   156–163
   Continuous assessment   161–162
   Criterion-referenced assessment   158–159
   End-of-course assessment   161–162
   Formative assessment   162–163
   Graded assessment   159–161
   Item analysis   194–198
   Norm-referenced assessment   157–158
   Summative assessment   162–163

Course characteristics – some basic features   23–40
   Course credits   37–39
   Course parameters   37–39
   Student enrolment   24–31
   Student registration   24–26

220   *Index*

    Study guides   27–31
    Study time   37–39

Course development process   **141–181**
    Stage 1: Development of course outline   141–166, 168–169
    Stage 2: Development of unit outlines   169–170
    Stage 3: Development of core content   171–176
    Stage 4: Development of materials in full   176–177
    Stage 5: Editing and layout   178

Course development process, first stage in   **141–166**
    Aims and objectives of course   144–147
    Assessment strategies   156–163
    Framework for course   142–156
    Functional analysis   144–146
    Hierarchical analysis   146–147
    Scheduling of process   178–180
    Structuring of course, a functional approach   148
    Structuring of course, a scenario-based approach   149–152
    Structuring of course, a project-based approach   152–154
    Structuring of course, other approaches   154–155
    Target group, characteristics of   143–144
    Target group, needs of   143–144

Course development process, principles underlying   **135–140**
    Quality assurance strategies   136–138
    Quality control strategies   138–139
    Supporting creative thinking   139–140
    Team work   136–140

Design features   **41–84**
    Activities   50–53
    Advance organisers   42–43, 64
    Aims, statements of   43–46, 64, 144–147
    Assessment strategies   70, 72–73, 75–78
    Checklists   58–60
    Objectives   58–60, 144–147
    Projects   50–53
    Signalling devices   50
    Summaries   58, 74

Existing materials, making use of   **78–84**
    No changes required   80
    Adjunct aids required   80–82
    Content needs restructuring   82–84

Frameworks for courses and study sessions   41–78
    Course, introduction to   63–70
    Course, conclusion to   71–78
    Course, framework for   60–79, 142–156
    Study session, introduction to   42–47
    Study session, conclusion to   58–60
    Study session, framework for   41–62

Institutional support   201–214
    A phased approach, advantages of   207
    Advantages of ODL, need to be aware of   204
    Cost effectiveness, factors determining   205
    Quality assurance mechanisms required   206, 212–214
    Quality control mechanisms required   206
    Support required for course development, estimation of   207–210
    Support required for course presentation, estimation of   210–212

Media, high technology forms of   99–104
    CDs   102
    Computer conferencing   89–93, 101
    Computers, student use of   99
    E-mails, use of   100
    Knowledge Media Institute   104
    Recent developments   103
    Video conferencing   102
    Websites, course-based   123
    Websites, institutional   123
    World Wide Web   103

Media, traditional forms of   94–99
    Audio cassettes   95
    Audio conferencing   97
    Cassettes   95
    Combination of media   87–88
    Faxes   97
    Home experiment kits   98
    Mass media   94
    Natural environment, use of   97
    Practical resources   97–99
    Printed material   94
    Radio   94
    Telephone   96
    Telephone-based links   96–97
    Television   95
    Video cassettes   96

222 Index

Media characteristics — 85–109
- Access to media — 105
- Appropriateness of media — 105
- Case studies, use of — 88–89
- Costs of media — 106
- Power of media — 86–87
- Selection of media — 104
- Skills required for use of media — 106

Quality assurance and control, collection of data for — 182–199
- Collection of data during Stage 1 of development process — 183–185
- Collection of data during Stages 2–5 of development process — 185–189
- Collection of data during presentation of course — 189

Quality assurance and quality control instruments — 186–198
- Assessment data — 194–198
- Course maintenance teams — 191
- Developmental testing — 186–187
- Interviews, open-ended — 191–192
- Item analysis — 194–198
- Questionnaires, varying formats for — 187–189
- Questionnaires, different forms of use for — 192–194

Quality assurance strategies — 182–198

Quality control strategies — 185, 189, 198

Schedules for course development — 70, 178–180

Student support — 110–132

Student support, academic and non-academic — 112–114, 119–120, 125–128
- Academic support — 113–114, 125–128
- Counselling — 112, 119–120, 128

Student support, centre-based forms of — 120–128
- Computer conferencing — 125–127
- Computer users, technical support for — 122–123
- Residential schools — 121–122
- Student newspapers — 121
- Websites, course-based — 123
- Websites, institutional — 123

Student support, selection of types of — 128–131
- Appropriateness of support — 129
- Continuity of support — 130
- Cost of support — 130

Ease of access to support	129
Skills required to use support	130

Tutor support, group-based forms of	**118–119**
Audio conferencing	119
Peer group support	119
Tutorials	118–119

Tutor support, individualised forms of	**116–117**
Ad hoc support	117
Regular support	117–118